FARMHOUSE KITCHEN II

A second book of recipes based on
the Independent Television series
presented by Dorothy Sleightholme

Edited by Mary Watts

**YORKSHIRE
TELEVISION**

£2.25

Published in Great Britain by

YORKSHIRE TELEVISION ENTERPRISES LTD

Television House, 32 Bedford Row,

London WC1R 4HE

Reprinted 1981 (twice)
Reprinted 1982
Reprinted 1983

ISBN 0 9501113 5 X

Printed in Great Britain by Spottiswoode Ballantyne Ltd,
Colchester and London

CONTENTS

ACKNOWLEDGMENTS

There are many original and innovatory recipes in this book as well as some which have been published before. Many of these are old favourites of ours and I am indebted to Messrs. Faber & Faber Ltd for permission to include some of Ursula Cavanagh's recipes, and to the Nutritional Science Research Institute of England, Mulberry Tree Hall, Brookthorpe, Gloucester, for the use of Elizabeth Shears' recipes. I am also grateful for the interest of the McCarrison Society, a group of members of the medical profession whose particular concern is the connection between nutrition and good health, and for the help and advice of the Long Ashton Research Station, Bristol.

Finally, I would like to thank Joyce Town for her work in organising and typing.

Mary Watts
Summer 1978

Cover Illustration: Mary Evans Picture Library

Text Illustrations: scarecrow motif and pp. 35, 158, 179– The Mansell Collection; pp. 58, 72–Mary Evans Picture Library; pp. 140, 164 – Radio Times Hulton Picture Library

INTRODUCTION

So many viewers of *Farmhouse Kitchen* have sent me recipes over the years that we have made a new book for them. There are over 350 recipes in this collection, including many of my old favourites.

We have spent many enjoyable hours trying and tasting all the recipes, and I would like to thank Mrs Judith Adshead, Mrs Stella Boldy, Mrs Pat Dixon, Mrs Margaret Heywood, Mrs Sybil Norcott, Mrs Anne Wallace, Mr Alan Briggs and Mr Dennis Rouston for helping me to do this and for contributing to this book.

I have always tried to share with you what I know about cooking and the preparation of wholesome, nourishing and economical meals. The cost of food is so high now that we have to be sure that what we buy and prepare is doing us good as well as filling us up. So I am pleased to include some of the work of Mrs Ursula Cavanagh and Mrs Elizabeth Shears who have a particular interest in nutrition. Mrs Jeannie Zacharova, who is planning a book on bread-making, has given us a preview of what it will contain, and Mrs Doreen Allars has let us choose from her large collection of preserves recipes.

Finally, I would like to say a special 'thank you' to the many thousands of cooks who watch my television programmes, and to those who have sent their recipes to me.

Dorothy Sleightholme

Yorkshire Television's *Farmhouse Kitchen* series is produced and directed by Mary and Graham Watts.

CHAPTER 1

SOUPS AND STARTERS

DOROTHY SLEIGHTHOLME'S SALT AND PEPPER MIX

For seasoning.

3 teaspoons salt to 1 teaspoon pepper. Using same proportions mix enough to fill a screw-top jar.

TO MAKE STOCK

Chicken-bone stock
Carcass of a chicken or any other poultry makes good stock. Put it in a large saucepan with plenty of water, an onion, a piece of carrot, leek, celery, parsley stalks or any vegetable stock or peelings that might otherwise get thrown out. Add 2 or 3 peppercorns, or a bay leaf. Simmer gently for at least an hour.
Strain off liquid, let it cool and then refrigerate or freeze it.

Beef bones
Put bones in a large saucepan with plenty of water and bring to boil. Add pieces of onion, carrot, leek, celery tops, parsley stalks, vegetable peelings and hard outer leaves. Add peppercorns, bay leaf, herbs. Any of these will enrich the stock. Simmer for at least an hour.

Ham bone
Simmer it with peppercorns and 1 or 2 cloves. The flavour is rich so use this stock with caution or add plenty of water.

Vegetable stock
Save the water in which vegetables are cooked. It will keep 24 hours in refrigerator.

SOUP MIX

Look in your store cupboard for lentils and legumes, cereals and grains such as split peas, dried peas, carlins (maple peas), chick peas, soya beans, butterbeans, red beans, mung beans, kidney beans, brown rice, barley, and wheat. Even wholemeal pasta goes in. Take a handful of each and mix them together in a large jar. Now you have the beginnings of a nourishing and satisfying soup – almost a meal in itself. But remember that the Soup Mix needs soaking for a day – or at least overnight – before you are going to eat it.

The Soup
1 handful Soup Mix
1 pint water
1½ pints vegetable or chicken or meat stock
½ teaspoon marjoram or basil
Salt
1 large onion
1 or 2 sticks celery
1 leek
1 carrot
A small piece of turnip
1 clove garlic (optional)
Some cauliflower
25 g/1 oz butter or margarine or good dripping
Pepper

Always put in onion but otherwise just use vegetables you have available. Tomatoes, fresh or tinned, can be used.

1. Put Soup Mix in the water to soak at least overnight.
2. Next day, put Soup Mix into a saucepan with its water and the stock, the herbs and some salt. Bring to the boil, cover and boil hard for 30 minutes. Then simmer till tender. The longer you soak the Soup Mix ingredients the less time they need to cook. Do not cook too long or they may go mushy. The soup is best if the beans, barley, etc., are still whole and recognisable.
3. Meanwhile, prepare vegetables. Peel onion and chop finely. Wash and chop up the celery, leek, carrot, turnip. Crush or chop up the garlic.
4. Break the cauliflower into very small florets. Chop up the stalk

and keep this separate from other vegetables.
5. Melt fat in a saucepan with tight-fitting lid.
6. Put in the onion and other vegetables, but not the cauliflower. Put on the lid and set pan on a very low heat. Let the vegetables 'sweat' in the pan for 10 minutes taking care they do not catch or burn.
7. Add vegetables to the Soup Mix.
8. Bring to the boil, add cauliflower and freshly ground black pepper to taste. Simmer gently for 5 to 10 minutes.

ARTICHOKE SOUP

450 g/1 lb Jerusalem artichokes
1 stalk celery
1 onion
1 tablespoon oil
600 ml/1 pint water
Salt
25 g/1 oz wholewheat or plain flour
400 ml/¾ pint milk
Black pepper
1 tablespoon chopped parsley

1. Wash and slice artichokes.
2. String and slice celery.
3. Peel onion and chop finely.
4. Put oil in a pan, add vegetables and sauté them for a few minutes – i.e., turn them over in the fat over moderate heat.
5. Stir in flour and let it cook for a minute.
6. Add water and a little salt. Bring to the boil, reduce heat, cover pan and let vegetables simmer until tender but not mushy.
7. If you like a creamy soup, sieve or liquidise, then return to pan.
8. Add milk and reheat the soup, but do not boil.
9. Add freshly-ground black pepper and chopped parsley and serve.

Isabel James,
McCarrison Society

BACON AND SPLIT PEA SOUP

1 sheet of bacon ribs, plain or smoked
Water
1 large onion
1 carrot
1 potato
2 sticks celery
A little seasoning
225 g/8 oz split peas, yellow or green, or both

1. Put bacon ribs in a large saucepan, cover with water, bring to the boil and boil for a few minutes, then pour water away. This removes excess salt.
2. Meanwhile, peel and chop the onion, scrub and grate the carrot and the potato. Finely slice the celery.
3. Pour 1·7 litres/3 pints fresh, cold water over the ribs and add rest of ingredients.
4. Bring to the boil, stirring occasionally. Put lid on pan, lower heat and cook gently for 1 to 1½ hours. This can be done in pressure cooker, in which case cook under maximum pressure for 30 minutes.
5. Remove bacon ribs and strip off any meat.
6. Sieve or liquidise the soup.
7. Serve the soup either with the meat chopped and added or save the meat for another meal.

Margaret Heywood,
Todmorden, Yorkshire

BARLEY BROTH OR MUTTON BROTH

To do this in the traditional way buy 450 g/1 lb scrag end of neck of mutton, cut it up small (discarding fat) and cook slowly, with the bones, in 1·2 litres/2 pints water for 2 hours. Use the stock and meat in the broth as below.

75 g/3 oz barley kernels or pearl barley

600 ml/1 pint water
2 onions
1 large carrot
1 or 2 sticks celery
1 small parsnip or turnip
25 g/1 oz butter or margarine
1 litre/1½ pints mutton, vegetable
or chicken stock
A bouquet garni or bunch of fresh
herbs such as parsley, thyme and
rosemary
Salt
Black pepper

1. Put barley in water to soak
overnight.
2. Peel onion and chop finely.
3. Scrub and finely chop or grate
the carrot and parsnip or turnip.
4. Cut up the celery very fine.
5. Melt the butter or margarine in a
large saucepan with a well-fitting
lid, put in the vegetables, cover the
pan tightly and let the vegetables
'sweat' over a very low heat for 10
minutes.
6. Add soaked barley with its
water, the stock and bouquet garni
or bunch of fresh herbs (or a pinch
of dried mixed herbs) and a little
salt. Bring back to the boil.
7. Simmer for 20 to 30 minutes
until barley is soft. Remove
bouquet garni.
8. Add a little black pepper just
before serving.

CREAM OF CARROT SOUP

450 g/1 lb carrots
2 medium-sized potatoes
1 onion
25 g/1 oz butter
850 ml/1½ pints chicken stock
1 small orange
1 bay leaf
¼ teaspoon salt
Pepper
Pinch of nutmeg
2 tablespoons thick cream
Chopped parsley or chives, to
garnish

1. Scrub carrots, peel potato and
onion. Slice them all thinly.

2. Melt butter in a pan, add
vegetables, cook gently for 3 or 4
minutes.
3. Add stock.
4. Add grated orange rind and
juice, bay leaf, salt, pepper and
nutmeg.
5. Simmer soup for about 20
minutes until vegetables are
tender.
6. Allow to cool slightly and
remove bay leaf.
7. Sieve or liquidise.
8. Return soup to pan, check
seasoning and reheat.
9. Remove pan from heat, stir in
cream and serve with a sprinkling
of parsley or chives.

CELERY SOUP

1 medium-sized head of celery
1 small onion
40 g/1½ oz butter or margarine
40 g/1½ oz wholewheat or plain
white flour
1 litre/1½ pints vegetable or
chicken stock (see page 8)
A bouquet garni, or sprig of
parsley, thyme and marjoram or
bay leaf tied together
300 ml/½ pint milk
Salt and pepper
2 tablespoons single cream

1. Chop up celery, including inner
leaves. Save a few chopped leaves
for garnish. Chop up the onion.
2. Melt butter or margarine in a
saucepan with a well-fitting lid.
Add vegetables.
3. Stir vegetables for 1 minute then
put lid on the saucepan. Turn heat
down very low and let the
vegetables 'sweat', without
browning, for 10 minutes.
4. Stir in the flour and let it cook
for 1 minute.
5. Add stock and bouquet garni.
Bring to the boil and simmer until
vegetables are tender but not
mushy. Remove bouquet garni.
6. If you prefer a creamy soup, put
it through liquidiser or through a
sieve. Return it to pan.

7. Add milk, a little salt and pepper. Reheat.
8. Just before serving stir in finely-chopped celery leaves and cream.

Isabel James,
McCarrison Society

GAME SOUP

1 onion
1 carrot
1 stick celery
50 g/2 oz butter
1·2 litres/2 pints game stock, from carcasses of 2 game birds (see page 8)
1 bay leaf
Salt and pepper
25 g/1 oz margarine or butter
25 g/1 oz plain flour
2 teaspoons redcurrant jelly
2 tablespoons sherry or red wine
2 teaspoons lemon juice

1. Peel and chop onion. Scrub and chop carrot. Wash and slice celery.
2. Melt butter in a large pan and sauté – i.e., lightly fry – the vegetables, turning them over in the hot fat for 2 or 3 minutes until lightly browned.
3. Add stock, bay leaf, salt and pepper and simmer for 1 hour.
4. Finely chop any meat picked from the carcasses.
5. Make a brown roux with the margarine and flour: i.e., melt margarine, stir in flour and fry till light brown.
6. Strain the soup and gradually stir it into the roux. Bring to the boil and cook for 2 or 3 minutes.
7. Add the meat and reheat. The soup may now be liquidised if a smooth texture is preferred.
8. Add the redcurrant jelly and lemon juice and sherry or wine. Reheat and serve at once.

Anne Wallace,
Dunlop, Scotland

TOMATO SOUP

450 g/1 lb fresh ripe tomatoes, or a 400 g/14 oz tin
1 large onion
25 g/1 oz green pepper
25 g/1 oz butter, margarine or good bacon dripping
½ to 1 litre/1 to 1½ pints chicken stock
Pinch of basil (optional)
1 bay leaf
Salt
Black pepper
½ teaspoon sugar (barbados preferred)
1 tablespoon chopped parsley
1 dessertspoon chopped mint

1. If fresh tomatoes are used, peel them. To do this, put them in a bowl and cover with boiling water. Wait 15 seconds then pour off hot water and cover with cold. Wait half a minute and skins will be easy to remove. Chop up tomatoes finely.
2. Peel onion and chop finely.
3. Chop green pepper very small.
4. Melt fat in a large saucepan. Fry onion and green pepper for 2 to 3 minutes until softening but not brown.
5. Add tomatoes, stock, basil and bay leaf. Bring to the boil and simmer for 10 to 15 minutes.
6. Test seasoning, adding a very little salt if necessary, plenty of freshly-ground black pepper and sugar.
7. Just before serving add chopped parsley and mint.

To make a meal of this soup add a handful of brown rice, brown macaroni or fancy pasta when soup comes to the boil. Make sure rice or pasta is cooked before serving.

CHILLED AVOCADO SOUP

Delicious and nutritious.
You need an electric blender or liquidiser.

600 ml/1 pint chicken stock (stock cube will do)
2 ripe avocado pears

11

About a 10 cm/4 inch length of cucumber
1 teaspoon lemon juice
275 g/10 fluid oz natural yoghurt
Salt and pepper

1. Prepare stock and allow to cool.
2. Halve the avocado pears, peel off skins and remove stones. Dice the flesh.
3. Dice the cucumber leaving skin on.
4. Put avocado, cucumber and a little stock in electric blender and liquidise. Pour out into a bowl.
5. Add remaining stock and stir in lemon juice and yoghurt. Season to taste with salt and pepper.
6. Chill well. Serve with hot toast.

UNCOOKED SOUPS

Many vegetables make delicious hot or cold soup even though they have not been cooked. If you can get organically grown vegetables, so much the better.
You need an electric liquidiser.

Artichoke
450 g/1 lb Jerusalem artichokes
450 g/1 lb potatoes
1 stick celery
600 ml/1 pint milk, preferably goat's milk
Seasoning, try herb salt or kelp powder and paprika
1 tablespoon chopped parsley
A little butter

1. Scrub the artichokes and potatoes and grate them.
2. String the celery and grate or slice it.
3. Put vegetables in the liquidiser with milk and seasoning and blend till smooth. Eat it as soon as possible, either hot or cold.
4. **To eat cold.** Chill the soup and garnish with parsley.
5. **To eat hot.** Heat a little butter in a pan. Pour in the soup and heat but do not cook. Stir in the parsley just before serving.

Watercress
450 g/1 lb potatoes
1 small onion
1 bunch watercress
1 pint milk, preferably goat's milk
Seasoning, try herb salt or kelp powder and paprika

1. Peel onion and grate with potatoes.
2. Wash watercress thoroughly and cut it up small.
3. Put vegetables, milk and seasoning into liquidiser and blend till smooth.

Beetroot
6 raw beetroot
2 tablespoons chopped chives
2 cartons soured cream
Seasoning, try herb salt or kelp powder and paprika

1. Wash and shred beetroot.
2. Chop the chives.
3. Put beetroot, chives and seasoning in liquidiser with $1\frac{1}{2}$ cartons of soured cream. Blend until smooth.
4. Pour into soup bowls and chill.
5. Serve with remaining soured cream swirled on top and a sprinkling of chopped chives.

Elizabeth Shears,
author of 'Why Do We Eat'

CROÛTONS

Very good with soup.

Bread
Oil, butter or margarine for frying

1. Cut slices of wholemeal or white bread into very small cubes.
2. Heat a little fat in a frying pan, tip in the bread cubes and fry gently, turning them over in the fat until they are golden brown.
Serve straight away while piping hot.

FRESH HERB AND GARLIC BREAD

Use any of these herbs and then try your own ideas.

Parsley or chives or thyme

50 g/2 oz butter
A fresh crusty loaf, French bread or wholemeal or even crusty bread rolls

1. Chop the herb finely – 2 tablespoons is enough.
2. Soften the butter but do not melt it. Mix in the herb.
3. Slice loaf into thick pieces without quite cutting through the bottom crust.
4. Spread one side of each slice with herb butter.
5. Wrap loaf in greaseproof paper and foil and put it in a moderate oven, Gas 3, 325°F, 160°C, for 15 to 20 minutes until butter has melted and soaked into the bread. Eat hot with soups or cold meat and salad, or omelettes.

Garlic Bread
½ to 1 clove garlic
A little salt
1 tablespoon chopped parsley
50 g/2 oz butter

1. If you do not have a crusher put garlic on a small plate with a sprinkle of salt. Use a palette knife or an old-fashioned table knife with a flexible rounded blade and crush garlic to a cream.
2. Mix garlic and parsley into butter.
3. Now use it as described above.

GRILLED GRAPEFRUIT

For 4 people

25 g/1 oz demerara sugar
15 g/½ oz butter
2 grapefruit
4 teaspoons sherry
2 glacé cherries

1. Mix sugar and butter together.
2. Cut grapefruit in half and prepare in the usual way removing core with scissors.
3. Put a teaspoonful of sherry in each grapefruit.
4. Spread sugar mixture over each grapefruit.
5. Put them under moderately hot grill for 3 to 5 minutes.

Serve at once with half a cherry on top.

HONEY COCKTAIL

Juice of 1 large or 2 small oranges
Juice of 2 lemons
2 tablespoons honey
2 eggs, separated
Glacé cherries on cocktail sticks, to decorate

1. Put orange and lemon juice in a bowl, add honey and egg-yolks. Whisk until light and creamy in colour.
2. Whisk egg-whites in another basin until very stiff. Fold carefully with a metal spoon into egg and honey mixture.
3. Divide into glasses.
4. Decorate with glacé cherries on cocktail sticks.

Serve at once.

Mrs Emily Williams,
Moggerhanger, Bedfordshire

PASTA COCKTAIL

For 6 people

40 g/1½ oz small pasta shapes
1 crisp eating apple
2 sticks celery

Sauce
4 tablespoons mayonnaise (see page 60)
1 tablespoon tomato sauce
1 tablespoon cream
2 teaspoons lemon juice
A dash of Tabasco sauce

To serve and garnish
Lettuce leaves
Lemon twists or paprika

1. First cook the pasta in boiling, salted water until tender. Strain in colander and pour cold water through it to rinse away excess starch. This prevents pasta sticking together.
2. Now prepare the sauce by mixing together all the ingredients.
3. Slice the celery.
4. Core, quarter and chop the apple.

5. Mix cold pasta, celery and apple into the sauce.

6. Line small dishes or sundae glasses with lettuce leaves and fill with the cocktail.

7. Garnish with twists of lemon or sprinkle with paprika – or both.

**Anne Wallace,
Dunlop, Scotland**

COUNTRY LOAF

**100 g/4 oz pig's liver
1 onion
2 sticks celery
75 g/3 oz wholemeal breadcrumbs
350 g/12 oz pork sausage meat
1 clove garlic
Salt
Pepper
1 egg-yolk**

1. Cut liver into strips, put it in a pan and pour boiling water over it. Simmer for 2 or 3 minutes. Then drain off water.

2. Peel onion and cut it up coarsely.

3. Cut up celery.

4. Mince liver, onion and celery.

5. Add breadcrumbs and combine with the sausage meat.

6. Add salt, pepper and crushed garlic. (To crush garlic, see page 66.)

7. Bind with beaten egg-yolk and make sure it is thoroughly mixed.

8. Pack into a greased ½ kg/1 lb loaf tin. Cover with greaseproof paper and foil.

9. Stand loaf tin in a small roasting tin and pour in cold water to come half-way up sides of tin. This is known as a water bath.

10. Cook in a moderate oven, Gas 4, 350°F, 180°C, for 1½ hours.

Serve cold, like pâté.

Mrs Edith Griffiths

PÂTÉ OF GAMMON, PIG'S LIVER AND SAUSAGE

**225 g/8 oz raw gammon
225 g/8 oz sausage meat
1 clove garlic
½ teaspoon mixed herbs
1 teaspoon dried parsley
1 small onion
Black pepper
Salt
225 g/8 oz pig's liver
1 tablespoon brandy
125 g/4 oz streaky bacon rashers
3 bay leaves**

1. Mince gammon coarsely and put in a large bowl.

2. Add sausage meat.

3. Add crushed garlic.

4. Add herbs.

5. Add peeled and grated onion, with pepper and salt.

6. Mix together well.

7. Liquidise the liver with the brandy and add to mixture.

8. Mix it all up again really well.

9. Remove rinds from bacon and cut rashers into suitable strips to line a ½ kg/1 lb loaf tin.

10. Spoon the mixture into the tin and lay the bay leaves on top.

11. Cover with greased, greaseproof paper and a piece of foil to hold it in place.

12. Stand loaf tin in a small roasting tin and pour in enough cold water to come half-way up sides.

13. Cook in the centre of a moderate oven, Gas 4, 350°F, 180°C, for 1½ hours.

This pâté freezes well, but do not keep longer than a week or two: garlic does not freeze well and may give it an 'off' flavour.

**Mrs Hylda Rodwell,
Keighley, W. Yorkshire**

See also Courgettes, page 69

CHAPTER 2

FISH

COD COOKED IN WINE WITH TOMATOES

Coley can also be used for this dish.

450 g/1lb ripe tomatoes, or
400 g/14 oz tin
1 clove garlic
½ level teaspoon salt
1 medium-sized onion
1 tablespoon oil
15 g/½ oz margarine
1 level tablespoon plain flour
4 tablespoons dry white wine or dry cider
1 tablespoon chopped parsley
Salt and Pepper Mix *(see page 8)*
4 cod steaks

1. If using fresh tomatoes, skin and slice them. (To skin *see page 66*.)
2. Peel garlic and crush it. (*See page 66*.)
3. Peel onion and slice thinly.
4. Heat 1 tablespoon oil with the margarine in a frying pan. Add onion and garlic and fry until onion is soft but not brown.
5. Stir in flour and let it sizzle a minute without browning.
6. Stir in wine or cider, tomatoes and 1 level tablespoon of parsley. Bring to the boil stirring, and transfer to a shallow, ovenproof dish.
7. Wash the cod steaks and pat dry. Arrange them on the tomato mixture.
8. Brush with oil and sprinkle on Salt and Pepper Mix.
9. Cover dish. A piece of greased, greaseproof paper will do.
10. Bake in centre of a moderately hot oven, Gas 5, 375°F, 190°C, for 25 to 30 minutes. Remove cover, sprinkle with remaining parsley and serve hot.

FISH AND RICE SALAD

For 4 people

225 g/8 oz natural brown rice
450 g/1 lb salmon, tuna or white fish such as cod
225 g/8 oz mushrooms
3 hard-boiled eggs
1 small onion or 2 shallots
50 g/2 oz chopped parsley
Sea salt
Pepper
Pinch of garlic powder
4 tablespoons salad cream or mayonnaise *(see page 60)*

1. Put rice in 1·1 litres/2 pints cold water. Bring to the boil, cover and cook gently for 35 minutes. Then drain and allow to cool.
2. Cook fish in enough boiling, salted water just to cover it. Then let it cool.
3. Meanwhile, chop the mushrooms, the hard-boiled eggs and the onion.
4. Remove skin and bones from fish and flake it into a bowl.
5. Add rice, mushrooms, eggs, onion, parsley, salt, pepper and garlic powder. Mix well.
6. Stir in mayonnaise.

Serve with green salad or garden peas.

Ursula Cavanagh, author of 'The Wholefood Cookery Book'

HADDOCK AND PRAWN PILAFF

For 4 people

2 eggs
225–350 g/8–12 oz fresh haddock fillet
1 medium-sized onion
1 small red pepper, or 200 g/7 oz can of red peppers
25 g/1 oz butter or margarine
225 g/8 oz brown or white rice
About 600 ml/1 pint chicken stock (stock cubes will do)
1 level teaspoon ground turmeric
50 g/2 oz peeled prawns
75 g/3 oz sultanas
50 g/2 oz blanched almonds

1. Hard boil the eggs for 12 minutes. Drain and cool in plenty of cold water.

2. Put haddock in a shallow pan and just cover with water. Poach gently (that is, bring to boil and allow just to simmer) for 5 to 10 minutes.
3. Peel and finely chop onion. Remove core and seeds from the fresh pepper and chop it finely. If using tinned peppers, discard liquid and cut them into neat pieces.
4. Strain liquid from fish into a measuring jug.
5. Melt butter or margarine in a large saucepan. Fry onion and fresh red pepper gently for 5 minutes until just softened, but not brown.
6. Add the rice, stir to prevent sticking and allow to cook for 2 to 3 minutes.
7. Add the fish liquid and most of the chicken stock. Add the turmeric.
8. Bring to the boil, then lower heat. Let it simmer for 12 to 20 minutes until rice is tender and has absorbed nearly all the liquid. Brown rice takes longer to cook than white and more stock may be required.
9. Remove skin and bone from fish and flake the flesh.
10. Shell and chop hard-boiled eggs.
11. Add tinned peppers, haddock, eggs, prawns, sultanas and almonds to rice and mix gently. Cook gently for about 5 minutes until heated through.

Stir very carefully to prevent sticking and to avoid breaking up fish. Serve at once.

SMOKED HADDOCK PANCAKES

This dish could be made with other fish.

For 4 people

4 thin pancakes (*see page 76*)
225 g/8 oz smoked haddock
A little water

Sauce
25 g/1 oz butter
25 g/1 oz wholewheat flour
300 ml/½ pint warm milk
Pepper
2 tablespoons cream or top of the milk
1 tablespoon finely grated cheese

1. Prepare pancakes and keep them warm.
2. Wash the fish well and poach it gently in a little water. Then remove skin and break it into small flakes. Keep it warm.
3. **For the sauce:** melt butter in a pan, add flour and let it sizzle a minute. Add warm milk gradually and bring to the boil.
4. Let it simmer for 2 or 3 minutes then stir in cream and pepper to taste.
5. Pour half of this sauce into a jug to use later.
6. Mix fish into rest of sauce and fill the 4 pancakes.
7. Roll up the pancakes and lay them in a warmed ovenproof dish.
8. Pour remaining sauce over the pancakes, sprinkle on the cheese and put dish under a hot grill for 2 or 3 minutes to colour the top.

STUFFED HERRINGS

For 4 people

4 herrings
Sea salt
Pepper
225 g/8 oz cooking apples
1 dessertspoon grated onion
50 g/2 oz chopped parsley
1 teaspoon barbados sugar
50 g/2 oz fresh wholewheat breadcrumbs
25 g/1 oz melted butter

1. Scale, gut, wash and trim heads and tails from fish. Cut each one open to backbone from belly to tail. Press out flat and remove backbone from tail to head.
2. Sprinkle with salt and pepper.
3. Peel and grate the apples.
4. Mix apple, onion, parsley and

sugar with 40 g/1½ oz of the breadcrumbs. Season well.
5. Spread this stuffing over herrings and roll them up from head to tail.
6. Grease an ovenproof dish and lay the rolled herrings in it.
7. Sprinkle with rest of breadcrumbs and pour over melted butter.
8. Bake in a moderately hot oven, Gas 5, 375°F, 190°C, for 30 to 35 minutes. Allow the extra 5 minutes if herrings are large.

Serve hot with peas or beans and mashed potatoes.
Serve cold with sliced tomatoes or tomato salad (see page 63).

Ursula Cavanagh, author of 'The Wholefood Cookery Book'

MACKEREL BAKED WITH APPLES AND CIDER

3 small or medium-sized mackerel
150 ml/¼ pint dry cider
Salt and pepper
225 g/8 oz cooking apples
1 level tablespoon chopped parsley

1. Clean the mackerel thoroughly and wipe them.
2. Make 3 diagonal cuts in the flesh on each side.
3. Arrange fish in a shallow ovenproof dish. Pour over the cider and add a shake of salt and pepper.
4. Leave to soak for 3 hours in the cider marinade. Turn the fish over once.
5. Preheat oven to moderately hot Gas 4, 350°F, 180°C.
6. Peel, quarter and core apples. Cut the quarters into small pieces.
7. Sprinkle apple pieces round the fish, pushing them down into the cider. Cover dish.
8. Put dish on centre shelf of oven and cook for 15 minutes.
9. Spoon the juices over fish and apple and return to oven for a

further 10 to 15 minutes.
10. Sprinkle with parsley.

COLD SPICED MACKEREL

For 6 people

6 small mackerel
Salt and pepper
150 ml/¼ pint malt vinegar
150 ml/¼ pint water
½ level teaspoon pickling spice
2 bay leaves
1 medium-sized onion

The fishmonger might clean and fillet the mackerel for you, in which case start at paragraph 3.

1. Trim tail and fins from the mackerel with a pair of scissors. Cut off head. Cut along the belly. Clean out inside.
2. Rinse and pat dry on soft kitchen paper. Open out flat on a board, skin-side down. Remove backbone.
3. Sprinkle fish with a little salt and pepper.
4. Roll up fish from tail to head and place them close together in a fairly deep, ovenproof dish.
5. Pour over malt vinegar and water, then sprinkle with pickling spice and add bay leaves. Peel and slice onion and spread over fish.
6. Cover dish with a lid or greaseproof paper and foil and put in a cool oven, Gas 1, 275°F, 140°C, for 1½ hours.
7. Remove from oven and allow to cool in the liquid.

Serve with boiled potatoes or brown bread and butter.

AUNT NELLIE'S MUSTARD SAUCE

To serve with cold meats or with oily fish such as mackerel.

1 egg
1 level tablespoon dry mustard, or more if you like more 'bite'

1 level tablespoon sugar
4 tablespoons milk
4 tablespoons malt vinegar

1. Beat egg well in a basin.
2. Add mustard and sugar and mix well.
3. Add milk and vinegar. Mix all together.
4. Stand basin over a saucepan of simmering water. Do not let water touch basin. A double saucepan can be used instead.
5. Stir sauce until it thickens.

May be kept in a covered jar in the fridge.

Miss Joan Parkinson,
Ovenden, Nr. Halifax

PILCHARD CURRY

Enough for 2 or 3 people, but easy to make in smaller quantities.

2 medium-sized onions
1 tablespoon oil or 15 g/½ oz butter
1 tablespoon curry powder
1 green pepper
1 teaspoon curry sauce (optional)
Pinch of salt
A large can, about 450 g/1 lb, pilchards in tomato sauce
1 tablespoon water, or wine if you have it

1. Peel and chop onions.
2. Heat oil or butter in a frying pan and fry onions for a minute or two.
3. Sprinkle curry powder over the onion and continue frying gently till onion is soft.
4. Remove core and seeds from the green pepper, chop up the flesh and add it to the pan.
5. Stir in the curry sauce and a small pinch of salt.
6. Tip the pilchards out of the can on top of the onion mixture.
7. Rinse out the can with a tablespoon of water or wine and pour over the fish. Cover pan and let the curry simmer until it is heated right through.

Serve with brown rice or white rice boiled with a pinch of turmeric.

You can adapt this dish to include what you have available. Try 2 or 3 sticks celery instead of green pepper. Or add 2 tablespoons sultanas with the green pepper, or 2 tablespoons desiccated coconut or a little finely chopped crystallised ginger. Alternatively, sultanas, coconut and crystallised ginger may be served separately in little dishes.

Ann Bridger,
Wallingford, Berkshire

PILCHARD PIZZA

Sconebase
100 g/4 oz self-raising flour
Pinch of salt
40 g/1½ oz margarine
50 g/2 oz grated cheese
2 to 3 tablespoons milk

Filling
1 small onion
50 g/2 oz mushrooms
15 g/½ oz butter or margarine
A 210 g/7½ oz can of pilchards in tomato sauce
50 g/2 oz grated cheese
1 skinned tomato (see page 66)

1. Sift flour and salt together.
2. Rub in margarine.
3. Mix in 50 g/2 oz of the grated cheese.
4. Add sufficient milk to make a soft but not sticky dough.
5. Roll out lightly, on a floured board, to fit a pie-plate.
6. **For the filling:** peel and finely chop the onion.
7. Chop mushrooms.
8. Melt 15 g/½ oz butter or margarine and fry onions for 2 or 3 minutes.
9. Add mushrooms and fry 2 or 3 minutes more.
10. Spread this mixture lightly over the scone base.
11. Then arrange pilchards nicely on top and pour sauce from tin over top.
12. Sprinkle with grated cheese.
13. Cut tomato into slices and put them on top.

14. Bake in a moderately hot oven, Gas 5, 375°F, 190°C, for 20 to 25 minutes.

**Mrs A. E. Phillips,
Selsey, W. Sussex**

PILCHARD SNACK

For 4 people

**4 standard eggs
225 g/8 oz tomatoes
A 225 g/8 oz can pilchards in tomato sauce
Salt and pepper
75 g/3 oz Cheddar cheese, grated
Sprigs of watercress, to garnish**

1. Hard boil eggs for 10 minutes; crack and leave to cool in cold water. Shell and cut in halves, lengthwise.
2. Meanwhile, skin tomatoes and cut into thin slices. (To skin *see page 66*.)
3. Carefully lift egg-yolks out of whites with a teaspoon. Put them in a basin and mash with a fork.
4. Add contents of can of pilchards and mix well. Taste and season with salt and pepper.
5. Pile mixture into egg-whites and arrange on an oven-proof plate.
6. Place tomato slices, overlapping, around edge of plate. Sprinkle eggs and tomatoes with grated cheese.
7. Put under a moderately hot grill until cheese is bubbling and eggs are hot.

Garnish with sprigs of watercress.

CREAMED PRAWNS

For 4 people

**100 g/4 oz mushrooms
50 g/2 oz butter
40 g/1½ oz wholewheat flour
Sea salt
Pepper
150 ml/¼ pint milk
150 ml/¼ pint single cream
225 g/8 oz cooked prawns
3 teaspoons sherry
50 g/2 oz chopped parsley**

1. Slice mushrooms and fry gently in the butter.
2. Stir in flour, salt and pepper.
3. Add the milk and cream, stirring all the time over low heat until thick and creamy.
4. Add prawns and sherry and reheat.
5. Sprinkle with parsley and serve.

**Ursula Cavanagh,
author of 'The Wholefood Cookery Book'**

PRAWN PILAFF

For 2 to 3 people
If you have a shallow pan suitable for frying and for the table, use it for this dish. Easy to make in an electric frying pan.

**1 onion
1 green pepper
350 g/12 oz fresh tomatoes
300 ml/½ pint water
150–175 g/5–6 oz long grain brown or white rice
Pinch of salt
50 g/2 oz butter
100 g/4 oz peeled prawns
Black pepper
A little sugar**

1. Peel and cut up onion.
2. Remove core and seeds from pepper and cut up flesh.
3. Skin tomatoes (to skin *see page 66*).
4. Cut up half the tomatoes roughly. Cut the rest into thick slices.
5. Bring ½ pint water to boil in a saucepan, add salt and shower in the rice. Bring to the boil. Turn heat very low and cover pan. Allow to cook very gently: brown rice for about 25 minutes, white for about 12 minutes.
6. Meanwhile, using the oven-to-table pan, melt butter, add onion and green pepper and fry gently for 2 to 3 minutes until softening but not brown.
7. Add roughly chopped tomatoes and prawns. Season lightly with

salt and black pepper. Cover and cook gently for 2 to 3 minutes.
8. Drain any liquid from the rice. Tip rice into the prawn mixture, forking it over gently to mix.
9. Arrange tomato slices in a circle on top and sprinkle them with a few grains of sugar and a little more black pepper. Cover and reheat gently (4 to 5 minutes should be enough).

Serve at once with green peas. Frozen peas may be added, for decoration, at same time as prawns or later with tomatoes.

SARDINE POTATO PIE

225 g/8 oz mashed potatoes
225 g/8 oz fresh tomatoes, or 1 small can
2 small onions
Large can of sardines
15 g/¼ oz margarine
2 tablespoons chopped parsley
50 g/2 oz grated cheese
Pepper and salt

1. Prepare the mashed potatoes.
2. Skin and slice the tomatoes. (To skin see page 66.) If using tinned tomatoes, drain off excess liquid into a cup and cut them up roughly.
3. Peel and grate onions.
4. Break up sardines into smaller pieces.
5. Grease a small pie dish with a little of the margarine.
6. Put a layer of tomato in bottom of dish, then a layer of sardine, a little onion, parsley, grated cheese and a sprinkling of salt and pepper.
7. Continue with similar layers till ingredients are used.
8. Spread mashed potatoes on top, mark with a fork and dot with margarine.
9. Bake in a moderately hot oven, Gas 6, 400°F, 200°C, for 30 minutes.

Mrs Reenie Lynn,
Skegness, Lincolnshire

TROUT STUFFED WITH MUSHROOMS

For 4 people

4 fresh river trout
225 g/8 oz mushrooms
1 medium-sized onion
40 g/1½ oz butter
2 tablespoons chopped parsley
Salt and pepper
2 lemons
Extra parsley, to garnish

1. Heat the oven to moderate Gas 4, 350°F, 180°C.
2. Cut along the belly of the fish and remove intestines (or ask the fishmonger to do this for you). Wash fish thoroughly.
3. Clean mushrooms and chop finely.
4. Peel onion and chop finely.
5. Melt butter in a frying pan, add onion. Fry until soft but not brown, about 3 minutes.
6. Add mushrooms and cook for 2 minutes longer.
7. Stir in chopped parsley and seasoning.
8. Strain contents of pan through a sieve and save liquid for later.
9. Divide mushroom mixture into 4 and stuff fish.
10. Place fish on individual pieces of foil lined with greased, greaseproof paper.
11. Mix mushroom liquid and juice of 1 lemon and pour it over the fish. Add seasoning to taste.
12. Close the foil securely round the fish and put the packages into a shallow roasting tin.
13. Bake in a moderate oven Gas 4, 350°F, 180°C, for 25 to 30 minutes.
14. When cooked, unwrap and serve on a large dish, garnished with lemon wedges and parsley sprigs.

COLD TROUT WITH CUCUMBER SAUCE

For 4 people

4 Rainbow trout
1 lemon

21

1 bay leaf
Sprig of parsley, sprig of fresh
thyme and a few peppercorns
Slice of onion and of carrot

Sauce
½ small cucumber
Salt and pepper
300 ml/5 fluid oz natural yoghurt

1. Clean out the trout, trim the
tails but leave the heads on. Wash
well.
2. Cut a wedge from the lemon and
place it with the bay leaf, parsley,
thyme, peppercorns, onion and
carrot in a shallow pan. Add water
to a depth of 4 cm/1½ inches.
3. Bring to the boil, cover and
simmer for 2 to 3 minutes.
4. Add trout, cover and poach
gently for 5 minutes. Remove pan
from heat and leave trout to cool in
the stock.

To make the sauce
5. Peel and finely dice the
cucumber.
6. Cover with a plate and leave to
stand for 15 to 20 minutes.
7. Drain off excess water.
8. Stir cucumber into the yoghurt
and add seasoning to taste.

To serve the dish
9. When trout is quite cold, remove
it from liquor, drain and arrange
on a serving dish.
10. Cut rest of lemon into wedges
and use to garnish the fish.
11. Serve sauce separately.

MERLAN PUDDING

Merlan or merling is another name
for whiting.

For 2 people

You need a 600 ml/1 pint pudding
basin or plain mould.

100 g/4 oz cooked whiting
50 g/2 oz fresh white breadcrumbs
Salt and pepper
1 teaspoon grated lemon rind
150 ml/¼ pint milk
50 g/2 oz butter
1 beaten egg
1 teaspoon chopped parsley

Parsley sauce *(see below)*

1. Flake the fish and put it in a
bowl.
2. Mix in the breadcrumbs, salt,
pepper and lemon rind.
3. Heat milk in a small pan with
40 g/1½ oz of the butter, but do not
let it boil. Pour over fish mixture.
4. Add beaten egg and mix well.
5. Grease the pudding basin or
mould with the last 10 g/½ oz
butter. Sprinkle parsley in bottom
of basin.
6. Spoon mixture into the basin.
Cover with a piece of greased,
greaseproof paper pleated across
middle. Put over this, loosely, a
sheet of foil and press it firmly
under rim of basin.
7. Steam pudding for 45 minutes to
1 hour. If you do not have a
steamer, stand basin on a trivet or
upturned saucer in a saucepan.
Pour in enough boiling water to
come halfway up sides of basin.
Keep water on the boil and
replenish with more boiling water
if necessary.
8. Turn pudding out on to a
warmed dish and serve with
parsley sauce.

Parsley Sauce
25 g/1 oz butter
25 g/1 oz flour
½ teaspoon Salt and Pepper Mix
(see page 8)
300 ml/½ pint milk
1 teaspoon lemon juice
A nut of butter
2 tablespoons chopped fresh
parsley

1. Melt butter in saucepan, stir in
flour and cook 1 minute.
2. Add salt and pepper and milk.
Stir until boiling and cook 1 to 2
minutes.
3. Remove from heat, beat in lemon
juice and a nut of butter. Stir in
the parsley.

*[See also Chapter 7 for Smoked
Haddock and Cottage Cheese Flan,
Salmon and Cucumber Flan, Tuna
Plait]*

CHAPTER 3

POULTRY, GAME AND RABBIT

TO PLUCK POULTRY AND GAME

Poultry

This is best done as soon after killing as possible, because the feathers are more easy to pull before the flesh stiffens. There is no quick way: the feathers must be pulled out a few at a time until the job is done. You can plunge the bird into hot (not boiling) water for about one minute and then pluck it at once. But do not leave it long in the water as the skin becomes tender and may be torn as the feathers are pulled. Sometimes, fine hairs remain and these can be removed by singeing. A lighted taper does the job efficiently. Move it quickly over the body so as not to scorch the bird.

Game

Game, such as pheasant and grouse, has tender skin that is easily torn. Be particularly careful over the breast.

TO CLEAN AND TRUSS POULTRY OR GAME BIRDS

1. To remove leg sinews, make a circular incision about 2·5 cm/ 1 inch below the hock joint, taking care not to cut into the sinews. Break the legs and pull off the feet (a loop of strong twine may help here).
2. Trim the extreme portions of the wings.
3. Place the bird on the table breast down and head away from you. With the finger and thumb take up the skin between the shoulders, cut a strip of skin about 12 mm/½ inch wide from that point to half-way up the neck. Sever the neck-bone at the shoulder and the skin half-way up the neck.
4. Remove the crop and wind-pipe.
5. Put your finger in the opening and by circular movement loosen the lungs and other organs.
6. Place the bird neck down, grasp the tail in one hand. Then take the knife and make an incision midway between the tail and the vent. Cut around the vent. Place the bird back down and tail towards you, feel inside and remove the fat around the abdomen. Then feel for the gizzard – it will be something firm to grasp – and draw gently. All the internal organs will come out.
7. Save the neck, gizzard, liver and heart for stock. These should be wrapped in greaseproof paper. The gizzard should be split, emptied and the inner tough skin peeled off. Take care not to break the gall bladder, a tiny greenish bag, in removing the liver.
8. Clean the bird thoroughly with a damp cloth or kitchen paper.
9. **To tie up.** Fold the flap of skin over the back and fold the wings back over this.
10. Take a trussing needle threaded with strong white string about 26 cm/18 inches long. With back downwards pull the legs back towards the head and press down firmly. Pass the needle through the body where the legs join the body.
11. Then turn the bird over and pass the needle through the joint of one wing, across the back of the bird and through the other wing. Now tie the two strings and cut off.
12. With the back downwards again, and keeping the tail towards you, pass the needle and thread through the loose skin underneath and near the tip of the breast bone. Leave the string above the legs. Turn the bird on its breast. The two ends of string are then brought round the legs, crossed and tied tightly round the tail. The trussing complete, strings should not be cut to stuff the bird. All stuffings can be put in at the neck end.

CHICKEN AND ALMONDS

1 boiling fowl, or roasting chicken, jointed
600 ml/1 pint water
4 tablespoons oil
2 small onions
2 small carrots
2 bay leaves
2 sprigs of thyme
3 or 4 peppercorns
Pinch of salt
Slice of lemon including peel
100 g/4 oz blanched almonds
3 sticks celery
100 g/4 oz mushrooms
1 good clove of garlic
Small piece of fresh ginger
1 dessertspoon soy sauce
1 dessertspoon dry sherry
1 dessertspoon cornflour
Salt
Black pepper
Spring onions and finely chopped parsley or fresh coriander, to garnish

1. Put giblets, neck and wing tips in a pan with water. Cover and simmer gently to make stock.
2. Heat 2 tablespoons oil in a heavy pan and brown the chicken joints all over.
3. Add 1 peeled onion, 1 scrubbed carrot cut into quarters, a bay leaf, a sprig of thyme, peppercorns, salt and slice of lemon and pour in a cupful of the stock. Put on a well-fitting lid.
4. Bring slowly to the boil and let the chicken steam in the stock till tender. If it is a boiling fowl it may take an hour, depending on its age. If it is a young roasting chicken, 30 to 40 minutes may be enough.
5. Take joints out of pan and remove the flesh.
6. Return the bones to the pan of stock, add fresh onion and carrot and herbs. Continue cooking until stock is rich.
7. Meanwhile, prepare the other ingredients. Cut almonds in slices. Slice the celery. Cut mushrooms in half or quarters. Crush the garlic. Chop the ginger finely.
8. Heat 2 tablespoons oil in pan and fry almonds until golden brown. Lift them out of the fat on to a paper bag to drain.
9. Toss celery and mushrooms, garlic and ginger in the fat for a minute or two.
10. Add soy sauce and sherry. Then add chicken flesh and one strained cupful of the chicken stock. Cook over moderate heat for 5 minutes.
11. Put cornflour in a cup and blend it with a little chicken stock. Add this to the chicken and stir as it thickens. Add almonds. Season with a little more salt if necessary, and some freshly-milled black pepper.
12. Serve at once. Do not overcook at this stage.

Garnish with spring onions and finely-chopped parsley or fresh coriander.
Serve with Indian Fried Rice (see page 74).

**Betty Yeatman,
Adelaide, South Australia**

CHICKEN FAVOURITE

For 4 people

A 1½ kg/3½ lb chicken with giblets

Stuffing
25 g/1 oz butter
50 g/2 oz chopped onion
50 g/2 oz mushroom stalks
Chicken liver and heart
3 tablespoons wholemeal or white breadcrumbs
Pinch of tarragon
Salt and pepper
1 beaten egg

To finish
25 g/1 oz butter
1 tablespoon oil
½ teaspoon salt
50 g/2 oz breadcrumbs, soft not dried
Pinch of tarragon

1. Chicken is divided into 4 even-sized pieces as follows. Cut legs from body including body-flesh behind breast. Cut breast away from carcass, with the wing.
2. Remove outer, bony wing joint.
3. With a pointed, sharp knife remove bones from legs.
4. Wipe the four pieces of chicken and cut a pocket in each of the breasts.
5. **To make the stuffing**: melt butter in a frying pan.
6. Add onion and let it fry gently.
7. Chop mushroom stalks and toss them in with onion.
8. Finely chop the chicken liver and heart. Add these to pan and toss all together over moderate heat for 3 or 4 minutes.
9. Put breadcrumbs in a bowl with tarragon, salt and pepper.
10. Add contents of pan and half of the beaten egg.
11. Mix well. Then stuff the cavities in the chicken pieces and secure with poultry pins or small skewers.
12. **To finish and cook the chicken**: melt 25 g/1 oz butter and beat it into the remaining egg with the oil and salt.
13. Mix breadcrumbs and tarragon together on a sheet of paper.
14. Dip stuffed chicken pieces into egg-mixture, and pat them into the crumbs to coat well.
15. Lay crumbed chicken pieces on a baking tray.
16. Bake in a moderately hot oven, Gas 5, 375°F, 190°C, for about 1 hour.

Very good served with sweetcorn and broccoli. (Try the next recipe to use up the chicken.)

CHICKEN RICE

A recipe to use chicken remaining from previous recipe.

1. First cook the chicken carcass, wing bones and remaining giblets in a large pan with 2 litres/2½ pints water, salt, bay leaf, and a few peppercorns. Cover pan, bring slowly to the boil and simmer for 1 hour or more.
2. Remove meat from bones.
3. Strain the stock.
4. Now proceed with the dish.

1 tablespoon oil
25 g/1 oz butter
1 chopped onion
175 g/6 oz brown rice
1 chopped green pepper
2 skinned and chopped tomatoes
(to skin see page 66)
1 pint chicken stock
1 teaspoon turmeric
Salt and pepper
Chicken pieces
Chopped parsley

1. Heat oil and butter in a frying pan with lid.
2. Fry onion lightly. When soft, but not brown, add rice and fry for a minute.
3. Add green pepper, tomatoes, stock, turmeric, salt and pepper.
4. Cover pan and cook gently till rice is almost tender – about 20 minutes.
5. Fork in chicken and cook till rice is done and chicken is hot.
6. Sprinkle liberally with chopped parsley just before serving.

Anne Wallace,
Dunlop, Scotland

CHICKEN WITH TOMATO RICE

For 4 people

2 medium-sized onions
25 g/1 oz butter
225 g/8 oz long-grain rice
A 400 g/14 oz can of tomatoes
600 ml/1 pint chicken stock (a stock cube will do)
2 teaspoons Worcestershire sauce
1½ level teaspoons Salt and Pepper Mix (see page 8)
4 chicken joints
2 teaspoons oil
225 g/8 oz packet of frozen mixed vegetables
Watercress, for garnish

1. Peel and slice onions.
2. Melt butter and fry onions to soften but not brown.
3. Add rice, stir it in and cook for 1 or 2 minutes to absorb fat.
4. Add tomatoes, stock, Worcestershire sauce, salt and pepper. Bring to the boil and pour into a large shallow casserole.
5. Place a rack over casserole – rack from grill pan, or a cooling wire will do.
6. Brush chicken joints with oil, place them on rack, sprinkle with salt and pepper.
7. Put into a moderately hot oven, Gas 6, 400°F, 200°C, and cook for 40 minutes.
8. Remove from oven and stir frozen vegetables into the rice. Replace rack on top.
9. Return to oven and cook 15 minutes more.
10. Arrange rice and chicken on a warmed dish and garnish with watercress.

CHICKEN WITH TOMATOES AND YOGHURT

For 4 people

1 large onion
25 g/1 oz plain flour
1 level teaspoon salt
1 level teaspoon paprika
4 chicken joints
25 g/1 oz margarine
A 400 g/14 oz can of peeled tomatoes
150 ml/¼ pint water
1 level teaspoon sugar
150 g/5 fluid oz natural yoghurt
1 tablespoon chopped parsley

1. Peel and thinly slice onion.
2. Mix flour, salt and paprika together.
3. Trim chicken joints and coat in seasoned flour.
4. Melt margarine in a large frying pan. Fry chicken joints until lightly browned, then lift out into a 2 litre/3½ pint shallow casserole.
5. Fry onion for 2 minutes in remaining fat.
6. Stir any remaining flour into pan. Add tomatoes, water and sugar. Bring to boil, stirring, and pour over chicken.
7. Cover and cook on centre shelf of moderately hot oven, Gas 5, 375°F, 190°C, for 1 hour until chicken is tender.
8. Just before serving, spoon yoghurt over chicken joints and sprinkle with chopped parsley.

PARSLEY AND LEMON STUFFING

Very good with chicken.

50 g/2 oz butter
Finely-grated rind and juice of one lemon
75 g/3 oz fresh brown or white breadcrumbs
4 tablespoons finely-chopped parsley
Pinch of thyme or marjoram
Salt and freshly milled pepper

1. Melt butter in a saucepan over a low heat and add lemon juice.
2. Put all the other ingredients into a basin and mix well.
3. Stir in lemon juice and melted butter until it is well incorporated and the stuffing is moist.
4. Spoon into breast or body of bird.

CHICKEN SALAD

To cook the chicken
1 chicken
1 small onion
A piece of carrot
A piece of celery
1 small bay leaf
4 peppercorns
A little salt

For the salad
1 green pepper
3 sticks celery
1 eating apple
Lettuce

The dressing
4 juniper berries

1 large teaspoon curry powder
¼ teaspoon tarragon
¼ teaspoon chervil
2 teaspoons lemon juice
3 large tablespoons mayonnaise
(see page 60)

1. Put the chicken, with its giblets inside, into a close-fitting pan. Put in the vegetables, bay leaf and peppercorns and salt. Add water just to cover.
2. Bring it to the boil, put on lid and let it poach – i.e., simmer gently – for 45 minutes to 1 hour, until it is cooked.
3. Take out chicken, remove meat and dice it quite small. Let it cool.
4. **To prepare dressing and salad:** crush the juniper berries. Mix them with curry powder, tarragon, chervil and lemon juice. Leave this for 5 minutes.
5. Remove core and seeds from green pepper and cut it up small.
6. Slice celery.
7. Quarter and core the apple, but do not peel it. Cut it up small.
8. Add curry and herbs mixture to the mayonnaise and mix well.
9. Mix together chicken, green pepper, celery, apple and dressing.
10. Lay lettuce leaves on a serving dish and spoon the chicken mixture on to them.

Don't forget to return chicken carcass to pan, with extra water if necessary, and simmer for another hour to make good chicken stock. Strain and refrigerate or freeze.

**Mrs M. Lucie-Smith,
London S.W.3**

CREAMED CHICKEN WITH MUSHROOMS AND BUTTER BEANS

For 4 people

175 g/6 oz butter beans
Water
1 small onion
2 tablespoons cooking oil
100 g/4 oz small white mushrooms
½ small green pepper
½ small red pepper
175–225 g/6–8 oz cooked chicken flesh
1 glass sherry
2–3 tablespoons double cream
Seasoning
Finely-chopped parsley, to garnish

White Sauce
25 g/1 oz butter
25 g/1 oz flour
300 ml/½ pint milk
Seasoning

1. Soak butter beans overnight in cold water.
2. Next day, put them with their water in a saucepan, adding enough extra water to cover them well. Bring to the boil and boil hard for at least 30 minutes. Reduce heat and cook gently until tender, about 2 hours in all. Add more water if necessary.
3. Peel and finely chop the onion.
4. Heat the oil and sauté the onions – i.e., stand the pan over moderate heat and toss the onions in the hot oil until soft but not brown.
5. Wipe mushrooms with a damp cloth and slice them.
6. Remove core and seeds from green and red peppers and chop flesh finely.
7. Add mushrooms and peppers to onion and cook for 2 minutes.
8. Cut chicken flesh into bite-sized pieces and add these to pan.
9. Add sherry, cream and seasoning. Bring to the boil, stirring. Then simmer gently for 3 minutes.
10. Drain cooked butter beans well and remove any loose outer skins. Add beans to the chicken mixture.
11. **To make the white sauce:** melt butter in a small pan. Add flour and stir over low heat for 1 minute. Remove from heat and gradually stir in the milk. Bring to the boil and cook for 2 or 3 minutes, stirring all the time. Season to taste.
12. Mix white sauce into chicken

mixture. Re-heat and adjust seasoning.
13. Turn it out of pan into a warmed serving dish and sprinkle with finely-chopped parsley.
Serve with a green vegetable.
Freezes well.

**Jean Welshman,
Malton, E. Yorkshire**

MARROW RINGS STUFFED WITH CHICKEN AND MUSHROOMS

1 marrow
150 ml/¼ pint water
100 g/4 oz cooked chicken
1 small onion
Half a green pepper
1 tablespoon cooking oil
100 g/4 oz mushrooms
2 tomatoes
100 g/4 oz sweetcorn (optional)
100 g/4 oz peas (optional)
300 ml/½ pint chicken stock (a stock cube will do)
1 dessertspoon cornflour
Pepper and salt
15 g/½ oz butter or margarine
Small sprigs of parsley

1. Cut marrow into thick rings. Peel and remove seeds.
2. Put rings into a casserole dish, add water, cover dish.
3. Put casserole into a moderate oven, Gas 4, 350°F, 180°C, and cook marrow while you prepare the filling.
4. Cut up the chicken into small pieces.
5. Peel onion and chop finely.
6. Slice green pepper, discarding core and seeds.
7. Heat oil in a large pan, fry onion and pepper gently till soft but not brown.
8. Add chicken and chopped mushrooms and toss together over low heat for 3 or 4 minutes.
9. Add chopped tomatoes (but save a few slices for decoration). Add sweetcorn and peas. Stir together

for 3 or 4 minutes.
10. Mix cornflour with a tablespoon of the stock. Add to the rest of the stock. Pour this into chicken mixture. Add salt and pepper if necessary.
11. Stir over low heat until it thickens slightly.
12. Take casserole from oven and drain off any liquid (keep it for making soup). Fill each marrow ring with chicken mixture. Lay a slice of tomato on each and dot with butter or margarine.
13. Cover casserole again and return it to the oven to cook for 20 minutes more.
14. Put a little sprig of parsley on each portion just before serving.

**Mrs Phyllis E. Roche,
Normanton, W. Yorkshire**

CHICKEN OR TURKEY MOULD

For 4 people

125 g/4 oz natural brown rice
300 ml/½ pint milk
300 ml/½ pint chicken stock
225 g/8 oz cold, cooked chicken or turkey
1 rasher cooked bacon
225 g/8 oz mushrooms
1 teaspoon chopped parsley
Sea salt
Pepper
2 tomatoes, to garnish

1. Cook rice in milk and stock for 25 to 35 minutes or until all the liquid is absorbed. Do not rinse rice after cooking.
2. Meanwhile, chop up the chicken and bacon and slice the mushrooms. Mix them into the rice.
3. Stir in parsley and seasoning and pour into a wetted 600 ml/ 1 pint pudding basin. Leave to set.
4. Turn out on to a plate and garnish with slices of tomato.

**Ursula Cavanagh,
author of 'The Wholefood Cookery Book'**

DEVILLED TURKEY

For 6 people, but easy to make in smaller or larger quantities.

900 g/2 lb cold, cooked turkey
1 green pepper
125 g/4 oz mushrooms
1 clove of garlic, or a pinch of garlic powder
25 g/1 oz butter
1 tablespoon vegetable oil
4 tablespoons dry white wine
2 tablespoons sauce diable or chilli sauce
300 ml/½ pint turkey stock
Sea salt
Pepper
1 tablespoon wholewheat flour
150 ml/5 fluid oz single cream

1. Dice the turkey and put it in a casserole.
2. Core, seed and slice green pepper.
3. Slice mushrooms.
4. Crush the garlic (see page 66)
5. Heat butter and oil in a pan and sauté – that is, lightly fry for a few minutes – the green pepper, mushrooms and garlic.
6. Stir in wine, sauce diable, garlic powder, if used, and all but 2 tablespoons of the stock. Add salt and pepper. Bring to the boil and pour over turkey pieces.
7. Cover casserole and cook in a moderately hot oven, Gas 5, 375°F, 190°C, for 1 hour.
8. Mix flour to a smooth paste with remaining cold stock and stir into casserole.
9. Add cream, check seasoning and return to oven for a further 10 minutes.

Serve with natural brown rice.

Ursula Cavanagh,
author of 'The Wholefood Cookery Book'

CHOOSING A DUCK

If buying fresh duck the best time of the year is June and early July. Choose a bird with a plump breast. Even a plump duck has a shallow breast and will not feed as many people as a chicken of the same weight. A 1·5 kg/3½ lb bird will feed 4 people adequately. Traditionally, young birds are roasted with sage and onion stuffing, and served with apple sauce, new potatoes and green peas.
Allow 15 minutes for each 450 g/1 lb and 15 minutes over. Remember to weigh the stuffed bird and to calculate cooking time on stuffed weight.

ROAST DUCK WITH ORANGE SAUCE

For 4 people

A 1·3–1·5 kg/3–3½ lb duck
Rind of 1 orange
25 g/1 oz butter
150 ml/¼ pint stock

1. Put the thinly-pared rind of the orange with 15 g/½ oz of the butter inside the duck.
2. Spread remaining butter over the breast.
3. Put into a hot oven, Gas 7, 425°F, 220°C, and immediately reduce heat to moderate, Gas 4, 350°F, 180°C. Roast the duck for 1 hour, basting several times.

Orange Sauce

2 oranges
50 g/2 oz butter
35 g/1¼ oz cornflour
400 ml/¾ pint brown stock (half a beef stock cube will do)
Salt and Pepper Mix (see page 8)
2 tablespoons sherry

1. Finely grate the zest from one of the oranges. Squeeze the juice from both and add the zest to the juice.
2. Melt butter in a small pan. Blend in cornflour and let it sizzle a little.
3. Remove from heat and stir in the stock. Bring to the boil, stirring, and let it boil for one minute.

Season with Salt and Pepper Mix.
4. Stir in orange juice with rind
and the sherry.

Heat through but do not boil.

See also Orange Stuffing, page 48

APPLE AND PRUNE STUFFING

For goose or duck or, as a change,
for pork.

20 prunes, soaked overnight
1 stick celery
Liver of the bird
350 g/12 oz peeled and sliced
apple, or left-over apple sauce
50 g/2 oz cooked brown rice
1 dessertspoon finely-chopped
parsley
Grated rind and juice of ½ lemon
A grating of nutmeg
Salt and pepper
Pinch of brown sugar
1 lightly-beaten egg

1. Stew prunes gently till tender
and let them cool.
2. Meanwhile, slice the celery
finely.
3. Chop up the liver.
4. Cut prunes in halves and
remove stones.
5. Mix prunes, apple and rice.
6. Add celery and liver.
7. Blend in parsley, lemon rind and
juice.
8. Season with nutmeg, salt,
pepper and brown sugar.
Note: sugar is not necessary if
using apple sauce.
9. Bind together with egg.

Sybil Norcott,
Irlam, Nr. Manchester

CHOOSING A GUINEA FOWL

The average weight of a guinea
fowl dressed for the table is
1·3–1·5 kg/3–3½ lb. It should look
firm in texture with a plump
breast. One bird is usually enough
for 4 people.

Its taste is something between
pheasant and chicken. However, it
is eaten fresh like chicken and not
hung to become 'gamey' like
pheasant. The meat is slightly
darker than chicken.

ROAST GUINEA FOWL

Choose a good-quality roasting
fowl. If the bird is frozen, thaw out
in refrigerator.
Stuff with veal forcemeat.

Veal Forcemeat
40 g/1½ oz butter
100 g/4 oz wholemeal or white
breadcrumbs
2 teaspoons chopped parsley
1 teaspoon mixed herbs, dried or
fresh
Grated rind of ½ lemon
Salt, pepper and a few grains of
cayenne pepper
1 beaten egg
A little milk if necessary
2–3 rashers of fat bacon, or 2 good
tablespoons lard or dripping, to
prepare bird for oven

1. Put butter to soften in a warm
place and then cream it.
2. Mix together breadcrumbs,
parsley, mixed herbs, lemon rind
and seasoning.
3. Mix in the creamed butter,
beaten egg and enough milk to
make a crumbly mixture that just
holds together. Milk may not be
required.

**To stuff and cook the guinea
fowl**
1. Stuff the forcemeat into the neck
or body cavity of the bird and tie it
up with skewers and string.
2. Weigh the stuffed bird and
calculate cooking time by allowing
20 minutes to the 450 g/1 lb and 20
minutes over.
3. Put it in a roasting tin and cover
well with fat bacon, lard or
dripping. Cover the breast with
greaseproof paper and foil.
4. Roast in a moderate oven, Gas 4,
350°F, 180°C. Remove the paper

and foil for the last 15 minutes.
Serve with bread sauce (see
following recipe), watercress and
pieces of lemon.

**Stella Boldy,
Sykehouse, N. Humberside**

BREAD SAUCE

**1 onion
4 cloves
300 ml/½ pint milk
50 g/2 oz wholemeal or white
breadcrumbs
Pepper and salt
Pinch of powdered mace
25 g/1 oz butter
1 tablespoon cream or top of the
milk**

1. Peel onion.
2. Stick cloves into onion.
3. Put onion in a saucepan with
the milk and bring slowly to the
boil.
4. Put breadcrumbs in a small pie
dish.
5. Pour milk over breadcrumbs
including onion and cloves.
6. Season with pepper and salt
and a pinch of powdered mace.
7. Stir in the butter and cream or
top of the milk.
8. Put in the coolest place in the
oven for 15 minutes while meat is
cooking.
Alternatively, put the
breadcrumbs into a small
saucepan with onion and cloves
and pour on milk. Final cooking
may then be done on lowest heat
on top of stove, simmering very
slowly for 15 minutes. This can be
done in advance. It keeps warm
without harm for an hour or so.

**Stella Boldy,
Sykehouse, N. Humberside**

ROAST PHEASANT

Enough for 4 to 5 people

Hen birds are more tender and
tasty, but cock birds are bigger.

**1 pheasant
100g/4 oz stewing beef, cheaper
cut
3 or 4 rashers streaky bacon**

The trimmings
Bread sauce *(see previous recipe)*
**Breadcrumbs fried in butter
Brown gravy
Watercress**

1. Pluck, draw and truss the bird
(see page 24).
2. Put piece of stewing beef inside
bird. This keeps the bird moist
during cooking. It is not served up
with the bird but do not throw it
away: with the carcass it will
make good stock.
3. Spread bacon over bird and put
it in a roasting tin.
4. Roast in a moderate oven, Gas 4,
350°F, 180°C, for 45 minutes to 1
hour.
5. Remove on to a warmed serving
dish and keep hot.
Serve garnished with bunches of
fresh watercress, potato crisps,
braised celery or Brussels sprouts.

Bread Sauce
(See previous recipe)
This may be cooked in the cooler
part of the oven with the meat.

Fried Breadcrumbs
**25 g/1 oz butter or margarine
50 g/2 oz wholemeal or white
breadcrumbs**

1. Heat butter or margarine in a
frying pan.
2. Tip in breadcrumbs and stir
them around in the hot fat until all
are nicely browned.
Serve them hot in a small warmed
dish.

Brown Gravy
Make this in the roasting tin when
pheasant is taken out on to
warmed serving dish.

1. Sprinkle 25 g/1 oz wholemeal or
plain flour into the roasting tin
and stir it into the fat and meat
juices. Let flour cook for a minute
on a low heat.

2. Pour in hot water, or water in which vegetables have been cooked. Stir well until gravy thickens, adding more water if necessary, to make a fairly thin gravy. Boil for 2 or 3 minutes. If too pale it may be darkened with a few drops of gravy browning.
3. Taste and add salt and pepper if necessary. Strain into warmed gravy jug.

CHESHIRE POTTED PIGEON

3 pigeons
Salt and pepper
A dash of Worcestershire sauce
2 to 3 tablespoons melted butter

Pigeons are plucked and drawn like poultry (see page 24).

1. Clean the pigeons.
2. Put them in a pan, cover with water and boil until the meat is leaving the bones.
3. Remove from heat and, when cool enough to handle, carefully remove all bones.
4. Put bones back into saucepan and boil until water has reduced to about 1 cupful.
5. Mince the meat finely.
6. Season with salt, pepper and Worcestershire sauce. Moisten with stock from the bones and a little of the melted butter.
7. Press into pots and run a layer of melted butter over the top to seal each jar.

Will keep in a fridge or cold place for one month. Once open it should be used in a day or two.
Sybil Norcott,
Irlam, Nr. Manchester

A HORSERADISH DRESSING

150 ml/¼ pint yoghurt
2 teaspoons grated horseradish or
3 dessertspoons horseradish sauce
Grated zest of ½ lemon and

1 teaspoon of juice
1 tablespoon chopped parsley
Salt and black pepper

1. Mix all ingredients together.
2. Allow to stand for a few hours to infuse and mellow.

Serve with red meats, game, smoked mackerel, or as a tangy sauce for hot cauliflower.
Sybil Norcott,
Irlam, Nr. Manchester

TO GUT, SKIN, CLEAN AND JOINT A RABBIT

Gutting

1. A rabbit must be gutted as soon as possible after it is killed. Do this before you tackle the skinning.
2. Start with a very sharp, pointed knife and plenty of newspaper.
3. Lay the rabbit on its back on the newspapers with its head towards you.
4. Feel for the lower edge of the breastbone and make first incision here, just through the skin. Then, without removing knife, cut through the skin from this point straight down to the base of the tail.
5. Pick the rabbit up, forelegs in one hand, hind legs in the other, turn it over so that the intestines can drop out on to the newspaper.
6. Feel inside the rabbit for any other organs, separating liver and kidneys and keeping them aside.
7. Wrap up the other guts and throw them away.

Skinning

8. Start with hindquarters. Work the skin off the body up to the backbone and down hind legs. You will be able to pull legs out of the skin.
9. Cut off the feet at heel joint. Cut off the tail.
10. Now work up the backbone and round rib cage.
11. Pull the skin up over head. The forelegs will pull out of the skin.

12. Cut off the front feet at first joint above foot.
13. Where neck joins head cut through backbone. Head and complete skin will then come away.

Cleaning
14. First make a slit between hind legs so that any remaining excrement can be washed out under cold running water.
15. Cut the membrane which encloses heart and lungs inside rib cage. Remove these and wash rabbit out thoroughly under cold running water.
16. A rabbit, particularly a wild rabbit, should be soaked in well-salted water for 1 hour before it is cooked. This may be done before or after jointing.

Jointing
17. Cut off the hind legs where they join backbone.
18. Make another joint, called the saddle, out of the next section of backbone up to the start of the ribs.
19. Divide the forepart of the animal down the backbone to make 2 joints, each with a foreleg, shoulder and section of rib-cage.

CASSEROLED RABBIT WITH RICE AND TOMATO

For 4 to 5 people

1 rabbit, jointed (see above)
100 g/4 oz ham or bacon
1 large onion
50 g/2 oz good pork or beef dripping
100 g/4 oz long grain brown or white rice
1 small can tomatoes
300 ml/½ pint stock
1 sprig of thyme
1 bay leaf
Salt and pepper

1. Soak rabbit joints in salted water for 30 minutes. Pat dry.

2. Dice the ham or bacon.
3. Peel and finely chop the onion.
4. Heat dripping in a large frying pan, add rabbit joints and brown on both sides. Transfer them to casserole.
5. Add ham or bacon, onion and rice. Stir gently until onion is beginning to brown and fat is absorbed.
6. Add tomatoes, ½ the stock, the herbs and salt and pepper if necessary. Bring to the boil.
7. Pour this over the rabbit. Add rest of stock so that rabbit is just covered.
8. Put on the lid and cook in a moderately hot oven, Gas 4, 350°F, 180°C for 1½ to 1¾ hours until rabbit is tender. Remove stem of thyme and bay leaf before serving. Serve with Carrots in a Casserole (*see page 68*) or buttered cabbage.

RABBIT WITH MUSTARD

For 4 to 5 people

1 rabbit, jointed
100 g/4 oz bacon, in the piece or 2 thick slices
6 small onions
25 g/1 oz bacon fat or dripping
2 level tablespoons wholemeal or plain flour
600 ml/1 pint chicken stock (a stock cube will do)
1 level dessertspoon French mustard
Salt
Freshly-ground black pepper
3 tablespoons cream or natural yoghurt
1 level tablespoon chopped parsley
15 g/½ oz soft butter, to thicken sauce
15 g/½ oz plain flour, to thicken sauce

To prepare and joint a rabbit, see page 33. Or, when you buy the rabbit, ask for this to be done for you.

1. Soak rabbit joints in salted water for 2 or 3 hours, then drain and pat dry ready for use.
2. Remove rind and cut bacon into small pieces.
3. Peel onions.
4. Heat fat in a large saucepan, fry bacon and onions for 2 or 3 minutes. Transfer them from pan to a plate.
5. Brown rabbit joints in the fat and lift out on to the plate.
6. Stir 2 tablespoons flour into fat and juices now in pan and cook, stirring, for 1 to 2 minutes.
7. Remove pan from heat and gradually blend in stock and mustard. Return pan to heat and boil stirring constantly. Keep stirring while it simmers for 1 to 2 minutes.
8. Return rabbit, bacon and onions to pan. Season to taste with salt and black pepper.
9. Cover pan and simmer for 1 hour.
10. Remove rabbit joints and arrange them on a warmed dish.

11. If sauce needs thickening, strain it into a small pan, spreading contents of strainer over rabbit. Blend together the 15 g/$\frac{1}{2}$ oz of butter and flour and whisk in small bits into the sauce. Bring to the boil and cook for 2 minutes.
12. Stir cream or yoghurt and parsley into sauce and pour over rabbit joints. Serve.

OLD CHESHIRE RABBIT BRAWN

2 pig's trotters
Water
1 large rabbit
Salt and pepper
Ground allspice

1. Put pig's trotters in a saucepan, cover with cold water and boil gently for 1$\frac{1}{2}$ hours.
2. Meanwhile put rabbit into cold, salted water for $\frac{1}{2}$ hour to whiten the flesh. Then discard water.

3. Put rabbit in pan with pig's trotters, adding more water to cover. Boil together for 2 hours, or until flesh is tender and leaves bones easily. Add more water from time to time if necessary.

4. Remove from heat and allow to cool until it can be handled.

5. Remove all the bones. Cut the meat in small pieces and season to taste with salt, pepper and allspice.

6. Strain the liquid and return it with meat to the pan. Bring to the boil.

7. Rinse 2 moulds with cold water – pudding basins, casserole or soufflé dishes will do.

8. Put the brawn into the wetted moulds. Leave to set overnight.

Serve turned out on a plate with lettuce and tomatoes.

**Sybil Norcott,
Irlam, Nr. Manchester**

See also Savoury Fritters, pages 77–78, and Chicken Soufflé, page 79

CHAPTER 4

MEAT

TO SALT A PIECE OF BEEF

An excellent brine for silverside or brisket. It is worth doing a large piece while you are about it: a 1·8–2·7 kg/4–6 lb piece is ideal. A piece of frozen meat can be done straight from the freezer without thawing.

Brine
4 litres/7 pints water
680 g/1½ lb coarse salt
450 g/1 lb dark brown sugar (barbados)
50 g/2 oz saltpetre
1 bay leaf
1 sprig of thyme
10 crushed juniper berries
10 crushed peppercorns

1. Put all brine ingredients in a large saucepan, bring to the boil and boil hard for 5 minutes. Then leave to cool.
2. Strain the brine into a crock or a polythene bucket. Put it in a cool place.
3. Immerse the meat and leave it for 7 to 10 days or longer, depending on weight of meat.

The brine may, of course, be used again.

To cook the Salt Beef
2 onions
2 or 3 cloves
2 or 3 carrots
A bouquet garni (see page 66)
5 or 6 peppercorns

1. Take meat out of brine and rinse in cold water. If it has been in brine over 10 days steep it in plenty of cold water overnight but no longer.
2. Put meat in a pan, cover with cold water and bring to the boil. If water tastes very salty throw it away and start again with fresh water.
3. Add the onions stuck with cloves, sliced carrots, bouquet garni and peppercorns to the pan.
4. Bring slowly to the boil, cover pan and just simmer. Allow 30 minutes to the ½ kg/1 lb and 30 minutes over.

Eat either hot or cold. If eaten cold press it lightly in a tight fitting dish. Keep the liquid for stock.

SWEET AND SOUR BEEF

1 green pepper
450 g/1 lb top rump
50 g/2 oz butter
1 clove garlic
100 g/4 oz mushrooms

Sauce
50 g/2 oz sugar
300 ml/½ pint stock
3 tablespoons vinegar
2 tablespoons sherry
½ teaspoon soy sauce
1 level tablespoon cornflour
2 tablespoons water

1. Remove seeds from the pepper, cut it into small pieces and boil for 5 minutes. Drain.
2. Cut beef into thin strips and fry in butter for 5 minutes, turning frequently.
3. Meanwhile, make the sauce. Use a small pan and dissolve the sugar in the stock. Add vinegar, sherry and soy sauce.
4. Blend cornflour with the water and add this to the sauce. Bring to the boil and cook gently for 2 minutes.
5. Crush garlic and slice mushrooms. Add these to the beef and cook for 5 minutes more.
6. Add the drained pepper to the beef and mushrooms. Add the sauce and heat thoroughly.

Serve with boiled brown or white rice.

**Judith Adshead,
Mottram St. Andrew, Cheshire**

BEEF AND HARICOT CASSEROLE

Enough for 6

175 g/6 oz haricot beans
675 g/1½ lbs chuck steak

100 g/4 oz lean bacon
1 large onion
2 carrots
2 medium tomatoes
2 cloves garlic
50 g/2 oz good dripping
Bouquet garni, or a bunch of fresh
herbs such as parsley, thyme and
marjoram
300 ml/½ pint red wine
Salt and pepper
A little beef stock
Finely-chopped parsley

1. Soak the beans in cold water
overnight.
2. Trim beef and cut into 2·5 cm/
1 inch squares.
3. Remove rinds and cut bacon
into 1·2 cm/½ inch strips.
4. Peel and slice onion. Scrub and
slice carrots into ½ inch cubes.
5. Skin tomatoes (see page 66).
Remove pips and cut flesh into
strips.
6. Crush the garlic (see page 66).
7.Melt dripping in a heavy flame-
proof casserole and fry bacon
until golden. Remove from pan.
8. Fry meat until well-browned.
9. Return bacon to the casserole
and add onion and carrots,
tomatoes, garlic, bouquet garni,
wine and seasoning.
10. Bring up to boiling point.
Cover with greaseproof paper and
the lid and cook very gently for 1½
hours.
11. Meanwhile, boil the soaked
beans in water for about 1 hour.
12. Drain the beans, saving the
liquid, and add them to the
casserole. Stir. Add some beef
stock if needed, or some of the
haricot liquid. Continue cooking
until meat and beans are
tender–about 1 hour more. Adjust
the seasoning.
13. Remove bouquet garni. Pile
meat and vegetables with the
sauce on to a hot serving dish.
14. Sprinkle with finely-chopped
parsley.
This dish freezes well.

**Jean Welshman,
Malton, E. Yorkshire**

BEEF GOULASH

For 4 people

680 g/1½ lb stewing steak
225 g/8 oz onions
75 g/3 oz dripping
1·1 litres/2 pints stock
2 green peppers
225 g/8 oz tomatoes
1 teaspoon caraway seeds
1 clove of garlic
450 g/1 lb potatoes
1 teaspoon paprika powder
Sea salt
Pepper
1 small carton natural yoghurt

1. Cut meat into cubes.
2. Peel and slice onions.
3. Fry onions in dripping for 2 or 3
minutes.
4. Add meat, turning it over in fat
and cook for about 5 minutes until
it is sealed all over.
5. Add 850 ml/1½ pints stock, cover
pan, bring to the boil and cook
gently for ½ hour.
6. Chop green peppers, discarding
core and seeds. Chop tomatoes.
7. Add these to meat with caraway
seeds and garlic. Simmer for a
further ½ hour.
8. Peel and dice potatoes and add
with paprika and salt and pepper
to taste.
9. Add more stock or water to
cover potatoes and simmer for a
further ¾ hour.
10. Just before serving, stir in
yoghurt.

**Ursula Cavanagh,
author of 'The Wholefood Cookery
Book'**

BEEF AND ORANGE STEW

675 g/1½ lb stewing steak
225 g/8 oz onions
25 g/1 oz good dripping
25 g/1 oz flour
2 carrots
2 small turnips
1 clove garlic
Salt

2 oranges
1 litre/1¾ pints boiling water
2 or 3 beef stock cubes
150 ml/¼ pint cider

1. Trim meat and cut into cubes.
2. Peel and chop onions.
3. Melt dripping in a large pan and fry beef and onions gently. Add flour and stir.
4. Scrub carrots, peel turnips, dice them and stir into pan.
5. Crush garlic (see page 66) and add it to the pan.
6. Thinly peel oranges and blanch the rind in a small pan with ½ pint of the boiling water – that is, simmer for 2 or 3 minutes, then lift it out of the pan. Cut it into thin strips. Squeeze the juice from oranges.
7. Add half of the sliced rind and the orange juice to the stew pan.
8. Dissolve the stock cubes in remaining pint of boiling water and add this stock and the blanching water to the stew pan.
9. Bring stew to the boil and simmer gently for about 2 hours until the meat is tender.
10. Add cider. Check seasoning, adding salt if necessary and some freshly-ground black pepper. Cook for 10 minutes.

Serve the stew garnished with the remaining slices of orange rind.

A PAN STEW

For 2 people
Can be cooked in an electric frying pan.

225 g/8 oz skirt of beef
1½ tablespoons sherry
1½ tablespoons soy sauce
1 large onion
1 clove garlic
2 sticks celery
2 medium-sized carrots
100 g/4 oz mushrooms
2 teaspoons cornflour
300 ml/½ pint stock
2 tablespoons cooking oil
Salt and pepper

1. Cut beef into pencil-thin strips about 3·7 cm/1½ inches long.
2. Mix sherry and soy sauce in a basin. Put in the beef and turn it over in this marinade. Leave it for at least 2 hours, turning meat over from time to time.
3. Peel and slice onion.
4. Crush garlic (see page 66).
5. Wash, trim and finely slice the celery.
6. Scrub carrots and cut them into matchstick-sized pieces.
7. Wipe mushrooms and, if large, cut them up.
8. Blend cornflour into a little of the stock then stir in the rest of the stock.
9. Heat oil in a large frying pan or shallow pan. Add meat and cook fairly quickly, turning with a spatula, until almost cooked – about 10 minutes. Push to one side.
10. Fry onion and garlic until soft but not brown. Add celery and carrot and fry for 5 minutes, adding more oil if necessary.
11. Add mushrooms and fry for 2 minutes.
12. Mix contents of pan together, adding stock mixture and any remaining marinade. Simmer for 10 minutes. Taste for seasoning and add salt and pepper if necessary.

Serve with brown rice and green vegetables.

STEAK AND KIDNEY PUDDING

Filling
25 g/1 oz beef dripping
100 g/4 oz chopped onion
450 g/1 lb lean pie beef, cut into cubes
100 g/4 oz ox kidney, trimmed and cut slightly smaller than the beef
1 level tablespoon flour seasoned with 1 teaspoon Salt and Pepper Mix (see page 8)
450 ml/¾ pint water

2 teaspoons Worcestershire sauce
100 g/4 oz mushrooms

Suet Crust
225 g/8 oz self-raising flour
½ teaspoon salt
100 g/4 oz shredded suet
7 tablespoons water

Note: you can use a pressure cooker (trivet removed) for this. It saves 1½ hours' cooking time.

1. Melt dripping in pan, add onion, cook 1 minute.
2. Mix beef and kidney into seasoned flour, coating well. Add to pan and stir over heat to seal – it will change colour.
3. Add water and Worcestershire sauce, stir until boiling.
4. Cover and simmer for about 2 hours until meat is tender. Stir occasionally. Or pressure cook.
5. Pour off all but 3 tablespoons of the gravy and mix the sliced mushrooms with the meat.
6. Make the suet crust mixing flour, salt, suet and water to a soft but not sticky dough.
7. Lightly grease a 1·2 litre/2 pint heat-proof basin.
8. Roll out pastry on a floured board to a round, about 35 cm/ 14 inches across.
9. Cut away a segment exactly a quarter of the circle. Shape it back into a ball (it will be used for the lid).
10. The large piece of pastry will now fit the basin. Press it in lightly.
11. Tip the meat mixture into the pastry-lined basin.
12. Roll out the lid to fit. Dampen edges and fit it on top.
13. Cover with a layer of greaseproof paper, lightly greased, with a 2·5 cm/1 inch pleat in it. Cover loosely with a piece of foil and press in round rim of basin to seal.

Either pressure cook:
(a) Place pudding on trivet in pressure cooker with 1¼ pints of water.

(b) With lid on, allow to steam 15 minutes.
(c) Put on control valve at lowest pressure and pressure cook for 25 minutes. Reduce at room temperature (7 to 8 minutes).

Or steam:
Place on top of steamer. Cook 1¼ hours, keeping water boiling.

Or:
If you have neither of these, stand basin on a trivet or upturned saucer in a large saucepan. Pour in boiling water to come halfway up side of basin. Boil for 1¼ hours. Keep pan replenished with boiling water. Do not let it go off the boil or pudding may be heavy.

Serve with gravy and green vegetables.

BOBOTIE

From a 19th century cookery book.

1 to 2 thick slices of bread
150 ml/¼ pint milk
1 medium-sized onion
1 tablespoon oil
1 tablespoon butter
50 g/2 oz sultanas or raisins
¼ kg/1 lb minced beef
25 g/1 oz shredded almonds
2 teaspoons wine or cider vinegar
2 teaspoons sugar
1 tablespoon curry powder
½ teaspoon salt
½ teaspoon mixed herbs
Black pepper
2 teaspoons lemon juice
2 beaten eggs

1. Soak slices of bread in milk and squeeze out. Keep the milk for later.
2. Peel and chop onion. Using a large pan, fry it in oil and butter till softening, but not brown. Remove from heat.
3. Add soaked bread, sultanas, beef, almonds, vinegar, sugar, curry powder, salt, herbs, pepper, lemon juice and 1 tablespoon of the beaten egg. Mix well.

4. Spread mixture in an ovenproof dish.
5. Mix remaining egg and milk. Pour it over the mixture.
6. Bake in a moderate oven, Gas 4, 350°F, 180°C, for 1 to 1½ hours.

Serve hot in portions or cold cut in fingers for a buffet.

**Sybil Norcott,
Irlam, Nr. Manchester**

CHILLI CON CARNE

For 4 people

**1 onion
1 clove garlic
Pinch of salt
25 g/1 oz good dripping
450g/1 lb minced beef
1 level tablespoon flour
A 225 g/8 oz can tomatoes
2 level tablespoons tomato pureé
½ level teaspoon chilli powder
Pinch of dried marjoram or oregano
A 225 g/8 oz can of baked beans**

1. Peel onion and chop it finely. Crush garlic with a little salt.
2. Melt dripping in large saucepan, add onion and garlic then beef. Fry slowly until beef is browned.
3. Stir in flour and cook for 1 minute.
4. Add can of tomatoes, tomato pureé, chilli powder and marjoram or oregano.
5. Bring to the boil, stirring. Cover pan and simmer for 30 minutes, stirring from time to time. Add a little water if mixture is too thick to stir.
6. Add beans and cook for 5 minutes more.

Serve with green vegetables or a green salad.

MEAT LOAF

**1 small onion
450 g/1 lb minced beef
225 g/8 oz beef sausage
Pinch of mixed herbs
Salt and pepper
1 beaten egg
2 hard-boiled eggs (optional)**

1. Peel and chop or grate onion.
2. Thoroughly mix onion, minced meat, sausage meat, herbs and seasoning.
3. Bind with beaten egg.
4. Grease a ½ kg/1 lb loaf tin and fill it with mixture. If using hard-boiled eggs, put in half the meat mixture then the eggs and pack the rest of the meat on top.
5. Cover with a layer of greaseproof paper and then foil, tucking edges in under rim of tin.
6. Bake in the middle of a moderately hot oven, Gas 4, 350°F, 180°C, for 1 hour. After ½ hour, remove paper and foil.
7. When cooked, pour off the juices and turn loaf out on to a plate.

Serve hot with potatoes in jackets or roast potatoes and vegetables or cold with salad.

The same meat mixture can be used for beefburgers.

Beefburgers
1. Take tablespoonfuls of raw mixture and, using a floured board, shape into flat cakes, 2 cm/¾ inch thick. Sprinkle with more flour if too sticky to handle.
2. Melt 25 g/1 oz lard or dripping in a frying pan. When hot put in beefburgers. Brown on one side, turn and lower heat to cook slowly. Cook 7 to 8 minutes altogether.

**Margaret Heywood,
Todmorden, Yorkshire**

BEEF CURRY

Made with home-mixed curry powder.

Curry Spices
**2 cloves or ¼ teaspoon ground cloves
2 teaspoons coriander seeds, or 1½ teaspoons ground coriander
1 teaspoon ground cummin seed
1 teaspoon turmeric
½ to 1 teaspoon chilli powder
1 teaspoon ground ginger
¼ teaspoon powdered cinnamon**
You can crush cloves between 2

spoons. Coriander seeds need a pestle and mortar.
Measure the spices carefully on to a plate and then mix them with a knife.

The Curry

Can be made a day in advance. Flavour is better if it is made, left as long as 24 hours and then reheated.

675 g/1½ lb braising steak
225 g/8 oz onions
350 g/12 oz fresh tomatoes, or
400 g/14 oz can
3 to 4 cloves garlic
2 level teaspoons salt
2 to 3 tablespoons cooking oil
Curry spices as above
1 level tablespoon plain flour
300 ml/½ pint beef stock or water, or dissolve 25 g/1 oz creamed coconut in 300 ml/½ pint boiling water

Side Dishes

Diced cucumber mixed with plain yoghurt
Sliced bananas sprinkled with lemon juice
Sultanas
Finely-sliced fresh onion rings
Poppadoms (can be bought from oriental shops with a variety of flavours)
Mango chutney, or home-made Sweet Mixed Pickle (see page 153)

1. Cut beef into even-sized small pieces.
2. Peel and chop onions.
3. Skin tomatoes (see page 66). If using can of tomatoes, drain juice and use it to make up quantity of stock.
4. Crush garlic (see page 66).
5. Heat oil in a heavy saucepan and gently fry the spices for 2 minutes
6. Add meat, fry gently on all sides until brown. Remove from saucepan on to a plate.
7. Add onion and garlic and gently fry to soften the onion.
8. Stir in flour. Let it cook for a minute.

9. Add chopped or canned tomatoes. Cook for about 2 minutes. Return meat to pan.
10. Add stock, bring to the boil, cover pan and simmer for about 1 hour, or until meat is tender and sauce is reduced to a thick gravy.

Serve with a dish of plain boiled brown or white rice and as many side-dishes as you can.

Jill Smith,
Cambridge

A MILD CURRY

Made with a little meat and a lot of vegetables.

Serves 2

Curry Spices

1 clove
1 level teaspoon ground coriander
½ teaspoon turmeric
½ teaspoon ginger
¼ teaspoon cinnamon
¼ teaspoon ground mace
¼ teaspoon ground nutmeg
¼ teaspoon paprika

The Curry

125–175 g/4–6 oz cold cooked beef, pork, or lamb
1 large onion
1 tablespoon dripping
1 large clove garlic
A 225 g/8 oz can tomatoes
A very little salt
1 small carrot
1 leek
1 tablespoon sultanas
1 tablespoon flaked almonds

To serve

175 g–225 g/6–8 oz brown rice

1. First measure curry spices on to a plate and mix well together. The clove may be crushed between 2 spoons. Grind or grate freshly as many spices as you can: the flavour is better.
2. Cut meat into small cubes, removing fat and gristle.
3. Peel onion and cut it into large chunks.

43

4. Melt dripping in a heavy, flame-proof casserole. Put in onion and meat and stir in curry spices. Cook gently for 5 minutes, stirring from time to time. If you don't have a casserole suitable for oven and stove top, use a heavy frying pan and when onion, meat, and curry spices have fried transfer them to an ovenproof dish with a lid.

5. Stir in crushed garlic.

6. Break up tomatoes and add half of them. Add a very little salt.

7. Put lid on dish and put in a slow oven, Gas $\frac{1}{2}$, 250°F, 120°C for 1 hour.

8. Meanwhile, scrub carrot and shred into fine rings. Slice the leek, into halves, wash well and cut up.

9. Sprinkle sultanas and nuts over curry. Make a border of carrot slices, pile leek in the middle and pour over the rest of the tomato to moisten. Sprinkle on a few grains of salt. Replace lid and return casserole to oven. Cook for 30 minutes more.

10. At the same time, put rice on to cook. Bring 300 ml/$\frac{1}{2}$ pint water to boil, add a very little salt and the rice. Let it return to boiling point, cover pan, reduce heat and allow to cook gently for 20 to 30 minutes. Long-grain brown rice takes longer to cook than the round variety.

Serve each helping on a bed of rice. Vegetables are crunchy, full of their own flavour and not swamped by the curry.

TO COOK AND PRESS AN OX-TONGUE

1 ox-tongue, salted by the butcher
2 large onions
2 large carrots
1 stick celery
1 bay leaf, sprig of thyme and parsley
5 peppercorns

1. Put tongue to soak in plenty of water for 24 hours. Change water at least twice. This draws out excess salt.

2. Put tongue in a large saucepan and cover with fresh water. Bring slowly to the boil.

3. Peel onion and cut up roughly. Scrub and chop carrot. Slice celery.

4. When tongue reaches boiling point skim off the scum, add vegetables and herbs and peppercorns. Simmer for 3 to 4 hours or until the little bones at root of tongue are easily pulled out.

5. Allow to cool in the liquid.

6. Remove tongue on to a dish, skin it and trim off bone or gristle at the root and some of the excessively fatty bits.

7. Curl tongue round and fit it tightly into a straight-sided dish or cake tin. It needs to be a tight fit to make a neat finished product.

8. Find a plate that will just fit inside the dish or tin. Press it in and put a heavy weight on top.

9. Leave it until the next day to set.

10. Turn it out on to a plate to serve.

Save the stock for soups but use it carefully as it may be salty and strongly flavoured.

FOLDS OF TONGUE

With savoury rice and cheese filling and fresh tomato sauce.

Enough for 4 people, but easy to make in larger or smaller quantities.

1 small red or green pepper
25 g/1 oz butter
1 teaspoon chopped capers
2 tablespoons cooked brown rice
Salt and pepper
75 g/3 oz grated cheese
4 slices of cooked tongue

Sauce
675 g/1$\frac{1}{2}$ lb ripe tomatoes, or a
400 g/14 oz can of tomatoes
1 onion
1 clove garlic
1 bouquet garni (see page 66) or
a bunch of fresh herbs such as
thyme, parsley, basil and marjoram

1 teaspoon sugar
1 teaspoon tomato purée
½ teaspoon salt
Freshly-ground black pepper

1. Blanch the pepper. To do this, cut it in half, remove core and knock out seeds. Cook in boiling salted water for 3 minutes. Drain off hot water and refresh with cold. Drain again. Chop finely.
2. Melt butter in a pan, add chopped capers, rice, peppers, seasoning and 50 g/2 oz of grated cheese.
3. Stir with a fork over a low heat until cheese has just melted. Do not leave it. If it is over-cooked cheese will turn to indigestible strings.
4. Divide mixture roughly into 4. Put a layer on one half of each slice of tongue.
5. Fold over other half on top and lay them slightly overlapping down centre of a fireproof dish.
6. To make sauce, first skin the tomatoes (see page 66) and chop them. Crush garlic.
7. Put all sauce ingredients into a pan, bring to the boil, then simmer gently, stirring occasionally, until thick and mushy. Adjust the seasoning. Remove bouquet garni or bunch of herbs.
8. Pour sauce over folds of tongue.
9. Sprinkle with rest of the cheese and place under a hot grill until cheese is golden brown.
Freezes well.

**Mrs Jean Welshman,
Malton, E. Yorkshire**

LIVER AND BACON CASSEROLE

For 6 people

700 g/1½ lb ox liver
300 ml/¼ pint milk or milk and water mixed
6 rashers bacon
2 tablespoons flour
2 teaspoons salt
1 teaspoon pepper

1 large onion
50 g/2 oz butter or margarine
400 g/14 oz tinned tomatoes
2 tablespoons tomato purée

1. Put slices of liver in a bowl with the milk for one hour to soak and draw out the slightly strong taste.
2. Remove bacon rinds, halve and roll the rashers.
3. Peel and chop onion.
4. Drain milk from liver. Pat each piece dry and toss in flour seasoned with salt and pepper. Discard the milk.
5. Fry onion in the butter or margarine until soft but not brown.
6. Add liver to the frying pan and fry quickly on both sides to seal. This is very important because it keeps the natural juices and flavour in the meat.
7. Put liver and onions into a casserole dish.
8. Chop the tinned tomatoes and mix well with tomato purée. Pour over liver and onions.
9. Place bacon rolls on top.
10. Cook, uncovered, in a moderately hot oven, Gas 5, 375°F, 190°C for 30/40 minutes.

**Judith Adshead,
Mottram St. Andrew, Cheshire**

LIVER PATTIES WITH APPLE AND ONION

Nourishing, economical, tender and tasty.

For 3 or 4 people

225 g/8 oz ox liver
1 medium-sized onion
1 medium-sized apple
1 well-rounded tablespoon porridge oats or flake meal
1 level tablespoon bran (optional)
100 ml/4 fluid oz beef stock
(½ stock cube will do but let it cool before using)
Salt
1 tablespoon oil

1. Wash and skin liver and cut into pieces. Liquidise or put

45

through middle disc of mouli-sieve or medium-coarse cutter of mincer. It is difficult to mince liver but you can blanch it first as follows: put it in a saucepan. Just cover with boiling water and bring to boiling point. Turn down heat, simmer for 2 to 3 minutes. Drain off water.
2. Peel onion and chop finely. Add to liver.
3. Peel and grate apple. Stir into liver and onion.
4. Mix in the porridge oats or flake meal, bran and stock. Season with a little salt.
5. Heat oil in frying pan.
6. Put large spoonfuls of liver mixture into pan and fry 4 to 5 minutes on each side.

**Mrs W. Gordon,
Glasgow**

TRIPE IN BATTER WITH ONION SAUCE

**450 g/1 lb tripe
Salt
Milk
Water
1 tablespoon flour
Pepper**

**Batter
100 g/4 oz plain flour
¼ teaspoon salt
1 egg
1 dessertspoon oil
125 ml/¼ pint milk
Deep fat or oil for frying**

**Onion Sauce
225 g/8 oz onions
25 g/1 oz butter
25 g/1 oz flour
A bare 300 ml/½ pint milk
Seasoning**

1. Although tripe is blanched, or partially cooked, when bought it may need to be cooked again before being used. If it will cut with a knife it is cooked enough. If not, put it in a pan, add a little salt and cover with mixed milk and water. Put lid on pan and cook until tender.

2. Drain the tripe, pat dry and cut into strips, about 3 × 7 cm/ 1½ × 3 inches.
3. Season flour with salt and pepper and toss in it the strips of tripe.
4. **The batter.** Put flour and salt in a bowl. Make a well in centre and drop in egg.
5. Add oil and milk gradually, beating well.
6. Dip tripe strips in batter and deep fry. Drain on kitchen paper.
7. **The onion sauce.** Peel and chop onions finely.
8. Melt butter and fry onions till soft but not brown.
9. Stir in flour and cook 1 minute.
10. Gradually stir in milk, bring to the boil and cook for 2 or 3 minutes.

YORKSHIRE PUDDINGS

Made with wholewheat flour. Enough for 9 or 10 small, light puddings.

**50 g/2 oz plain wholewheat flour
Pinch of salt
1 egg
150 ml/¼ pint milk
2 tablespoons water
Dripping**

1. Mix flour and salt.
2. Make a well in the centre. Drop in egg and mix to start drawing in flour.
3. Add milk and water gradually, beating all the time to avoid lumps in the flour.
4. Put a knife-end of dripping in each patty tin and put them in a hot oven, Gas 7, 425°F, 220°C, for 5 minutes to get really hot.
5. Give pudding mixture a final hard whisk with egg beater and pour at once into the tins.
6. Put straight in the oven for 20 to 30 minutes until puffy and golden brown. It will cook in a moderately hot oven, Gas 5, 375°F, 190°C, but will take the full 30 minutes. Try not to open oven for first 10 minutes.

ROAST HAND OF PORK WITH BRAISED ONIONS

It is more economical to buy a hand of pork at the weight given because there is a larger proportion of meat to bone and it is better value than buying a smaller joint. Cooking as suggested ensures that the skin is crisp: this is nicer hot than cold. The pork can be eaten cold and is moist for sandwiches. See Pork Oaties for using up the last of the joint.

1·8–2 kg/4–4½ lb hand of pork (ask the butcher to score skin finely)
15 g/½ oz pork dripping
1 small teaspoon salt
Medium-sized onions, 1 for each person
Water
1 to 2 tablespoons wholewheat or plain flour

1. Preheat oven to moderately hot, Gas 6, 400°F, 200°C.
2. Rub dripping over pork and sprinkle on the salt.
3. Place joint on a small trivet or rack in a large roasting tin and put in the oven.
4. Cook for 30 minutes. Reduce heat to moderate, Gas 4, 350°F, 180°C, and cook for 2 to 2½ hours depending on weight of meat.
5. Peel onions and put them whole into saucepan with water to cover. Boil for 20 minutes. Then drain, saving water for the gravy.
6. Put onions in the fat around the meat for the last ½ hour of cooking time. Turn them over in fat once or twice to brown evenly.
7. When meat and onions are done, set them on a warmed dish and keep hot.
8. **To make the gravy.** Pour nearly all fat off sediment in roasting tin into a basin. Stir flour into remaining fat in tin and let it sizzle for 1 minute. Pour in onion water and any other vegetable water, stir till gravy thickens, boil for 2 to 3 minutes and season to taste. If you like smooth gravy, strain it into a warm jug.

PORK OATIES

1 medium-sized onion
1 medium-sized apple
225 g/8 oz cold pork
100 g/4 oz wholemeal breadcrumbs
1 level teaspoon dried sage
½ teaspoon salt
A good shake of pepper
1 beaten egg
A little wholewheat flour
50–75 g/2–3 oz oatmeal
Pork dripping, from joint

1. Peel onion and cut up roughly. Peel, core and quarter apple.
2. Mince together pork, onion and apple.
3. Combine pork mixture with breadcrumbs, sage, salt and pepper.
4. Add half the beaten egg and mix it in well to bind all together.
5. With floured hands, make 8 or 12 balls. Flatten them into round cakes. Chill them for at least 30 minutes.
6. Flour them lightly, brush with beaten egg and coat with oatmeal.
7. Put 2 tablespoons dripping into frying pan and make it hot. Fry the oaties for 6 minutes on each side.

Serve with baked beans, green peas or grilled tomatoes.

FRENCH ROAST PORK

1 teaspoon sea salt
½ teaspoon grated nutmeg
2 tablespoons vegetable oil
1 boned hand of pork
1 wineglass of cider
50 g/2 oz barbados sugar
1 cooking apple
1 tablespoon wholewheat flour
40 g/1½ oz butter

1. Mix salt and nutmeg with oil.
2. Rub this mixture all over the meat and put it in a roasting tin.
3. Put in a hot oven, Gas 8, 450°F, 230°C, for 10 minutes.

4. Reduce heat to moderate, Gas 4, 350°F, 180°C, and add cider and sugar. Roast at this temperature for 2 hours, basting frequently.

5. Just before serving meat, core apples and cut into segments. Dip them in flour and fry in butter till golden brown.

6. Put meat on a warmed dish and decorate with apple.

Ursula Cavanagh, author of 'The Wholefood Cookery Book'

ORANGE STUFFING

Try it with roast pork, including roast belly pork, poultry and loin of mutton.

75 g/2½ oz fresh brown or white breadcrumbs
1 level tablespoon chopped fresh mixed herbs, parsley, chives and thyme
1 level tablespoon finely-chopped fresh sage leaves
Salt and black pepper
25–40g/1–1½ oz margarine
2 level tablespoons finely-chopped onion
Grated rind and juice of 1 large orange
1 egg

1. Mix the crumbs in a bowl with the herbs and seasoning.
2. Melt margarine and fry onion to soften without browning.
3. Add onion to the crumbs with the grated orange rind and juice.
4. Mix in egg. The mixture should be of moist consistency. Add extra orange juice or a few drops of water to moisten if necessary.

GAMMON AND APRICOT PIE

225 g/8 oz dried apricots
1 gammon rasher, 2·5 cm/1 inch thick
1 teaspoon dripping
25 g/1 oz sultanas
Pepper
2 or 3 tablespoons gravy or stock
6 potatoes

1. Soak apricots in water over-night.
2. Lightly brown gammon on both sides in the dripping in a frying pan.
3. Lay rasher in a large oven-proof dish.
4. Arrange apricots and sultanas on top. Sprinkle with pepper and pour the gravy over.
5. Peel and slice potatoes and lay them on top to cover.
6. Cover with a piece of greased, greaseproof paper.
7. Bake in a moderate oven, Gas 4, 350°F, 180°C, for 1 hour.

Sybil Norcott, Irlam, Nr. Manchester

PORK CASSEROLE

For 4 people

You need a shallow casserole dish with a well-fitting lid.

450 g/1 lb pork fillet (tenderloin)
25 g/1 oz lard
4 rashers bacon
1 large onion
1 cooking apple
A little salt
Pepper
6 dried juniper berries
2 large potatoes
300 ml/½ pint cider
50 g/2 oz butter

1. Cut pork into 4 to 6 pieces and fry in lard till brown on each side. Place in casserole dish.
2. Grill bacon lightly and place on top of pork.
3. Peel and chop the onion and the apple and place on top of pork and bacon.
4. Season with a little salt and some pepper.
5. Add crushed juniper berries (crush with the back of a knife).
6. Peel and slice potatoes and place on top.
7. Pour on the cider.
8. Cut a piece of greaseproof paper 12 mm/½ inch larger than casserole dish. Spread this with the butter and put it butter-side down over

the potatoes. Cover with tight-fitting lid to ensure it is well sealed.

9. Cook in a slow to moderate oven, Gas 2 to 3, 310°F, 160°C, for 1½ hours.

**Judith Adshead,
Mottram St. Andrew, Cheshire**

PORK IN A CASSEROLE WITH TOMATO AND MUSHROOMS

For 2 or 3 people

225 g/8 oz shoulder of pork, or fillet
25 g/1 oz butter
1 large onion
25 g/1 oz flour
300 ml/½ pint stock
2 tablespoons tomato purée
2 bay leaves
Pepper and salt
75 g/3 oz mushrooms

To serve
100 g/4 oz brown or white rice
100 g/4 oz peas

1. Cut meat into even-sized slices.
2. Melt butter in a frying pan, add meat and let it brown on both sides. Lift it out into a casserole dish.
3. Peel and slice onion. Fry it gently in pan until soft but not brown. Lift out of pan with a draining spoon and arrange it over the meat.
4. Add flour to pan, cook for 1 minute.
5. Gradually pour in stock, stirring as it thickens. Bring to boil.
6. Add tomato purée, bay leaves, pepper and salt. Mix well and pour it over the meat.
7. Put lid on casserole and put in a moderate oven, Gas 4, 350°F, 180°C, for ¾ hour.
8. Meanwhile, remember to put rice on to cook, allowing 25 to 35 minutes for brown rice and 10 to 12 minutes for white rice.
9. Wipe mushrooms and cut them

up if necessary into even-sized pieces.

10. Add them to casserole and let it cook another 15 to 20 minutes.

Serve each helping on a bed of rice with lightly-cooked green peas.

**Mrs Margaret Ferns,
Loundsley Green, Derbyshire**

CRISPY PORK AND POTATO PIE

450 g/1 lb thin slices of belly pork
450 g/1 lb onions
1 carrot, 1 parsnip, 1 stick celery or 50 g/2 oz mixed, dried vegetables may be used
1 tomato (optional)
675–900 g/1½–2 lb potatoes
1 large cooking apple
Salt and pepper
600 ml/1 pint good stock
50 g/2 oz fresh wholemeal or white breadcrumbs
1 tablespoon mixed herbs
1 egg
1 tablespoon milk

1. Remove rinds from pork slices.
2. Peel onions and slice into rings.
3. Scrub and finely slice carrot, parsnip and celery, if used.
4. Remove skin and seeds from the tomato and chop it small.
5. Peel potatoes and cut into slices.
6. Peel and core apple and cut into rings.
7. Line bottom of a fairly shallow pie-dish with half of the potatoes.
8. Mix onion and apple rings together and lay them evenly on top of potatoes.
9. Mix the carrot and parsnip slices and lay these in dish. Or add mixed, dried vegetables.
10. Add chopped tomato.
11. Cover with rest of potatoes.
12. Season to taste with salt and pepper and sprinkle with a pinch of mixed herbs. Pour over the stock.
13. Mix rest of herbs into breadcrumbs.
14. Beat egg with the milk.
15. Coat each pork slice with egg

49

mixture and then herb and breadcrumb mixture.
16. Lay pork on top of potatoes.
17. Cook in moderately hot oven, Gas 5, 375°F, 190°C, for ½ hour. Reduce temperature to slow, Gas 2, 300°F, 150°C for 1 hour or until potatoes are cooked.

The pork will be brown and crisp. The herbs and vegetables absorb the fatty taste which so many people dislike in belly pork.

Mrs. J. Allison, Nottingham

SWEET AND SOUR PORK

For 4, but easy to cut down quantities.
Can be cooked in an electric frying pan.

450 g/1 lb boneless pork, either from shoulder or belly
2 tablespoons cooking oil
1 small green pepper
4 dessert apples
15 g/½ oz butter
1 tablespoon brown sugar
2 teaspoons soy sauce
2 tablespoons orange or pineapple juice
A dash of wine or cider vinegar or Worcestershire sauce
Salt and pepper

1. Cut pork into 1·5 cm/½ inch cubes.
2. Heat oil in large, frying pan or shallow pan, or electric frying pan. Fry pork quickly to seal all over. Lower heat and continue frying, turning meat over with spatula from time to time until brown and cooked. This will take about 20 minutes.
3. Meanwhile, remove core and seeds from green pepper and cut up small.
4. Just before they are required, peel and core apples and slice thinly.
5. Push meat to sides of pan. Melt butter in centre of pan. Add apples and fry over medium heat, turning them over until beginning to soften.
6. Sprinkle sugar over apples and push them to sides of pan.
7. Add green pepper and fry for 2 or 3 minutes.
8. Sprinkle with soy sauce, fruit juice and vinegar or Worcestershire sauce. Stir and check seasoning, adding salt and pepper if necessary.
9. Stir over medium heat for 2 to 3 minutes.

Serve with plain boiled brown rice (see page 74).

PIG'S HEAD BRAWN

1 pig's head, split in half
Water
Salt
1 tablespoon vinegar
8 black peppercorns
1 large onion, peeled
1 bay leaf
225 g/8 oz shin of beef (optional)
Half a rabbit (optional)
Pepper

1. With a sharp knife, take away ears and eyes. Scoop out brains. Chop off the snout. These bits are not used.
2. Wash the 2 halves in cold running water. Then put in a large bowl of water, adding 1 tablespoon of salt per pint of water. Leave to soak for 2 or 3 hours.
3. Drain away water. Put head into a large pan and cover with water.
4. Add vinegar, peppercorns, whole onion, bay leaf and 2 teaspoons salt.
5. If using shin of beef or rabbit, add it now. The addition of either of these helps to counteract the fat-content of the head.
6. Bring to the boil, cover pan and simmer until meat leaves the bones.
7. Turn off heat and leave meat in pan till cool enough to handle.
8. Lift all meat out into a large bowl.

9. Return pan of stock to heat and simmer until it is reduced by about half.
10. Remove all meat from bones. Chop it into small pieces but do not mince.
11. Strain over the meat enough of the reduced stock to 'float' the meat. Season with salt and pepper.
12. Return to a saucepan, bring to boil and simmer for 10 minutes.
13. Pour into a mould and set in a cool place.
14. Turn out on to a plate and serve with pickles and salads.

TOMATO LIVER

For 4 to 5 people

2 medium-sized onions
1 large green pepper
450 g/1 lb fresh tomatoes or a
425 g/15 oz can
25 g/1 oz butter
450 g/1 lb pig's liver
2 tablespoons flour
150 ml/¼ pint white wine or stock
Salt and black pepper
2 tablespoons cream (optional)

1. Peel and chop onions. Chop green pepper, removing core and seeds.
2. Skin and cut up tomatoes. (To skin see page 66.)
3. Melt butter and gently fry onion and green pepper.
4. Slice liver and dredge in flour.
5. Add to onion mixture, cook for 2 or 3 minutes, turning it over.
6. Add tomatoes, wine, or stock. Cover pan and simmer for 15 minutes.
7. Check seasoning. Add cream if required.

Mrs Alison Seymour,
Aston Tirrold, Oxon

TO MAKE PORK SAUSAGES

Makes about 2·25 kg/5 lbs sausages

Do not start this until you know you can get some sausage-skins. A butcher who makes his own sausages may sell you some. Some electric food mixers have a sausage-filling attachment. If you don't have one, the only alternative will be to use a large piping bag with large nozzle, but it will be difficult (see paragraph 6 below).

450 g/1 lb white or wholemeal bread
600 ml/1 pint water
1·3 kg/3 lb lean pork, from the shoulder
450 g/1 lb fat belly pork
25 g/1 oz salt
8 g/½ teaspoon pepper
6 g/¼ teaspoon ground mace
4 g/small pinch of ground ginger
2 g/tiny pinch of ground or rubbed sage

1. Cut bread into cubes and soak in the water for 1 or 2 hours.
2. Mince the meat using coarse blades of mincer.
3. Mix in the seasonings.
4. Squeeze water from bread thoroughly and discard water.
5. Mix all ingredients and put through mincer again, this time using fine blades.
6. Thread skins on to nozzle and fill. Link as desired.

Can be frozen.

Stella Boldy,
Sykehouse, N. Humberside

CUMBERLAND SAUSAGE

If you buy Cumberland Sausage it is usually long and thick. To be truly authentic you must try and get casings – or skins – that will give a thick sausage.

2 kg/4½ lb lean pork, from the shoulder
675 g/1½ lb fat belly pork
6 g/¼ oz powdered sage
Pinch of marjoram
25 g/1 oz white pepper
75 g/3 oz salt
100 g/4 oz soft breadcrumbs

To wash sausage casings, attach one end to the cold tap and run fresh water carefully through it. Then leave to soak in salted water overnight. Rinse and use. Some electric mixers have a sausage-filling attachment. Otherwise use a large piping bag and nozzle. Work the casing up over the nozzle, so that as you squeeze the bag sausagemeat is forced into the end of the casing. Casing gradually slides off nozzle as it is filled.

1. Mince the meat but not too finely. Cumberland Sausage is coarser than our usual sausages.
2. Thoroughly mix in all the other ingredients.
3. Test flavour by cooking a little in a greased frying pan.
4. Fill sausage casings and twist into links.

Will keep for weeks if hung from hooks in the ceiling.

SAUSAGES AND KIDNEYS IN A WINE AND MUSHROOM SAUCE

Lamb's liver can be used instead of kidneys. Easy to make in smaller or larger quantities

4 chipolata sausages
Cooking oil
4 lamb's kidneys or 225 g/8 oz lamb's liver
100 g/4 oz mushrooms
1 tablespoon flour
300 ml/1½ pints beef stock (a stock cube will do)
3 tablespoons red wine
1 dessertspoon tomato purée
25 g/1 oz butter
4 slices bread

1. Cook sausages gently in a very little oil. Lift them out of pan and keep them warm.
2. Meanwhile, remove skins from kidneys, cut them in halves, trim out the tubes. Or, skin liver and cut it into 4 even-sized slices.
3. Slice mushrooms coarsely.
4. Add mushrooms to sausage pan and fry gently, turning them over in fat for 2 or 3 minutes.
5. Stir in flour and cook for 1 minute.
6. Add stock, wine and tomato purée, bring to boiling point and simmer for 5 minutes. Keep it warm.
7. Cut bread into triangles or fancy shapes.
8. Melt butter and fry bread until brown and crisp. Lift it out on to a paper to drain and keep hot.
9. In same pan, quickly fry kidneys on both sides till brown. Do not overcook or they will be tough and rubbery.
10. Pour sauce into a warmed dish. Arrange sausages and kidneys on top with fried bread standing up in between.

Serve at once, before fried bread goes soggy in sauce.

Mrs Anne Hamblin,
Hilton, Derbyshire

TOAD-IN-THE-WHOLE

Made with a 'whole'-wheat batter.

40g/1½ oz dripping
675 g/1½ lb pork sausages

Batter
225 g/8 oz wholewheat flour
Pinch of sea salt
Pepper
2 eggs
200 ml/7 fluid oz milk
200 ml/7 fluid oz water

1. Start with batter. Mix flour, salt and pepper in a bowl, make a well in centre and drop in eggs.
2. Beat well, gradually incorporating flour and adding milk and water. Whisk for 4 to 5 minutes.
3. Put dripping in a large roasting tin and place in hot oven, Gas 8, 450°F, 230°C. Leave for 5 minutes to get smoking hot.

4. Pour in batter and space sausages evenly in it.

5. Bake for 40 minutes, reducing heat to moderately hot, Gas 6, 400°F, 200°C, if batter is browning too quickly.

Ursula Cavanagh, author of 'The Wholefood Cookery Book'

ROAST LAMB WITH APRICOT STUFFING

Remember to start this dish the night before serving.

50–75 g/2–3 oz dried apricots
50 g/2 oz butter or margarine
1 medium-sized onion
50 g/2 oz fresh wholemeal or white breadcrumbs
1 tablespoon chopped parsley
Salt and pepper
150 ml/¼ pint stock
1 egg-yolk
1 kg/2 lb boned shoulder of lamb
A little dripping

1. Put apricots to soak in water overnight.
2. Next day, drain and cut them up quite small.
3. Melt butter or margarine in a frying pan.
4. Peel and chop onion and lightly fry it until transparent but not brown.
5. Mix in the apricots, breadcrumbs, parsley, salt and pepper. Moisten with 1 to 2 tablespoons stock.
6. Beat egg-yolk and add it to stuffing with a little more stock, if necessary, to make it moist but not sticky.
7. Open out lamb, season with pepper and a very little salt. Spread stuffing over it.
8. Roll it up and secure with string to keep in the filling.
9. Put in roasting tin and dot with dripping.
10. Roast in a hot oven, Gas 8, 450°F, 230°C, for 10 minutes. Reduce to moderate temperature,

Gas 4, 350°F, 180°C, for a further 1 to 1¼ hours.

Mrs Emily Williams, Moggerhanger, Bedfordshire

HONEYED LAMB

For 2 people

½ small onion
15 g/½ oz butter
1 dessertspoon oil
2 teaspoons flour
¼ teaspoon mustard powder
Salt and pepper
A 200 g/7 oz slice of lamb from fillet end of leg
200 ml/7 fluid oz apple juice
2 teaspoons honey
½ beef stock cube
1 carrot, cut in spirals
70 g/3 oz pasta
2 slices apple
1 teaspoon oil
Chopped parsley

1. Chop onion finely and fry in butter mixed with oil. Remove to a plate.
2. Sift mustard, salt, pepper and flour together and coat meat with it.
3. Fry meat to seal it all over. Remove to plate with onion.
4. Stir any surplus flour into pan and let it brown.
5. Add apple juice, honey and stock cube. Stir until it boils.
6. Replace onion and lamb in sauce, place carrot round, cover pan and simmer till meat is tender – about 40 to 45 minutes.
7. Meanwhile, put pasta on to cook in boiling salted water, allowing time to be ready with meat.
8. Five minutes before serving, add apple to meat, turning it over in the sauce.
9. Drain pasta and toss it in oil.
10. Arrange meat, carrot and apple on a hot serving dish, strain sauce over, leaving space on dish for pasta.
11. Add pasta to serving dish and sprinkle with chopped parsley.

Anne Wallace, Dunlop, Scotland

ÍNCED LAMB WITH ÀUBERGINES OR GREEN PEPPERS

Can be made with minced beef.

For 6 people

1 large onion
2 cloves garlic
225 g/8 oz mushrooms
4 tomatoes
10 tablespoons sunflower or soya oil
450 g/1 lb minced, uncooked fillet of lamb or lean shoulder
2 tablespoons chopped parsley
Sea salt
Black pepper
2 tablespoons tomato paste
6 tablespoons stock
4 unpeeled aubergines or 3 to 4 green peppers
50 g/2 oz wholewheat flour
6 tablespoons grated parmesan cheese

If using green peppers less oil will be needed (*see paragraph 8*).

1. Peel and finely chop onions and garlic.
2. Slice mushrooms.
3. Skin and slice tomatoes (to skin *see page 66*).
4. Fry onion and garlic in 4 tablespoons of oil. Add lamb and continue cooking, stirring all the time until it is brown.
5. Add mushrooms, tomatoes, parsley, salt and pepper to taste. Cook until onions are tender.
6. Dilute tomato paste with stock and add to meat mixture. Simmer for 10 minutes.
7. Meanwhile, slice unpeeled aubergines lengthwise and dust slices with flour. Or slice green peppers, discarding core and seeds.
8. Heat remaining 6 tablespoons oil in another pan. Fry aubergine slices on both sides in the hot oil, until soft and golden. Or fry green pepper gently till softening in 2 tablespoons oil. Drain on kitchen paper.
9. Line an oven-proof dish with some of the aubergine or green pepper. Spread a layer of meat mixture on top, sprinkle with some of the parmesan. Spread another layer of aubergine and so on until dish is full, ending with a sprinkle of parmesan.
10. Bake in a moderately hot oven, Gas 5, 375°F, 190°C, for ¾ hour until cooked and nicely brown on top.

Ursula Cavanagh,
author of 'The Wholefood Cookery Book'

SAUSAGE AND MUTTON ROLL

A good cheap dish for small households, nice hot or cold.

1 finely-chopped onion
1 teaspoon lard
350 g/12 oz pork sausagemeat
Salt and pepper
1 teaspoon dried mixed herbs
1 boned breast of lamb

1. Fry onion in lard until transparent.
2. Mix sausagemeat, onion, salt, pepper and herbs together.
3. Spread this stuffing on inside of breast of lamb, roll it up and tie securely with string. Then weigh it.
4. Place on a rack in a roasting tin and cook in a moderate oven, Gas 3, 325°F, 160°C, at 40 minutes to the ½ kg/1 lb.

Serve hot with vegetables, cold with salad or with chutney or pickles.

Mrs Hilda Whitney,
Wellingborough, Northants

PRUNE AND APPLE STUFFING

For breast of lamb.

40 g/1½ oz margarine
50 g/2 oz cooked prunes
1 apple
100 g/4 oz fresh wholemeal or white breadcrumbs

1 teaspoon chopped parsley
A small pinch of mixed herbs
Salt
Pepper

1. Melt the margarine.
2. Chop the prunes, removing stones.
3. Grate or chop the apple.
4. Mix all ingredients, binding with melted margarine.

**Mrs M. Clough,
Padgate, Cheshire**

FRIED STRIPS OF BREAST OF LAMB

Start this dish the day before you want to eat it. Buy a large breast of lamb – it has more lean meat on it.

**1 large breast of lamb
1 onion
1 small carrot or piece of turnip or parsnip
1 piece celery if you have it
Salt and pepper
Water
1 beaten egg
2 oz dried breadcrumbs**

Try serving this with a sweet and sour sauce (see next recipe).

1. Put lamb in a saucepan.
2. Peel onion and chop coarsely. Scrub the other vegetables and cut them up.
3. Add vegetables to pan with salt and pepper and cover with water.
4. Bring to the boil and simmer for about 2 hours until meat is tender. Or pressure cook with 300 ml/$\frac{1}{2}$ pint of water for 30 minutes.
5. Take meat out of liquor and put both aside to cool.
6. Next day, or when quite cold, cut bones and lumps of fat out of meat and cut lean meat into even-sized strips about 5 cm/2 inches long.
7. Dip slices of meat into beaten egg and coat in breadcrumbs.
8. Lift the dripping off the pan of stock and melt a little in the frying pan.

9. Fry the strips of breast of lamb gently till golden and warmed through.

The stock will make a good soup or even a small stew for another time.

**Mrs V. Greatwood,
Castle Cary, Somerset**

A SWEET AND SOUR SAUCE

For breast of lamb, but also good with sausages, belly pork, pork chops and spare ribs.

**50 g/2 oz chopped pineapple, or 2 tablespoons pineapple jam
50 g/2 oz finely-chopped onion
1 tablespoon vinegar
1 heaped tablespoon sugar
$\frac{1}{2}$ tablespoon tomato purée or ketchup
1 dessertspoon cornflour
2 teaspoons soy sauce
300 ml/$\frac{1}{2}$ pint water
2 teaspoons oil**

1. Prepare pineapple and onion.
2. Blend together in a small pan vinegar, sugar, tomato purée, cornflour, soy sauce, and stir in the water.
3. Cook over low heat until thick.
4. Stir in the oil, pineapple and onion and cook for 5 minutes more.

Mrs Edith Griffiths

BREAST OF LAMB WITH BACON AND LEMON

**450 g/1 lb breast of lamb
Boiling water
100 g/4 oz bacon rashers
1 lemon
1 onion
A bunch of sweet herbs, such as thyme, parsley, marjoram, rosemary, mint
Stock
2 tablespoons dried breadcrumbs
1 tablespoon cornflour
A little gravy browning (optional)**

Salt and pepper
300 ml/½ pint butter beans, to serve

1. Cover butter beans with water and soak overnight.
2. Remove skin from lamb. Put meat in a pan of boiling water and simmer for 5 minutes.
3. Lay meat in cold water.
4. Take rinds off bacon and cut it into smaller pieces.
5. Use half of the bacon to line a small stew pan.
6. Slice lemon thinly and lay slices over bacon.
7. Place lamb on top of bacon and lemon and lay rest of bacon over it.
8. Chop onion coarsely and add with the herbs and enough stock just to cover (use liquid from boiling meat).
9. Bring to the boil and simmer for 1½ hours.
10. Remember to put butter beans on to cook (in the water they have soaked in) 40 minutes before dish is to be served.
11. Put lamb on to a warmed dish, sprinkle with breadcrumbs and keep hot.
12. Strain stock left in stewpan.
13. Blend cornflour with 2 tablespoons cold water and stir into stock. Put over a low heat and stir as it thickens.
14. Colour the gravy with a little gravy browning and season to taste with salt and pepper.
15. Put butter beans round the meat and serve the gravy separately.

**Mrs Iris Elliott-Potter,
Roborough, Nr. Plymouth**

LAMB AND LENTIL HOT-POT

125 g/4 oz lentils
Boiling water
2 medium-sized onions
450 g/1 lb carrots
675 g/1½ lb middle neck of lamb

1 level tablespoon plain flour
40 g/1½ oz lard
2 beef stock cubes
1 tablespoon Salt and Pepper Mix
(see page 8)
Sprig of fresh rosemary or 1 teaspoon dried rosemary well crushed, or thyme
Chopped parsley

1. Place lentils in a basin, cover with boiling water. Leave for one hour then drain, reserving the water.
2. Peel and chop onions.
3. Scrub and thinly slice carrot.
4. Trim excess fat from meat.
5. Put flour on a plate or in a clean bag and thoroughly coat the meat.
6. Melt half of the lard in a large frying pan. Fry onions and carrots for 3 minutes. Lift them out into a casserole, saving fat in pan.
7. Add remaining lard to pan and put in the floured meat to fry until brown on both sides. Add to casserole.
8. Crumble the beef stock cubes into the casserole.
9. Make the lentil water up to 600 ml/1 pint with fresh cold water and pour this over. Add salt, pepper and rosemary or thyme.
10. Cover casserole and cook in centre of moderate oven, Gas 4, 350°F, 180°C, for 1¼ to 1½ hours until meat is tender.
11. Sprinkle with chopped parsley.

Serve with a lightly-cooked green vegetable.

SPICED LIVER

For 4 people, but easy to make in smaller or larger quantities.

450 g/1 lb lamb's liver
1 large onion
3 tablespoons cooking oil
4 tablespoons flour
½ teaspoon salt
¼ teaspoon ground black pepper
¼ teaspoon cinnamon

¼ teaspoon crushed cardamon seeds
¼ teaspoon ground cloves
½ teaspoon ground coriander
300 ml/½ pint stock or water

To serve
225 g/8 oz long grain brown or white rice
4 tomatoes
4 rashers bacon
225 g/8 oz can sweetcorn (optional)

1. Skin liver and cut into small cubes.
2. Peel and chop onion.
3. Heat oil in a frying pan and fry onion gently for 2 minutes.
4. Meanwhile, mix salt, pepper and all the other spices into the flour.
5. Toss liver in the spiced flour. Add it to frying pan and fry quickly, turning it over in the fat until it is brown on all sides.
6. Put rice on to cook in another pan.
7. Add stock to liver, stir until it boils. Reduce heat and simmer for 10 minutes, stirring occasionally.
8. Meanwhile, cut rinds off bacon and cut rashers into smaller pieces.
9. Cut tomatoes in halves or quarters.
10. Grill bacon and tomato.
11. Heat sweetcorn.
12. Arrange rice round edge of large, warmed serving plate with liver in the centre. Arrange bacon, tomatoes and sweetcorn decoratively on the same dish.

**Chris Kerton,
Heston, Middlesex**

KIDNEYS WITH A SHERRY AND CREAM SAUCE

For 4 people

8 lamb's kidneys
25 g/1 oz plain flour
Salt and pepper
A grating or pinch of nutmeg
25–50 g/1–2 oz butter

150 ml/¼ pint light stock
3 large tablespoons sherry
12 stuffed olives
3 tablespoons soured cream, or natural yoghurt

Note: If you cannot buy soured cream, mix ½ teaspoon lemon juice into fresh cream for a similar effect. Leave it for an hour or more before use.

1. Remove skins and core from kidneys.
2. Season flour with salt, pepper and nutmeg.
3. Toss kidneys in seasoned flour.
4. Warm butter in a pan, add kidneys, turn up the heat. Turn kidneys over in the hot butter until sealed and butter is absorbed.
5. Pour stock and sherry over kidneys and simmer for about 5 minutes, stirring occasionally.
6. Meanwhile, slice the olives.
7. Stir in olives and soured cream.
Serve with rice, green vegetables or a green salad.

**Mrs J. M. Clark,
Stratford-upon-Avon**

KIDNEYS WITH RICE

For 4 people

1 large onion
1 green pepper
500 g/1 lb lamb's kidneys
4 tomatoes, or 1 small can
1 clove garlic (optional)
Salt
1 tablespoon corn oil
25 g/1 oz butter
1 teaspoon soft brown sugar
1 teaspoon lemon juice
1 teaspoon vinegar
2 small teaspoons Tabasco sauce
225 g/8 oz long grain brown or white rice

If using brown rice allow 20 to 25 minutes to cook. White rice takes 10 to 12 minutes.

1. Peel and chop onion. Chop up green pepper, discarding core and seeds.

2. Skin, core and slice kidneys.
3. Skin and chop tomatoes (to skin *see page 66*).
4. Crush garlic with a little salt.
5. Heat oil and butter in a pan.
6. Cook onion and green pepper gently for 5 minutes.
7. Add kidneys and cook for 3 minutes, turning them over till they are brown on all sides.

8. Add tomatoes, garlic, sugar, lemon juice, vinegar and Tabasco sauce.
9. Cover pan and simmer gently for 10 minutes.
10. Arrange rice round a warmed dish. Pour kidney mixture into centre.

**Mrs Barbara Piper,
Balham, London**

Saturday Marketing.

CHAPTER 5

SALADS AND VEGETABLES

WHOLE EGG MAYONNAISE

Made in the liquidiser.

1 whole egg
½ teaspoon sugar
1 teaspoon salt
½ level teaspoon dry mustard
¼ level teaspoon pepper
2 tablespoons vinegar or lemon juice
300 ml/½ pint salad oil, olive or sunflower oil, if possible

1. Put all ingredients except oil into liquidiser. Switch it on.
2. Pour in 2 tablespoons oil through hole in lid and allow to blend.
3. As it blends, pour in rest of oil in a steady trickle.

Will keep in refrigerator in a screw-topped jar for a week or two.
If thinner mayonnaise is required mix in a little cream or top of milk when it is needed.

FRENCH DRESSING

3 tablespoons salad oil
1 tablespoon cider or wine vinegar
A squeeze of lemon juice
1 teaspoon sugar (try barbados)
¼ teaspoon salt
A knife-end of mustard
Freshly-grated black pepper

Combine all ingredients. Stir well immediately before using.

DRESSING WITHOUT OIL

The quantities may seem small but it is plenty for salad for 4 or 5 people if used as described below.

2 tablespoons top-of-the-milk
1 tablespoon wine or cider vinegar
½ teaspoon barbados sugar
¼ teaspoon salt
Freshly-milled pepper

Mix all ingredients together in a salad bowl and toss salad in it thoroughly just before it is to be eaten.

DRESSING WITHOUT VINEGAR

4 tablespoons good salad oil, such as olive or sunflower oil
1 tablespoon lemon juice
1 teaspoon barbados sugar or 2 teaspoons honey
A pinch of salt
Freshly-milled black pepper

Mix all ingredients together in a salad bowl and toss salad in it thoroughly just before it is to be eaten.

YOGHURT DRESSING

3 tablespoons yoghurt
1 tablespoon cider vinegar
A squeeze of lemon juice
1 teaspoon honey or barbados sugar
A little milk

Mix all ingredients together, adding milk if it is too thick. Toss the salad in the dressing.
Kate Watts,
London, N.W.11

APPLE AND CUCUMBER SALAD

1 small cucumber
2 medium-sized dessert apples
Lettuce leaves
Half a box of mustard and cress
2 to 3 radishes

Dressing
150 ml/¼ pint cream or natural yoghurt
½ teaspoon lemon juice
Salt and black pepper

1. First mix the dressing.
2. Cut cucumber in half lengthways. Remove and discard the centre. Dice up the rest.
3. Quarter, core and dice apple.
4. Mix half of the dressing with

the apple and cucumber.
5. Arrange lettuce round the serving dish and pile the apple and cucumber mixture in the centre.
6. Pour remaining dressing evenly over apple and cucumber.
7. Garnish with cress and thinly-sliced radish.

**Judith Adshead,
Mottram St. Andrew, Cheshire**

AVOCADO SALAD

A way to make one avocado pear go round at least four people.

French dressing (see page 60)
½ clove garlic
1 heaped tablespoon chopped parsley
2 tablespoons finely-chopped green pepper
About 5 cm/2 inches cucumber
½ bunch watercress
1 large avocado pear
1 green-leaved lettuce
50 g/2 oz small fresh mushrooms

1. Put French dressing into salad bowl and mix it up.
2. Crush garlic and mix it with parsley into the dressing.
3. Chop green pepper quite small and mix it into the dressing.

These are the only ingredients that should go into the dressing at this stage. The rest should be added immediately before salad is to be eaten. However, they may be prepared a little in advance.

4. Cut off 5 cm/2 inches of cucumber, wash and dry. Cut into 4 pieces lengthways then slice. Do not remove skin.
5. Wash and trim watercress.
6. Wash lettuce and shake it dry.
7. Wipe mushrooms and slice, but not too small.
8. Cut avocado pear in half lengthways, remove stone and peel off skin. Turn the halves cut-side down, cut into four or five pieces lengthways. Then cut across these to make large dice. Don't cut it up too small.

9. At the last minute, stir up the dressing again. Tip into it cucumber, watercress, avocado and mushrooms. Toss these about in the dressing.
10. With your fingers, break up lettuce into easy-to-eat pieces. Toss it into bowl and see that all is well-coated with dressing.

It must be eaten at once.

ROSY BEETROOT SALAD

1 medium-sized cooked beetroot
2 to 3 stalks celery
2 dessert apples
4 tablespoons French dressing (see page 60)

Prepare the French dressing before cutting up the fruit and vegetables.

1. Dice the beetroot.
2. Slice the celery.
3. Core but do not peel the apples, unless skins are tough. Dice them.
4. Mix all the ingredients together in the dressing until a delicate rosy pink.

**Judith Adshead,
Mottram St. Andrew, Cheshire**

BEETROOT RELISH

This keeps for about 1 month, preferably in the fridge. Easy to make in smaller quantities.

450 g/1 lb beetroot
225 g/8 oz horseradish
A pinch of salt
100 g/4 oz demerara
300 ml/½ pint wine or cider vinegar

1. Wash beetroot without damaging skin.
2. Boil in plenty of water. Or cook in pressure cooker.
3. Meanwhile, wash horseradish and grate it across the sticks. It is a good idea to do this out of doors or near an open window, as it will make you 'cry'.
4. Peel and shred the cooked beetroot on coarse side of grater.

5. Mix all the ingredients together and pack into jars with vinegar-proof lids.
This relish is ready to eat immediately.

**Mrs Doreen Allars,
Welbourn, Nr. Lincoln**

CELERY AND EGG SALAD

For 4 people

**2 small heads of celery
15 g/½ oz parsley
¼ onion
2 hard-boiled eggs
15 g/½ oz chopped walnuts
4 tablespoons mayonnaise**

1. Wash and slice celery.
2. Chop parsley.
3. Chop onion finely.
4. Chop up hard-boiled eggs.
5. Mix all together with walnuts and stir in mayonnaise.

**Ursula Cavanagh,
author of 'The Wholefood Cookery Book'**

COTTAGE CHEESE SALAD

Enough for 2, but easy to make in smaller or larger quantities.

**1 hard red apple
1 teaspoon lemon juice
225 g/8 oz cottage cheese
1 tablespoon seedless raisins
25 g/1 oz coarsely-chopped walnuts
Chopped chives
Chopped parsley
Salt
Black pepper
Lettuce leaves**

1. Quarter and core apple but do not peel. Cut up into small pieces and toss in lemon juice.
2. Combine apple with the cheese, raisins, walnuts, chopped chives and parsley. Season with a little salt and black pepper.

3. Spread out lettuce leaves and pile cheese mixture on top.

CRUNCHY SALAD

For 2

**A piece red pepper
2 stalks celery
1½ crisp eating apples
A few sliced nuts
Lettuce leaves**

**Dressing
1 dessertspoon wine or cider vinegar
4 dessertspoons salad oil
Pinch of salt, pepper and mustard
1 teaspoon honey**

1. Shake all dressing ingredients together in a jar till creamy.
2. Slice red pepper finely and blanch it. To do this, drop into a pan of boiling water, leave for 1 minute, then drain and cover with plenty of cold water. Drain and pat dry.
3. Chop celery and apple. Do not peel apple unless the skin is tough. Toss with nuts in the dressing.
4. Line a salad plate with lettuce leaves and pile the dressed salad on top.

**Anne Wallace,
Dunlop, Scotland**

JELLIED HAM RING

For this you need a ring mould.

**600 ml/1 pint tomato juice
15 g/½ oz gelatine (1 envelope)
Cucumber
Parsley
Cream cheese
Black pepper
Thin slices cold cooked ham**

If you have a ring mould you will be able to work out the quantities of the ingredients needed to fill it.

1. Heat tomato juice nearly to boiling point. Remove pan from heat, sprinkle in gelatine and stir to dissolve.

2. Pour a little into ring mould. Let it set.
3. Dice cucumber, chop parsley and mix them with some black pepper into the cream cheese.
4. Spoon cream cheese mixture on to slices of ham, roll them up and fit them into the ring mould.
5. Pour over rest of the gelatine and tomato juice.
6. Put in a cold place to set.
Turn out on to a plate.
Serve with a lettuce and tomato salad.

NEW POTATO SALAD

Can be made with left-over potatoes.

450 g/1 lb new potatoes
A little boiling water
1 very small onion
1 tablespoon salad cream or
mayonnaise (see page 60)
2 tablespoons milk or, if using a
bland mayonnaise, 1 tablespoon
milk and 1 tablespoon cider
vinegar
¼ teaspoon barbados sugar
Sea salt
Black pepper
Chopped parsley
Chopped mint

1. Scrub potatoes and put them in a pan with a good lid. Add a very little boiling water. Bring to the boil, turn heat very low. Simmer and steam potatoes for 10 to 12 minutes until done but still firm. Drain and cool.
3. Meanwhile, chop onion very small and put in a serving bowl with the salad cream and milk. If using bland mayonnaise add milk and vinegar.
4. Add sugar. Season with a very little salt and freshly-grated black pepper.
5. Stir in as much chopped mint as you can spare and a little chopped parsley.
6. Cut potatoes into quarters or thick rings and mix them into the dressing until the pieces are nicely coated with dressing.

RED CABBAGE SLAW

2 tablespoons sultanas
Juice of one lemon
50 g/2 oz walnuts
Red cabbage, 3 cups when
shredded
2 to 3 tablespoons French dressing
(see page 60)

1. Place sultanas in a small bowl with the lemon juice and leave for 2 hours to plump up.
2. Chop walnuts.
3. Prepare cabbage. Shred it finely, discarding the very fibrous part of the stalk.
4. Prepare French dressing.
5. Mix sultanas with the cabbage and walnuts.
6. Add dressing and toss all together.

Judith Adshead,
Mottram St. Andrew, Cheshire

TOMATO SALAD

Easy to make in a smaller quantity.

French dressing (see page 60)
1 tablespoon finely-chopped green
pepper
1 tablespoon freshly-chopped
parsley
1 tablespoon chopped fresh mint
1 tablespoon chopped chives
450 g/1 lb tomatoes

1. Prepare dressing in the salad bowl.
2. Prepare green pepper, parsley, mint and chives and mix into dressing. This may all be done in advance.
3. Skin tomatoes (see page 66), and slice them thickly.
4. At last minute, stir up dressing and herbs, put in the tomatoes. Toss them gently so that they are covered with the dressing and herbs.

WHOLEFOOD SPECIAL SALAD

Dressing

1 tablespoon apple cider vinegar
3 tablespoons sunflower or olive oil
1 teaspoon barbados sugar
Sea salt
Pepper
A pinch garlic powder

Salad

125 g/4 oz carrots
¼ onion
½ head celery
¼ Dutch cabbage
225 g/8 oz tomatoes
1 green pepper
1 dessert apple
50 g/2 oz chopped nuts
50 g/2 oz raisins
50 g/2 oz chopped parsley

1. First, mix together the dressing ingredients.
2. Wash and grate carrots.
3. Chop onion small.
4. Wash and slice celery.
5. Wash and slice cabbage.
6. Wash and chop tomatoes.
7. Wash green pepper, remove core and seeds and slice flesh.
8. Chop parsley.
9. Wash apple, leave unpeeled. Core and chop it.
10. Toss all ingredients together in the dressing.

**Ursula Cavanagh,
author of 'The Wholefood Cookery Book'**

SPROUTING

Elizabeth Shears, author of *Why Do We Eat*, published by the Nutritional Science Research Institute of England, writes:
'Sprouts are the richest source of vitamins known. They are a storehouse of vitamin A, C, D, E, F, K and the B complex. Proteins, fats and starches are also present in abundance. Sprouted legumes, seeds and grains contribute enough first-class protein to be classified as complete.
'Sprouted grains are known to improve the health. They are reputed to compare with fresh fruit in vitamin C content and troops in World War 1 suffering from scurvy were completely cured by sprouted seeds. Sprouting is not new; there are records of the riches obtained by sprouting as far back as 200 B.C. in China. They contain nutritive values not found in the dry seed state. Sprouting releases the abundant energy that is lying dormant in the dry seed and grain. Before this energy goes into making a full-sized plant the seed is eaten in its sprouted stage and thus retains its maximum strength.
'To achieve this remarkable crop you don't need a garden, soil or compost. You have no problems with weeds or insects. You can grow them at any time of the year and in any climate. There is no waste. One pound of seed will increase to six pounds easily: some much more. Keep this in mind when buying the seeds for sprouting. Alfalfa seeds do seem expensive when you buy them in a small packet. The seed is extremely small and will go a long way, not to mention the nutritive value to be gained from it. See directions for sprouting and germinating on the next page.
'The key to successful sprouting is, of course, the quality of the seed. Those seeds which do not sprout have had the life force killed. Others may sprout but are weak. The seeds ought, if possible, to be produced from plants that have not been in contact with chemical fertilisers or sprays. They must be grown in the best possible way to produce the full nutritive value. The variety of seeds and grains to sprout is endless. Alfalfa seeds and mung beans are two of the easiest to sprout successfully and two of the best to eat, so it is advisable to start with them. As

you gain experience you will be sprouting peas, radishes, sunflower seeds, wheat, oats, barley, rye, buckwheat, green lentils, sweetcorn and different types of beans and cress. Aduki beans taste just like sprouted nuts. The grains require a twenty-four hour soaking in warm water first.

'There is nothing you cannot eat sprouts with. Put them in scrambled egg, in an omelette just before it leaves the heat, in a mushroom risotto or a chicken pilaff. They would be good in any soup you like to name. The soup is cooked on a low heat and at the last moment you throw in a handful of any type of sprouts you have available; mung beans are some of the best. Add to party dips, to cereal and nut croquettes and to vegetable pasties. Sandwiches come alive with the use of fresh raw sprouts (alfalfa are ideal for this). Use in vegetable and fruit salads.

'The Chinese use soya and mung beans liberally in their cooking. They are delicious, whichever way you choose to eat them.'

TO SPROUT CHINESE BEANSHOOTS OR MUNG BEANS

Buy ½ kg or 1 lb good quality Mung beans, organically grown if possible. Health food shops usually sell them.
You need a clean glass jar with a wide neck, a piece of muslin to cover the neck of the jar, a rubber band to secure the muslin.
1. Put 1 or 2 tablespoons Mung beans in jam jar.
2. Fill jar with lukewarm water and leave beans to soak over-night.
3. Next day, pour off water and cover jar with muslin and rubber band.

4. Find a warm, not hot, dark place to leave jar and tilt it almost upside down so that water can drain out (see sketch, page 66).
5. Rinse beans 2 or 3 times each day in clear luke-warm water, shaking them up before putting almost upside down to drain again.
6. It takes about 3 days for beans to sprout. Then let them grow in daylight until sprouts are 1½ to 2 inches long rinsing and draining twice a day. The jar may be quite filled when beans are fully sprouted.
7. You will probably be eating the beans in about a week.
8. When they are ready to eat, put them in the refrigerator if you cannot eat them all at once.

To eat sprouted beans
They are best used raw in salads (either vegetable or fruit salads) or with cream cheese or egg in sandwiches.
You can also mix them at the last minute into scrambled egg or omelettes, in a pilaff, into soups. To cook and eat on their own toss them in a little butter in a pan over low heat for no more than 3 minutes.

TO GERMINATE WHEAT

Very good with salads, fruit salads and particularly with breakfast muesli.

1. Put 2 or 3 tablespoons of wheat in a wide-necked jam jar.
2. Fill up jar with tepid water and let wheat soak for 24 hours.
3. Cover jar with a piece of muslin or gauze secured with a rubber band.
4. Shake water out of jar. Fill it again with tepid water and drain out water.

5. Prop jar nearly upside down in a place where moisture drains out but air can easily enter.

Good drainage and good ventilation are important. Leave it in a warm, dark place.
6. Fill jar with tepid water once or twice a day, shake up wheat and drain again.
7. In 3 or 4 days there will be signs of germination and wheat is ready to use. Bring jar out into full daylight. Sprouts will go on growing. Continue to water and drain each day.

The flavour becomes stronger as the sprouts grow. If you prefer the mild, wheaty flavour put jar in fridge when sprouts are still tiny.

TO GROW YOUR OWN MUSTARD AND CRESS

For something green in your salad at any time of year.

A 25 g/1 oz packet of seed will give you several crops – much cheaper than buying the cress itself.
Use plastic trays used for pre-packed foods, saucers or any shallow containers.
1. Make a pad to fit the container from a piece of towelling, folded paper towel or cotton wool. This is the growing pad.
2. Fit it in the container and moisten thoroughly.

3. Grow cress seed first – it takes longer to germinate. Sprinkle cress seed thickly on the growing pad and set the container in a dark place.
4. 3–4 days later sow the mustard on a wet growing pad in another container. Put it in a dark place for 2 to 4 days. Keep growing pads moist.
5. Look at seeds daily to see if there is any sign of growth.
6. As soon as seeds start to grow bring them into full light. Keep growing pads moist.
7. Cut crop with sharp scissors when it is 2·5–5 cm/1–2 inches high.

TO MAKE A BOUQUET GARNI

Tie the following together firmly with a piece of strong cotton: half a bay leaf, a sprig of thyme and several sprigs of parsley, including stalks.
If dried herbs are used, tie up the following in a small piece of muslin: half bay leaf, 1 teaspoon parsley and $\frac{1}{2}$ teaspoon thyme. Other herbs may be used for particular dishes. Marjoram or basil are often used.
Herbs enhance almost any dish. For some sauces in particular it is better to use a bouquet garni than to spoil the appearance of the sauce with pieces of dried herbs.

TO CRUSH GARLIC

If you do not have a garlic crusher, simply peel the clove of garlic and put it on a small plate. Sprinkle with a little salt then crush the garlic with the end of a table knife. The salt helps reduce the garlic to a creamy pulp.

TO SKIN TOMATOES

Put the tomatoes in a basin and pour on enough boiling water to cover them. Leave for 10 to 15 seconds, drain and cover at once with cold water. Wait half a minute and the tomato skins will be easily removed.

For green tomatoes: prick them in several places with a fork. Then pour on boiling water. Leave for a few minutes. Skins will be easily removed.

STUFFED AUBERGINES

For 4 people

Allow half a large aubergine or one whole small one per person.

2 large aubergines (about 350 g/ 12 oz each)
1 medium-sized onion
4 tablespoons oil
100 g/4 oz streaky bacon
1 clove garlic (optional)
75 g/3 oz fresh wholemeal breadcrumbs
½ level teaspoon dried oregano
Pinch of dried thyme
Salt and pepper
2 tomatoes
25 g/1 oz finely-grated, well-flavoured cheese, preferably Parmesan
A little chopped parsley

1. Cut the ends off aubergines and halve lengthways. Cut out some of the flesh to leave 5–12 mm/¼–½ inch walls.
2. Roughly chop flesh and put aside.
3. Peel and chop onion.
4. Heat oil in a frying pan and quickly fry aubergine cases for ½ minute on the cut side. Lift them out into an oven-proof dish or roasting tin, leaving as much oil as possible behind in the frying pan.
5. Add chopped onion to pan and cook gently until beginning to brown.
6. Cut rinds off bacon and chop the rashers. Add to onion.
7. Cook for a minute and add aubergine flesh. Cook for 10 minutes, stirring occasionally.

8. Peel clove of garlic, chop finely and add to frying pan.
9. Mix breadcrumbs and herbs in a bowl and season well.
10. Drain fried mixture and add to the crumbs. Mix well.
11. Pour any remaining oil into aubergine cases.
12. Pile the filling mixture into aubergine cases.
13. Slice tomatoes and arrange on top.
14. Sprinkle with cheese.
15. Cover dish, foil will do, and bake in a moderate oven, Gas 4, 350°F, 180°C, for ¾ to 1 hour until aubergines are tender.
16. Sprinkle a little chopped parsley on to each aubergine and serve.

BROAD BEANS WITH BACON

Can be made in large or small quantities.

Broad beans
Rashers of bacon, or bacon pieces
1 small onion
¼ teaspoon oil
2 teaspoons cider or tarragon vinegar
½ teaspoon sugar
Freshly-ground black pepper
Salt

1. Prepare beans. If they are very young and tender do not pod them. String the pods and cut into 5 cm/2 inch lengths.
2. Take rinds off rashers and cut bacon into small pieces.
3. Peel and finely chop onion.
4. Put beans on to cook with a very little water in a pan with a good lid. As soon as they reach boiling point turn heat down and simmer and steam for 5 to 8 minutes. Broad beans are unpleasant if overcooked.
5. As soon as beans are on, put bacon on to fry briskly in oil for 1 minute, turning over in pan.
6. Add onion, reduce heat and let

it soften for 3 or 4 minutes.

7. Add vinegar, sugar and freshly-ground black pepper and cook slowly for 2 to 3 minutes, stirring.

8. Drain beans, throw them into pan, add a pinch of salt, toss them in the mixture and serve at once.

**Betty Yeatman,
Adelaide, South Australia**

GREEN BEANS IN SAVOURY SAUCE

**450 g/1 lb French or runner beans
Sea salt
1 onion
1 clove garlic
25 g/1 oz butter
1 tablespoon olive oil
2 tablespoons chopped parsley
20 g/¾ oz wholewheat flour
300 ml/½ pint milk
¼ teaspoon nutmeg
Pepper**

1. Leave French beans whole, just string if necessary. String and slice runner beans.

2. Cook beans in a very little boiling water, about 1 cm/½ inch in pan is enough, with a very little salt. Cover pan and just simmer for 8 to 10 minutes until tender.

3. Meanwhile, chop onion and garlic.

4. Melt butter with olive oil, stir in parsley, garlic and onion. Fry gently for 2 minutes.

5. Stir in flour and gradually add milk. Add nutmeg, season well and boil for 3 minutes.

6. Add drained beans. Heat through and serve.

**Ursula Cavanagh,
author of 'The Wholefood Cookery Book'**

ORANGE BEETROOT

For 4 people

**6 small cooked beetroot
25 g/ 1 oz butter
25 g/1 oz wholewheat flour**

**150 ml/¼ pint water
Grated rind and juice of 2 oranges
Sea salt
Pepper
2 teaspoons barbados sugar**

1. Slice the cooked beetroot into rounds.

2. Melt butter in a pan, stir in flour, then slowly add water, stirring all the time.

3. Add grated orange rind, then juice, salt, pepper and sugar. Stir until sauce thickens.

4. Stir in beetroot slices.

Serve hot or cold.

**Ursula Cavanagh,
author of 'The Wholefood Cookery Book'**

CABBAGE DELIGHT

**Cabbage
Onion and/or green pepper
Butter
Salt
Freshly-ground pepper**

Use as much cabbage as you need. Use 1 onion, 1 green pepper to 1 small cabbage.

1. Shred cabbage finely.

2. Peel and slice onion finely. Slice green pepper finely, discarding core and seeds.

3. Melt enough butter in pan to cover the bottom. Fry onion and green pepper gently until it just begins to soften.

4. Add cabbage and let it cook gently until tender but still crunchy. Shake pan freqently to stop it sticking or browning. Do not overcook.

5. Add salt and pepper to taste and serve at once.

**Sybil Norcott,
Irlam, Nr. Manchester**

CARROTS IN A CASSEROLE

Goes well with Casseroled Rabbit (*see page 34*)

450 g/1 lb carrots

Boiling water or light stock
¼ teaspoon salt
1 teaspoon butter
Pepper

1. Scrub or scrape carrots and cut them into 2·5 cm/1 inch pieces.
2. Put them in a small casserole with a well-fitting lid. Pour over boiling water or light stock just to cover.
3. Put in a moderate oven, Gas 3, 325°F, 160°C, for ¾ hour.
4. Just before serving, stir in butter and a shake of pepper.

CAULIFLOWER AND TOMATOES

1 medium-sized cauliflower
1 onion
1 clove garlic (optional)
Salt
450 g/1 lb tomatoes, or a 400 g/ 14 oz can
1 tablespoon oil
25 g/1 oz butter
1 tablespoon chopped parsley
Black pepper

Sauce
40 g/1½ oz margarine
40 g/1½ oz flour
300 ml/½ pint milk
100 g/4 oz grated cheese
25 g/1 oz dry breadcrumbs

1. Divide cauliflower into even-sized florets and put them in a saucepan. Pour in about 300 ml/ ½ pint of boiling water, bring back to the boil, cover the pan, turn down the heat and let cauliflower cook in this way for 7 minutes.
2. Drain off cauliflower water into a cup for later use and keep cauliflower warm.
3. Peel and chop onion. Crush garlic (see page 66).
4. Skin the tomatoes (see page 66), and cut into quarters.
5. Heat oil and butter in a frying pan and cook onion and garlic just to soften, not brown.
6. Add tomatoes, parsley, salt and black pepper and cook 1 to 2 minutes.

7. Now make the sauce. Melt margarine in a small saucepan. Stir in flour and allow it to cook for a minute.
8. Stir in 150 ml/¼ pint of cauliflower water and the milk. Bring to the boil, stirring, and cook for 3 minutes.
9. Add 75 g/3 oz of the cheese. Reheat but do not boil.
10. Spread tomato mixture over the base of an oven-proof dish. Lay florets of cauliflower on top, then pour the sauce over.
11. Mix the dry crumbs with rest of the cheese, and sprinkle on top.
12. Put dish under grill to brown.

This dish is good on its own, but don't overcook the cauliflower. If you think flower will be cooked before stalks are tender, split stalks as you do with Brussels sprouts.

COURGETTES

Nice as a starter or as a vegetable to accompany another dish.

For 4 people

450 g/1 lb courgettes
1 teaspoon chopped parsley
1 teaspoon chopped fresh tarragon
2 bay leaves
1 clove garlic
Sea salt
Pepper
Juice and grated rind of ½ lemon
5 teaspoons olive oil
4 teaspoons water

1. Trim courgettes and slice them into rings.
2. Put all the other ingredients in a saucepan and heat gently, stirring until well mixed.
3. Add courgettes, cover pan and bring to the boil. Reduce heat and simmer for about 10 minutes, until courgettes are tender but not overcooked.
4. Allow mixture to cool, chill it and serve with a green salad.

Ursula Cavanagh, author of
'The Wholefood Cookery Book'

LENTIL PUDDING

175–225 g/6–8 oz lentils
1 medium-sized onion
175 g/6 oz cheese
1 or 2 tomatoes (optional)

1. Cover lentils in water and soak overnight.
2. Next day, peel and finely chop onion.
3. Put lentils and water in which they were soaking into a large saucepan, add the onion and add more cold water, if necessary, to cover.
4. Bring to the boil, lower heat, cover pan and simmer until lentils are tender and have absorbed most of the water. Stir occasionally, but particularly towards end of cooking time. It will take only about 15 minutes.
5. Meanwhile, grate the cheese.
6. When lentils are done, drain off any excess liquid. Don't throw it away – you can use it in soup.
7. Stir 125 g/4 oz of the cheese into pan of lentils.
8. Turn it all out into a well-greased, 1 litre/2 pint pie-dish.
9. Sprinkle rest of cheese on top.
10. Bake in a moderately hot oven, Gas 6, 400°F, 200°C, for 15 to 20 minutes, or until cheese has melted and browned a little.

If using tomatoes, lay them overlapping in a row across the middle, 5 minutes before end of cooking time.

Mrs Grace Dix,
Downton, Wiltshire

LENTIL SAVOURY

175 g/6 oz lentils
75 g/3 oz lean bacon
175 g/6 oz carrots
1 onion
1 clove garlic
25 g/1 oz dripping
1 dessertspoon plain flour
150 ml/¼ pint red wine
300 ml/½ pint hot water, or use
450 ml/¾ pint chicken stock instead of wine and water

A bouquet garni (see page 66) or a bunch of fresh herbs such as thyme and parsley
Finely-peeled zest of ½ orange
25 g/1 oz butter

1. Soak lentils in water overnight. Then drain them.
2. Remove rinds and cut bacon into strips.
3. Peel carrots and cut into 7 mm/¼ inch dice.
4. Peel and chop onion finely.
5. Crush the garlic (see page 66).
6. Melt dripping in a pan and fry bacon over a low heat.
7. Add carrots and onion and continue cooking until onion is soft.
8. Stir in flour and mix well.
9. Slowly stir in wine and water.
10. Add lentils, crushed garlic, bouquet garni and herbs, and the orange peel cut in strips.
11. Bring to the boil stirring all the time. Lower heat, cover pan and let it just simmer for about 1 hour or until lentils are cooked. Add more boiling water if necessary.
12. Remove bouquet garni and orange peel. Season to taste. Stir in the butter. It should have the consistency of a thick, mushy cream.
13. Pour into a warmed serving dish.

Jean Welshman,
Malton, E. Yorkshire

MARROW STUFFED WITH MUSHROOMS

1 marrow, about 1 kg/2 lb
2 small onions
200 g/7 oz mushrooms
1 small tomato
25 g/1 oz butter or margarine
2 tablespoons wholemeal breadcrumbs
½ level teaspoon sage
Salt
Black pepper
A little hot water, if necessary

Use a dish that will be a tight fit for the marrow.

1. Peel marrow and cut off one end. Scoop out the seeds.
2. Peel onions and chop them finely.
3. Wipe mushrooms and chop them finely.
4. Skin and chop up the tomato. (To skin see page 66.)
5. Melt butter or margarine in a frying pan. Fry onions gently for 2 or 3 minutes until soft but not brown.
6. Add mushrooms and fry lightly for 2 or 3 minutes.
7. Mix together tomato, breadcrumbs, sage, a little salt and plenty of black pepper, freshly-milled if possible.
8. Add to this the mushroom mixture and combine it all. It may be best to mix it with your hands. It should feel firm. If it is too dry add 2 or 3 tablespoons hot water.
9. Stuff it into the marrow and replace the cut off end. Cover with well-greased, greaseproof paper and foil and put in a tight-fitting dish.
10. Cook in a moderate oven, Gas 3, 325°F, 160°C, for 2 hours or until marrow is soft all over.

**Mrs S. J. Collyer,
Camborne, Cornwall**

SAVOURY OATMEAL DUMPLING

**1 onion
1 carrot
100 g/4 oz chopped or grated suet
200 g/8 oz oatmeal
Salt and pepper
A little milk**

1. Peel and chop onion. Scrub and chop or grate carrot.
2. Mix onion, carrot, suet and oatmeal and season well with salt and pepper.
3. Add enough milk to make mixture soft but not sticky.
4. Turn dumpling into a greased bowl (a 2 litre/3 pint size is big enough). Tie a layer of greaseproof paper over the top and

put on a covering of foil.
5. Steam for 1 hour. If you do not have a steamer, stand basin on a trivet in a saucepan of boiling water and boil it for 1 hour. Water should come half-way up sides of basin. If replenishing, use boiling water.
Serve hot with brown gravy.

**Mrs Margaret Hussey,
Leeds**

SCALLOPED POTATOES

For 4 people

**725–900 g/½–2 lb potatoes
150 ml/¼ pint milk
25 g/1 oz butter
½ teaspoon Salt and Pepper Mix**
(see page 8)

1. Peel and thinly slice potatoes. Arrange them in a 1·2 litre/2-pint casserole.
2. Heat milk in a pan with butter, salt and pepper. Do not boil.
3. Pour over the potatoes. Cover dish (greaseproof paper and foil will do).
4. Cook on lower shelf of a moderately hot oven at Gas 5, 375°F, 190°C, for 1 hour. Remove cover for final 15 minutes to crisp top.

BAKED STUFFED TOMATOES

Enough for 2 people

**4 large firm tomatoes
1 tablespoon grated onion
100 g/4 oz grated cheese
1 thick slice wholemeal or white bread made into crumbs
50 g/2 oz chopped mushrooms (optional)
Salt and pepper
2 rashers bacon**

1. Stand tomatoes stalk end down, slice off rounded end and scoop out insides with a teaspoon.
2. Mix tomato pulp with onion, cheese, breadcrumbs, mushrooms

and seasoning. This forms a crumbly mixture.

3. Fill tomato shells, replace the tops.

4. Spread remaining mixture in a small, greased, oven-proof dish. Make 4 hollows in mixture and stand tomatoes in them.

5. Remove rinds from bacon. Cut rashers in halves. Stretch each piece on a board with back of a knife and make it into a roll.

6. Thread bacon rolls on a skewer. Lay these across tomatoes.

7. Bake in middle of a moderately hot oven, Gas 5, 375°F, 190°C, for 20 minutes.

8. To serve, remove skewer and arrange bacon rolls.

**Margaret Heywood,
Todmorden, Yorkshire**

TURNIPS WITH ORANGES

Particularly good with duck or pork.

For 4 to 6 people

**12 young turnips
2 oranges
Water
Salt
50 g/2 oz butter
Coarsely-ground black pepper**

1. Peel turnips.

2. Grate rind finely from one orange and squeeze juice from them both.

3. Put whole turnips with orange juice in a saucepan. Just cover with water and add a little salt. Bring to the boil, cover pan and simmer until tender, about 20 to 25 minutes.

4. Drain turnips, saving liquid for soup or gravy.

5. Put turnips into a warmed, buttered, heatproof dish. Put a dab of butter on each and sprinkle all over with grated orange rind and coarse black pepper.

6. Put under a hot grill for 2 minutes to melt butter and crisp and dry the orange rind and tops of turnips.

**Sybil Norcott,
Irlam, Nr. Manchester**

CHAPTER 6

RICE, PASTA, PANCAKES, FRITTERS, CHEESE AND EGG, SAVOURIES, SNACKS, AND SANDWICH SPREADS

TO COOK BROWN RICE

For 2 people

Allow 2 oz uncooked rice per person.
Once you have tried brown rice, which is very nourishing, you will probably prefer it to the refined white rice which has so little goodness.

100 g/4 oz brown rice
300 ml/½ pint boiling water
A few grains of sea salt

Some types of brown rice take longer to cook than others, but here is a method of cooking which you will be able to adapt to suit the rice you have.
1. Put rice in a pan which has a well-fitting lid and pour on the boiling water.
2. Add salt. Bring it back to the boil and give it a stir.
3. Turn heat down to low, put lid on pan and simmer for 20 minutes.
4. After 15 minutes, check to see that it is not getting too dry and add a little more boiling water if necessary. Cover and simmer again.
5. At 20 minutes, test rice: if centre is no longer hard, it is done.

The rice absorbs the water during cooking and, if it works out right, the rice is cooked and all the water absorbed at the same time. There is no waste of goodness in throwing excess water down the drain.

INDIAN FRIED RICE

Long grain white rice
1 onion
1 tablespoon butter or oil
1 teaspoon turmeric
1 teaspoon cummin
Salt and pepper
A little curry powder (optional)

1. Cook as much rice as required.
2. Peel and finely chop onion.
3. Heat butter or oil in a heavy frying pan and fry onion gently until softening but not brown.
4. Add turmeric and cummin and cook a little.
5. Stir in rice and heat gently.
6. Add salt and pepper and a little curry powder to taste.
Goes well with Chicken and Almonds (*see page 25*).

Betty Yeatman,
Adelaide, South Australia

LANDER MACCARONEN

A Swiss dish.

For 4 to 5 people

2 medium-sized potatoes
200 g/8 oz brown or white macaroni
2 small onions
50 g/2 oz butter
150 ml/¼ pint milk
100 g/4 oz grated cheese

1. Peel and cut potato into roughly even-sized pieces, about the size of walnuts.
2. Put potato into a pan of boiling, salted water and boil for 3 minutes.
3. Add macaroni and boil for 7 to 10 minutes.
4. While this is boiling, peel and slice onions and fry in butter until golden. Drain onions, leaving butter in frying pan.
5. Drain potatoes and macaroni and place in layers with the cheese in a warm serving dish.
6. Place onions on top.
7. Pour milk into the frying pan and bring to the boil. Pour it over the onions and serve immediately.

Judith Adshead,
Mottram St. Andrew, Cheshire

74

MACARONI FRITTERS WITH TOMATO SAUCE

Also a way to use up other left-over cooked pasta.

For 2 people

75 g/3 oz brown or white macaroni
or
100 g/4 oz cooked pasta cut up small
1 level tablespoon plain flour
2 tablespoons milk
2 eggs
50 g/2 oz grated Parmesan cheese
Salt and Pepper Mix *(see page 8)*
Oil for frying

Tomato Sauce
A 225 g/8 oz can of tomatoes
1 tablespoon oil
1 small onion, peeled and grated
A good pinch of sugar
Salt and Pepper Mix
Pinch of basil or ½ bay leaf
(optional)

1. Put macaroni on to cook, following directions on packet.
2. Put into a small pan all the tomato sauce ingredients, bring to the boil and simmer for 20 minutes. Crush tomatoes with a wooden spoon to thicken sauce. While sauce cooks continue with fritters.
3. Drain cooked macaroni and allow to cool a little.
4. Put flour in a bowl and gradually stir in the milk to make a smooth paste.
5. Add eggs, beat lightly with a fork to mix well.
6. Stir in the cheese, season and add macaroni. Stir well to mix.
7. Heat a little oil in a large frying pan. Put the mixture in four, large separate spoonfuls into the pan.
8. Cook gently for 2 to 3 minutes on each side.

Serve at once with the sauce. Sauce may be sieved if you prefer it smooth.

SPAGHETTI WITH HAM, BLACK OLIVES AND PARSLEY

Boiling water
Level teaspoon salt
350 g/12 oz brown or white spaghetti
100 g/4 oz cooked ham
50 g/2 oz firm black olives
2 tablespoons chopped parsley
300 ml/10 fluid oz single cream or
225 g/8 oz natural yoghurt
Black pepper

1. Fill a large pan, three quarters full of boiling water. Add the salt.
2. Gently work spaghetti into pan, moving it with a fork so that it does not stick together.
3. Cook spaghetti in the boiling water for 15 to 20 minutes. (10 to 12 minutes for white spaghetti.) It is done when a piece will break apart neatly between finger and thumb. This is called *al dente*. If it is overdone it will be mushy when mixed with other ingredients.
4. Meanwhile, chop up ham finely and remove stones from olives.
5. Drain spaghetti. Return it to pan with ham, olives, 1 tablespoon of parsley, the cream or yoghurt and plenty of freshly-milled black pepper. Toss over a medium heat until piping hot. Sprinkle remaining chopped parsley on top just before serving. Eat at once.

SPAGHETTI WITH MEAT SAUCE

Enough for 4 people but easy to make less or more.

2 medium-sized onions
2 medium-sized carrots
1 clove garlic
1 tablespoon oil
225 g/8 oz minced beef
2 tablespoons tomato purée, or
1 small can peeled tomatoes
Pinch basil or mixed herbs
A wine glass of red wine (optional)
300 ml/½ pint beef stock

50 g/2 oz mushrooms
15 g/½ oz butter or margarine
350 g/12 oz brown spaghetti, if
available
50 g/2 oz finely-grated cheese, to
serve

1. Peel and finely chop onions.
2. Scrub and chop carrots.
3. Peel and crush garlic (see page
66).
4. Heat oil in a large pan and fry
onions gently for 3 or 4 minutes.
5. Add meat and stir it around
over the heat until it separates and
colours.
6. Add carrot, garlic, tomato,
herbs, wine and enough of the
stock just to keep it moist.
7. Put lid on and let sauce simmer
gently for 30 minutes, stirring
occasionally and adding more
stock if necessary.
8. Chop up mushrooms.
9. Put spaghetti on to cook in
plenty of boiling, lightly-salted
water 15 minutes before it is
required.
10. Fry mushrooms lightly in
butter or margarine for 2 to 3
minutes and stir them into sauce
just before you serve it.
11. Put cheese in a small bowl and
serve separately.

WHOLEWHEAT
PANCAKES

100 g/4 oz wholewheat flour
½ level teaspoon sea salt
1 egg
300 ml/½ pint milk
A little butter, oil or a piece of
suet, to cook

1. Mix flour and salt in a bowl and
make a well in the centre.
2. Drop in the egg and begin to stir
it in, adding the milk slowly until
all flour is incorporated.
3. Beat mixture hard or whisk it
for 5 minutes. Put it in a jug.
4. Heat a frying pan and rub it
with butter, oil or suet.

5. Carefully pour mixture into
frying pan to make very thin
pancakes. Cook till golden brown
underneath and drying on top.
6. Toss or slip them over and cook
until golden brown.

SUET PANCAKES

175 g/6 oz flour (plain, self-raising
or wholewheat)
Pinch of salt
75 g/3 oz finely-grated beef suet
6 tablespoons milk
A little extra suet for frying, or a
little lard

1. Mix flour, salt, suet and milk to
a soft but not sticky dough.
2. Using a floured board, roll out
thinly – about as thick as a 50p
piece. Cut rounds about 8 cm/3
inches across.
3. Heat a frying pan and grease it
lightly with a piece of suet. Fry
pancakes until golden brown on
both sides.

Serve at once, very hot, with
golden syrup. Try also with butter,
treacle, marmalade, lemon curd or
Marmite.

Mrs Eva Hay,
Reigate, Surrey

SPINACH AND
WHOLEMEAL
PANCAKE ROLL

Enough for 4 or 5 people

Each part of this dish can be
prepared in advance and then
completed just in time for the
meal.

Pancake Batter
100 g/4 oz wholemeal flour
½ teaspoon salt
1 egg
150 ml/¼ pint milk
150 ml/¼ pint water
50 g/2 oz lard, for cooking batter

Filling
450 g/1 lb fresh spinach, or 225 g/
8 oz frozen leaf spinach

1 tablespoon finely-chopped onion
25 g/1 oz butter
100 g/4 oz cottage cheese
1 egg-yolk
$\frac{1}{4}$ teaspoon grated nutmeg
Seasoning

Tomato Sauce
1 onion
1 clove garlic
A 400 g/14 oz can of tomatoes
Pinch mixed herbs
1 level teaspoon barbados sugar
Seasoning

Basic White Sauce
15 g/$\frac{1}{2}$ oz butter
15 g/$\frac{1}{2}$ oz flour
150 ml/$\frac{1}{4}$ pint milk
Seasoning

To finish
50 g/2 oz grated hard cheese
First mix the batter
1. Mix flour and salt in a bowl and make a well in the centre.
2. Drop in the egg.
3. Mix milk and water together.
4. Beat egg into flour, gradually adding milk and water and beat thoroughly.
5. Leave to stand in a cool place for 20 minutes.

Next prepare the filling
1. Cook spinach in a very little water until it is tender.
2. Melt butter and fry onion until soft but not brown.
3. Sieve cottage cheese.
4. Drain and cut spinach and drain again very thoroughly as it must not be wet.
5. Mix together spinach, onion, cottage cheese, egg-yolk, nutmeg and seasoning.

Now make tomato sauce
1. Peel and chop onion finely.
2. Crush garlic (*see page 66*).
3. Mix all ingredients together in a small pan, bring to the boil, cover pan, lower heat and simmer for 20 minutes.

Back to the pancake roll
1. Melt the 50 g/2 oz lard in an oblong Swiss-roll type of tin

(approx. 23 × 30 cm/9 × 12 inches).
2. Pour in the batter.
3. Bake near top of a moderately hot oven, Gas 6, 400°F, 200°C, for about 10 minutes, or until the mixture is set and cooked, but not crisp.
4. Turn out on to a piece of greased, greaseproof paper.
5. Spread the spinach mixture over the cooked batter and roll up like a Swiss-roll.
6. Cut across the roll into slices 2·5 cm/1 inch thick. Lay these, slightly-overlapping, in an oven-proof serving dish.

The sauces and final preparation
1. Make the white sauce. Melt butter in a small pan, stir in flour and cook it gently for 1 minute.
2. Add milk gradually, stirring well, and bring to the boil. Let it cook 2 or 3 minutes and season to taste.
3. Mix together white sauce and tomato sauce. Pour over the spinach rolls.
4. Cover with grated cheese.
5. Bake in a hot oven, Gas 7, 425°F, 220°C, for 15 minutes.

This dish freezes well.

Jean Welshman,
Malton, E. Yorkshire

SAVOURY FRITTERS

Basic Fritter Batter
100 g/4 oz wholewheat or white self-raising flour
$\frac{1}{2}$ level teaspoon salt
Black pepper
1 large egg
150 ml/$\frac{1}{4}$ pint milk
A little lard, for frying

The Batter
1. Mix flour, salt and pepper in a bowl. Make a well in the centre and drop in the egg.
2. Gradually stir in half the milk using a wooden spoon. Mix well and beat until smooth, adding rest of milk. If using wholewheat flour add 1 tablespoon extra milk.

77

The Fillings
Bacon: Cut 225 g/8 oz streaky bacon into strips and fry until crisp.

Cheese: Grate 175 g/6 oz Cheddar cheese.

Tuna and parsley: Flake 200 g/7 oz tinned tuna and mix into it 2 tablespoons chopped parsley.

Sweetcorn: Drain a 200 g/7 oz can of sweetcorn with peppers.

Salami: Finely chop 100 g/4 oz or more.

Cold cooked chicken with mushrooms: Chop 50 g/2 oz mushrooms, fry for 2 minutes in 15 g/½ oz butter or margarine. Mix with 100 g/4 oz or more finely-chopped chicken.

The Fritters
1. Stir the filling of your choice into the batter or divide the batter and make a variety of fritters.
2. Heat a little lard in a frying pan. Add tablespoonfuls of mixture and fry until golden brown on both sides.

Serve with fresh watercress.

CRISPY BACON BITES

Makes 12 small balls. They are deep-fried and very tasty.

1 medium-sized onion
225 g/8 oz cooked bacon from a joint, or fresh rashers
25 g/1 oz bacon dripping
25 g/1 oz plain wholewheat or white flour
150 ml/¼ pint chicken stock
(½ stock cube will do)
Pepper
75 g/3 oz fresh wholemeal or white breadcrumbs
1 beaten egg
1 tablespoon tomato ketchup (optional)

1. Peel and roughly cut up onion. Cut up bacon.
2. Mince bacon and onion.
3. Melt dripping, stir in flour and cook for 1 minute.

4. Add stock and stir until boiling. Cook for 1 minute.
5. Remove from heat, add a good shake of pepper, 50 g/2 oz of the crumbs and half the beaten egg. Mix well. Mix in minced bacon and onion and tomato ketchup.
6. Make 12 small balls of mixture. Leave to become firm – 30 minutes in fridge is enough.
7. Brush balls with remaining beaten egg and roll them in rest of breadcrumbs.
8. Deep fry in hot fat for about 7 or 8 minutes. Drain on kitchen paper.

Serve with grilled tomatoes or baked beans.

HARVEST PUDDING

1 large onion, chopped
15 g/½ oz butter
100 g/4 oz fresh wholemeal or white breadcrumbs
1 teaspoon dried sage
3 tablespoons milk
Or **instead of the above, use 1 packet sage and onion stuffing prepared in a large bowl according to instructions**
50 g/2 oz grated cheese
100 g/4 oz cooked ham, chopped
2 large eggs, separated
Black pepper
Pinch of mustard powder

1. Fry onion in butter until soft.
2. Put breadcrumbs in a large bowl, mix in sage and fried onion, adding tablespoons of milk to moisten
Or prepare packet of sage and onion stuffing as indicated on packet and allow to cool.
3. Stir in cheese, ham, egg-yolks, some freshly-ground black pepper and the mustard powder. Mix well.
4. Beat egg-whites until stiff and fold them in lightly with a metal spoon.
5. Turn mixture into a greased oven-proof dish.
6. Bake in a moderately hot oven, Gas 5, 375°F, 190°C, for 35 minutes.

Serve with a lightly cooked green vegetable or a green salad.

SAVOURY BREAD AND BUTTER PUDDING

4 large slices wholemeal or white bread
Butter
Yeast extract
100 g/4 oz grated cheese
1 small onion, grated
2 beaten eggs
300 ml/½ pint milk
Salt and pepper
Pinch of dry mustard

1. Butter bread and spread lightly with yeast extract.
2. Cut bread into small cubes.
3. Grease an oven-proof dish.
4. Spread half of bread cubes in bottom of dish.
5. Cover with half of cheese, then onion.
6. Add rest of bread and finally rest of cheese.
7. Add milk and seasoning to beaten eggs and strain this over the pudding.
8. Bake in a moderate oven, Gas 4, 350°F, 180°C, for 35 to 40 minutes.

Margaret Heywood,
Todmorden, Yorkshire

CHEESE AND POTATO BAKE

For 1 person, but easy to make in large quantities.

1 large potato
About 25 g/1 oz cheese
Salt and pepper
A little butter or margarine

1. Boil potato in a little water.
2. Grate cheese.
3. Mash potato and mix in cheese, salt and pepper.
4. Grease a small oven-proof dish with a little butter or margarine, put in potato mixture, smooth top

and dot with tiny pieces of butter or margarine.
5. Cook in moderate oven, Gas 3, 325°F, 160°C, for 10 to 15 minutes.
Eat hot with bacon, fried egg, green salad, or cold meats.
Try also with one small sliced tomato arranged on top of potato and cooked with it (paragraph 5).

Mrs Hilda Whitney,
Wellingborough, Northants

CHEESE AND POTATO LUNCH

For 2 people

450 g/1 lb potatoes
75 g/3 oz margarine
2 tablespoons milk
Salt and pepper
100 g/4 oz porridge oats
1 teaspoon dry mustard
100 g/4 oz grated cheese

1. Simmer potatoes in a very little water. Drain and mash with 25 g/ 1 oz of the margarine, the milk, salt and pepper.
2. Grease a warmed pie-dish with a little of remaining margarine and put in mashed potato.
3. Melt rest of margarine.
4. Mix oats, mustard and cheese and stir in melted margarine.
5. Spread this mixture on top of hot potatoes and grill gently until topping is crisp and brown. Or bake in a hot oven, Gas 6, 400°F, 200°C, for 15 minutes.

Try these variations
Add 1 finely-chopped, lightly-fried onion, or chopped chives to potato.
Put a layer of skinned and sliced tomatoes under the topping.
Enough for 4 people if served with bacon, grilled ham, beefburgers or sausage.

Margaret Heywood,
Todmorden, Yorkshire

CHICKEN SOUFFLÉ

Base
1 medium-sized onion

2 rashers back bacon
15 g/½ oz butter or margarine
100 g/4 oz mushrooms

Soufflé
25 g/1 oz butter
25 g/1 oz plain flour
150 ml/¼ pint milk
225 g/8 oz cooked chicken
3 eggs
Salt and pepper

1. Preheat oven to moderately hot, Gas 5, 375°F, 190°C, and have the centre shelf ready.
2. Peel and slice onion.
3. Remove rind from bacon and cut rashers into pieces.
4. Melt 15 g/½ oz butter in a saucepan and add onion and bacon. Cook gently for 5 minutes until onion is soft.
5. Clean and quarter mushrooms. Add to pan and cook for 3 minutes.
6. Turn mixture into a greased soufflé dish or similar deep oven-proof dish.
7. **For the soufflé:** melt 25 g/1 oz butter in the saucepan and stir in flour. Cook for 2 minutes without browning.
8. Gradually add milk, stirring until thick. Remove from heat.
9. Chop chicken finely.
10. Stir chicken into sauce and remove from heat.
11. Separate egg-yolks from whites. Stir yolks into sauce with a little salt and pepper.
12. Stiffly beat whites until they will stand in peaks.
13. With a metal spoon, fold whites lightly into chicken mixture.
14. Pour into the soufflé dish over the mushroom mixture.
15. Put immediately into the oven for 30–35 minutes, until well-risen and golden brown. Try not to open oven during cooking.

Serve at once. A soufflé falls very soon after it is taken from oven into cooler air.

HAM AND CHEESE SOUFFLÉ

100 g/4 oz ham
1 small bunch chives
25 g/1½ oz butter
25 g/1 oz wholewheat or plain flour
150 ml/¼ pint milk
40 g/1½ oz Parmesan cheese
Salt
Black pepper
3 eggs, separated

1. Preheat oven to moderately hot, Gas 6, 400°F, 200°C, and have ready the centre shelf. Lightly butter a 1·2 litre/2 pint soufflé dish or similar straight-sided dish.
2. Chop up ham finely. Chop chives.
3. Melt butter in a saucepan. Stir in flour to blend smoothly with butter and cook for 2 minutes.
4. Gradually add milk, stirring until thick. Remove from heat.
5. Stir in ham, chives, most of cheese, a very little salt, black pepper and egg-yolks. Beat well together.
6. Whisk egg whites until stiff enough to stand up in peaks.
7. With a metal spoon, fold in egg whites.
8. Pour into soufflé dish and sprinkle remaining cheese on top.
9. Put straight away into oven and cook for 30 minutes without opening the door.

Serve immediately. A soufflé sinks almost as soon as it reaches the cold air.

HARD-BOILED EGGS IN CUCUMBER SAUCE

For 2 people

3 eggs
½ a cucumber
300 ml/½ pint milk
Salt and pepper
15 g/½ oz butter or margarine
15 g/½ oz flour

1. Slice cucumber, but not too thinly.
2. Put in a pan with milk and seasoning and simmer for 20 minutes.
3. When cucumber has cooked for about 10 minutes, put eggs on to hard-boil for 10 minutes.
4. Melt butter or margarine in a small pan. Stir in flour and let it sizzle for 1 minute.
5. When cucumber is cooked strain liquid and add it gradually to butter and flour, stirring over low heat as it thickens. Bring to the boil and cook for 2 or 3 minutes.
6. Shell hard-boiled eggs, cut in halves lengthways and lay them in a small, warmed dish.
7. Add cucumber to sauce, reheat and pour over the eggs.

Serve with thin slices of brown bread-and-butter.

Mrs M. Earl-Spyvee,
Cross-in-Hand, Sussex

KIDNEY SCRAMBLE

A snack for 4, but easy to make for any number.

4 lamb's kidneys
25 g/1 oz butter
¼ teaspoon Worcestershire sauce
1 level teaspoon tomato ketchup
¼ level teaspoon mustard
Salt and black pepper
4 large eggs
4 tablespoons single cream or top of the milk
4 slices buttered toast

1. Skin kidneys and cut out the core. Chop flesh finely.
2. Fry kidneys in half of the butter, turning them until lightly browned.
3. Stir in sauces and mustard. Season with salt and pepper.
4. Cook over moderate heat for a further 2 minutes, then keep warm.
5. Lightly beat eggs and cream together and season a little.

6. Melt remaining butter in a clean pan, and pour in the eggs. Cook over a low heat, stirring occasionally until just beginning to set.
7. Spoon egg on to toast and top with kidneys.

Serve at once with a crisp salad.

Mrs T. Birch,
Weston Zoyland, Somerset

KIDNEY TOAST

For 2 people

3 lamb's kidneys
25 g/1 oz butter
½ teaspoon chutney
½ teaspoon curry paste
1 tablespoon Worcestershire sauce
1 teaspoon grated lemon rind
Pinch of salt
Hot-buttered toast

1. Skin kidneys and remove core. Cut each kidney into about 8 pieces.
2. Melt butter in a pan, add chutney, curry paste, Worcestershire sauce and lemon rind and stir together over low heat.
3. When hot, stir in kidneys. Stir over low heat until kidneys are cooked and lightly browned— about 5 to 8 minutes.
4. Prepare toast.
5. Spread kidney mixture on hot toast and serve without delay as hot as possible.

Mrs Iris Tassell,
Bexhill-on-Sea, Sussex

SANDWICH SPREADS

Beef and Pickle

Put a few slices of cold, cooked beef in the liquidiser with 2 chopped pickled onions and 2 teaspoons horseradish sauce. Blend till smooth.

Cheese and Chutney

Mix grated, hard cheese with chutney.

Stella Boldy,
Sykehouse, N. Humberside

MORE SANDWICH SPREADS

Cheese and Egg

3 eggs
100 g/4 oz cheese
Salt and pepper
1 to 2 tablespoons salad cream

1. Boil eggs for 5 to 6 minutes and allow to cool.
2. Grate cheese.
3. Shell eggs and put them in a bowl. Mash them up with a fork and mix in grated cheese.
4. Add salt, pepper and salad cream to taste. Mix well together.

Miss Jill-Anne Dudgeon

Curried Egg

25 g/1 oz butter, softened
1 level teaspoon curry powder
A little salt
2 hard-boiled eggs

Soften butter without melting it and beat in curry powder and salt. Mix well with finely-chopped eggs.

Peanut Butter, Carrot and Cress

2 slices wholemeal bread
Peanut butter
Grated carrot
Mustard and cress

Spread peanut butter thinly on both slices of wholemeal bread. Fill with carrot and cress.

Sardine

Sardines
Dash of vinegar
Dash of Worcestershire sauce
Pepper

Mash sardines in a saucer, adding the other ingredients to taste.

Tomato Paste

Spread on toast or in sandwiches.

8 medium-sized tomatoes
1 small onion
100 g/4 oz margarine
1 beaten egg
50 g/2 oz grated cheese
100 g/4 oz brown or white breadcrumbs
Pepper and salt

1. Skin tomatoes (see page 66).
2. Cut up tomatoes quite small.
3. Peel and finely chop onion.
4. Melt margarine in a pan, add tomato and onion and cook gently until tender.
5. Mash, sieve or liquidise the mixture until smooth.
6. Put tomato mixture in pan, add beaten egg and stir over a low heat until mixture thickens. Do not let it boil.
7. Stir in cheese and breadcrumbs, and pot at once.

Will keep for several weeks in the refrigerator.

**Mrs M. Skipworth,
Louth, Lincolnshire**

Watercress and Cream Cheese

25 g/1 oz butter, softened
50 g/2 oz cream cheese
2 tablespoons chopped watercress
Salt
Black pepper

Soften butter without melting it. Beat it into cream cheese and beat in watercress. Season to taste.

CHAPTER 7

PIES AND PASTRIES

FLAKY PASTRY

200 g/8 oz plain flour (preferably strong plain flour)
Pinch of salt
75 g/3 oz butter or firm margarine
75 g/3 oz lard
½ teaspoon lemon juice
Approximately 125 ml/¼ pint cold water

1. Sift flour and salt into a bowl.
2. Cut up butter or margarine and lard and mix together well. Chill a little and divide into quarters.
3. Rub one of the quarters into flour and salt and mix to a pliable but not sticky dough with lemon juice and water. Cover and allow to rest 10 to 15 minutes in a cool place.
4. Using a floured board, roll out pastry 3 times as long as wide – about 7 mm/¼ inch thick.
5. Using a second quarter of fat, place in dabs over the top two-thirds of pastry.
6. Fold bottom third up, and top third down. Seal edges lightly with rolling pin. Turn, leaving pressed edges at top and bottom and at right-hand side. Wrap in greaseproof paper and put it to rest in the refrigerator or in a cold place for 10 minutes.
7. Repeat rollings with third and then fourth quarter of fat, then wrap and leave in a cold place for 1 hour, or overnight. If leaving it overnight, wrap a damp cloth round greaseproof covering to make quite sure it is still soft and has no crust when you need to use it.
8. Roll out and use as required, rolling out quite thinly unless recipe states otherwise.
Cook pastry at Gas 7, 425°F, 220°C. Reduce heat to Gas 5, 375°F, 190°C, if filling is not cooked.

SHORTCRUST PASTRY

225 g/8 oz plain flour
½ teaspoon salt

50 g/2 oz firm margarine (cheaper variety)
50 g/2 oz lard
2 full tablespoons water (use a measure)

1. Put flour and salt in a basin.
2. Rub in fats until mixture is like fine breadcrumbs.
3. Mix to a firm dough with the water. Do not be tempted to add more water unless your kitchen is very cold, and then only 1 teaspoon more.
4. Knead lightly until smooth and basin comes clean.

SWEET SHORTCRUST PASTRY

225 g/8 oz soft or fine plain flour
½ level teaspoon salt
125 g/5 oz firm margarine
1 egg-yolk
25 g/1 oz castor sugar
3 teaspoons water (use a measure)

1. Mix flour and salt in a bowl.
2. Rub in margarine until mixture is like fine breadcrumbs.
3. Mix together egg-yolk, sugar and water.
4. Mix to a firm dough with egg-mixture. Leave in a cool place for 15 minutes before rolling out.

CHEESE PASTRY

225 g/8 oz plain flour
½ level teaspoon salt
½ level teaspoon dry mustard
Pinch of cayenne pepper
75 g/3 oz firm margarine
75 g/3 oz finely-grated cheese
1 egg-yolk
2 tablespoons water (use a measure)

1. Sieve flour, salt, mustard and cayenne pepper into a bowl.
2. Rub in margarine.
3. Mix in cheese.
4. Mix egg-yolk with water and bind all together.
5. Knead until smooth. Wrap in greaseproof paper. Leave for ½ hour before rolling out.

WHOLEWHEAT PASTRY

For savoury flans, etc.

225 g/8 oz wholewheat flour
½ teaspoon salt
75 g/3 oz margarine
50 g/2 oz lard
3 tablespoons cold water (use a measure)

1. Mix flour and salt in a bowl.
2. Rub in fats.
3. Mix to a firm dough with water. Knead lightly till smooth and basin comes clean.

SWEET WHOLEWHEAT PASTRY

225 g/8 oz wholewheat flour
Pinch of salt
1 teaspoon dark brown barbados sugar
75 g/3 oz margarine
50 g/2 oz lard
3 tablespoons water (use a measure)

1. Mix together flour, salt and sugar.
2. Rub in fats.
3. Mix to a firm dough with the water. Knead lightly until smooth and basin comes clean.

WHOLEWHEAT CHEESE PASTRY

225 g/8 oz wholewheat flour
Pinch of salt
Pinch of dry mustard and cayenne pepper
100 g/4 oz butter, or firm margarine
75 g/3 oz finely-grated cheese
1 egg-yolk
3 tablespoons water (use a measure)

1. Mix together flour, salt, mustard and cayenne.
2. Rub in butter or margarine. Add cheese.

3. Mix egg-yolk with water and bind all together.
4. Knead until smooth. Cover and leave in a cool place for 15 to 20 minutes before rolling out.

MAKING FLANS

A few tips
First decide which kind of pastry you would like to use:

Shortcrust, page 84
Sweet shortcrust, page 84
Cheese, page 84
Wholewheat, this page
Sweet wholewheat, this page
Wholewheat cheese, this page

Next, how much pastry is needed for different sizes of flan ring or flan tin?

15 cm/6 inch	100 g/4 oz flour
18 cm/7 inch	
20 cm/8 inch	175 g/6 oz flour
23 cm/9 inch	
25 cm/10 inch	225 g/8 oz flour

Important
Traditionally, if a recipe calls for 8 oz pastry you have to make up a dough based on 8 oz flour. If any recipe in this book departs from this principle, what you have to do will be made clear.

TO BAKE A FLAN CASE BLIND

'Blind' means that the flan case is cooked or partly cooked before the filling is added.

1. Put flan ring or flan tin on a baking sheet.
2. Using floured board, roll out pastry to a round, 5 cm/2 inches wider than diameter of your flan ring or tin.
3. Cut a circle of greaseproof paper the same diameter as pastry and grease it.
4. Fit pastry into flan ring. Press in firmly and roll off surplus pastry with rolling pin.

5. Prick base of pastry all over.
6. Crumple up paper to make it easier to fit. Open it out and fit it, greased-side down, into flan.
7. Put in a layer of dried peas or haricot beans, about 1·5 cm/½ inch deep. (Save your baked peas and beans in a jar for the next flan you make – they cannot be eaten.)

Oven Temperatures and Times

Shortcrust
Hot, Gas 7, 425°F, 220°C, for 10 to 12 minutes. Remove beans and paper, switch temperature to moderate, Gas 4, 350°F, 180°C, and return for a further 7 to 8 minutes to set and bake right through.

Sweet shortcrust
Moderately hot, Gas 5, 375°F, 190°C, for 10 minutes. Remove beans and paper and return to oven for a further 10 to 15 minutes until golden and firm.

Cheese pastry
Moderately hot, Gas 6, 400°F, 200°C, for 17 to 20 minutes until set. Remove beans and paper and return to oven for 5 or 6 more minutes to dry out a little.

Wholewheat, savoury or sweet
In centre of hot oven, Gas 7, 425°F, 220°C, for 20 minutes until set. Or bake for 15 minutes, then remove beans and paper and bake for 10 minutes more. Reduce heat to moderately hot, Gas 5, 375°F, 190°C, if browning too quickly.

Wholewheat cheese pastry
In centre of hot oven, Gas 7, 425°F, 220°C, for 15 to 20 minutes until set. Remove beans and paper. Reduce heat to moderately hot, Gas 5, 375°F, 190°C, and bake for 10 minutes more.

If baking flan cases to store, remove flan ring for last 5 minutes. Cool on a wire rack and store in an air-tight tin.

CHESHIRE FIDGET PIE

150 g/5 oz shortcrust pastry (see page 84) **or wholewheat pastry** (see page 85)
450 g/1 lb cooking apples
225 g/8 oz onions
350 g/12 oz streaky bacon
Seasoning
100 ml/3 to 4 fluid oz stock or water

1. Make layers in a pie-dish of apple, onion and bacon until all is used. Season between layers with pepper and a very little salt.
2. Pour over the stock or water.
3. Roll out pastry on floured board.
4. Cover pie-dish with pastry.
5. Trim edges.
6. Re-roll trimmings and cut leaves to decorate pie.
7. Bake in a moderate oven, Gas 4, 350°F, 180°C, for 2 hours.

**Sybil Norcott,
Irlam, Nr. Manchester**

SAVOURY SAUSAGE FLAN

Enough for 5 to 6, but easy to make smaller quantities.

225 g/8 oz made-up shortcrust pastry (see page 84)

Filling
450 g/1 lb potatoes
25 g/1 oz margarine
1 medium-sized onion or
1 teaspoon mixed herbs
225 g/8 oz pork sausagemeat
1 level teaspoon Salt and Pepper Mix (see page 8)

1. Cook potatoes in a little salted water. Drain and mash well with margarine.
2. Using a floured board, roll pastry out 7 mm/¼ inch thick. Line a 20 cm/8 inch pie-plate or flan dish.
3. Peel and finely chop or grate onion and add it, or mixed herbs, to sausagemeat with salt and

pepper. Mix well.

4. Spread sausagemeat in uncooked pastry case.

5. Pipe potato to cover the sausage. Or spread it over, forking the top.

6. Bake in a hot oven, Gas 7, 425°F, 220°C, for 20 minutes. Reduce temperature to moderately hot, Gas 5, 375°F, 190°C, for 20 minutes more.

Delicious eaten hot or cold. Can also be made as individual tartlets. Freezes well.

**Pat Dixon,
Holmfirth, W. Yorkshire**

SAUSAGE CARTWHEEL FLAN

175 g/6 oz cheese pastry (see page 84)

Filling
1 medium-sized onion
15 g/½ oz margarine
225 g/8 oz skinless sausages
1 large egg
150 ml/¼ pint milk
Salt and pepper
50 g/2 oz grated cheese

1. Roll out pastry. Line a 20 cm/ 8 inch flan ring.

2. Peel and chop onion.

3. Melt margarine and fry onion gently until soft. Lift onion out of pan into flan case.

4. Lightly fry sausages in pan.

5. Cut 6 of the cooked sausages to fit in flan, like the spokes of a wheel. Put aside on a plate for a moment.

6. Cut up remaining sausages and trimmed ends and put these on top of onion.

7. Beat egg, milk and seasonings. Pour into flan.

8. Arrange the 6 sausages like a cartwheel in flan. Sprinkle cheese between the spokes.

9. Bake in a hot oven, Gas 6 to 7, 400° to 425°F, 200° to 220°C, for about 35 minutes.

SAUSAGE AND APPLE TURNOVERS

Makes 6 turnovers

275 g/10 oz wholewheat pastry (see page 85)

For the Filling
450 g/1 lb sausagemeat
2 lamb's kidneys (optional)
1 medium-sized onion
225 g/8 oz cooking apples
Salt and pepper
A little milk, to glaze

1. First make the pastry.

2. **The filling:** put sausagemeat in the mixing bowl. Remove skin from kidneys. Cut them in half along the round edge. Take out the white core. Cut up kidneys into 7mm/½-inch pieces. Add them to sausagemeat.

3. Peel and grate onion. Grate apple without peeling it.

4. Mix onion and apple into sausagemeat with a little salt and pepper.

5. Prepare a large space, lightly floured, for rolling out pastry. Divide dough into two pieces. Work each piece lightly into a brick-shaped lump. This will make it easier to roll out as required.

6. Roll out each piece into a rectangle 15 cm × 46 cm/ 6 inches × 18 inches.

7. Divide each piece into 3 equal portions. Each portion will be 15 cm/6 inches square, and there will be six portions.

8. Place even quantities of filling on to each square.

9. Brush edges of pastry with water. Fold them corner to corner to make triangles. Press edges together to seal well.

10. Brush each turnover with milk and make 3 cuts in the top of each one to let out the steam.

11. Lift them on to a large baking sheet. Bake on centre shelf of a moderately hot oven, Gas 6, 400°F, 200°C, for 45 minutes when they will be golden brown and cooked. Serve either hot or cold.

CHEESE SAUSAGE ROLLS

Cheese Pastry
100 g/4 oz plain flour
Pinch of dry mustard
Salt
Pepper
A few grains cayenne pepper
50 g/2 oz butter
50 g/2 oz grated hard cheese
1 egg-yolk
2 teaspoons cold water
A little milk

Filling
200 g/8 oz sausagemeat

1. Sieve flour, mustard, salt, pepper and cayenne pepper into a bowl.
2. Rub butter or margarine into flour mixture.
3. Mix in grated cheese.
4. Bind together with the beaten egg-yolk mixed with 2 teaspoons of cold water.
5. Using a floured board, roll pastry out into a long strip about 6–8 cm/2½–3 inches wide.
6. Place sausagemeat in a long roll down the centre.
7. Damp one edge of pastry and roll up sausagemeat, pressing lightly to seal the join. Cut sausage rolls into desired lengths.
8. Place on a baking sheet. Brush a little milk round the basin used for egg-yolk and use this to glaze sausage rolls.
9. Bake in a moderately hot oven, Gas 6, 400°F, 200°C, for about 15 minutes until golden brown.

**Stella Boldy,
Sykehouse, N. Humberside**

BAKED SAVOURY ROLLS

Enough for 3 to 4 helpings (very filling)

First, choose a filling

Minced Meat
1 small onion
25 g/1 oz dripping or lard
225 g/8 oz minced meat, cooked or uncooked
Salt and pepper
A little water
1 small carrot
1 small potato

1. Peel and chop onion finely.
2. Melt fat, add onion and meat and fry till browning.
3. Season and, if necessary, add a little water to make a moist paste.
4. Grate carrot and potato and mix them into the meat. Leave it to cool.

Bacon and Mushroom
2 to 3 rashers bacon
1 onion
50 g/2 oz mushrooms
3 to 4 tomatoes
A little dripping
Salt and pepper

1. Remove rinds and cut up bacon.
2. Peel and chop up onion.
3. Slice mushrooms.
4. Skin and chop tomatoes. (To skin *see page 66*.)
5. Fry bacon and onion for 2 or 3 minutes, adding a little dripping if necessary.
6. Add mushrooms and tomatoes and cook 2 or 3 minutes more. Season to taste. Allow to cool.

Cheese and Onion
175 g/6 oz grated cheese
1 grated onion
Salt and pepper

Mix cheese and onion and season lightly.

Pastry
100 g/4 oz self-raising flour
¼ teaspoon salt
50 g/2 oz shredded suet
3 to 4 tablespoons cold water.

1. Sift flour and salt into a bowl and mix in suet.
2. Add enough water to mix to a pliable dough.
3. Using a floured board, shape pastry into a rectangle. It will be

easier then to roll out to about 20 × 25 cm/8 × 10 inches.

4. Brush edges with water, 1·5 cm/½ inch is enough.

5. Spread on the filling, up to the damped edges.

6. Roll it up lightly like a Swiss roll. Press edges to seal.

7. Put roll on to a greased baking sheet.

8. Bake in middle of a moderately hot oven, Gas 5, 375°F, 190°C, for about 30 minutes until crisp and brown.

**Margaret Heywood,
Todmorden, Yorkshire**

SMOKED HADDOCK AND COTTAGE CHEESE FLAN

For 4 people

You need a 20 cm/8 inch flan ring on a baking sheet or a flan tin with removable base.

Pastry
175 g/6 oz wholewheat flour
¼ level teaspoon salt
100 g/4 oz margarine
2 tablespoons cold water (use a measure)

Filling
175 g/6 oz smoked fillet of haddock or other smoked fish
Water or milk and water to cook fish
25 g/1 oz butter
1 small onion
50 g/2 oz mushrooms
2 eggs
3 tablespoons milk
100 g/4 oz cottage cheese
Freshly-ground black pepper
Juice of ½ lemon
Salt
Chopped parsley

1. Put flour and salt in a bowl, rub in margarine and mix to a firm dough with water. Leave it to rest for 5 to 10 minutes.

2. Roll it out on a floured board to a round about 25 cm/10 inches across. Cut a circle of greaseproof paper about 25 cm/10 inches across and grease it lightly on one side. Fit pastry into flan ring. Roll off surplus pastry with a rolling pin.

3. Bake it 'blind' – i.e., the flan case is partly cooked before filling goes in. (*See pages 85–6, paras. 5–7.*)

4. Bake in centre of hot oven, Gas 7, 425°F, 220°C, for 10 minutes. Remove beans and paper and bake another 10 minutes. If pastry is browning too quickly, reduce heat to Gas 5, 375°F, 190°C.

5. Remove from oven but leave pastry in flan ring on baking sheet. Lower oven temperature to Gas 2, 300°F, 150°C.

6. **The filling:** put fish in a shallow pan with water, or milk and water, just to cover. Bring to boil, cover pan and simmer 8 minutes or until cooked.

7. Peel and finely chop onion. Slice mushrooms.

8. Melt butter and fry onion gently till soft. Add mushrooms and cook for 1 or 2 minutes.

9. Drain fish when cooked and flake it.

10. Combine fish, onion and mushrooms and spread over base of flan.

11. Beat together eggs and milk, then beat in cottage cheese, pepper and lemon juice. A little salt may be added, but remember the fish is salty.

12. Pour this mixture over fish and put flan straight into cool oven, Gas 2, 300°F, 150°C, and cook for 40 minutes until filling is set and golden on top.

Serve hot or cold, sprinkled with chopped parsley.

SALMON AND CUCUMBER FLAN

Shrimps or prawns may be used instead of salmon.

For 4 people

Shortcrust pastry made up with 100 g/4 oz flour (*see page 84*). Or, use a ready-baked 18 cm/7 inch flan case.

Filling
25 g/1 oz margarine
25 g/1 oz plain flour
1 level teaspoon mustard
1 level teaspoon sugar
Good pinch salt
A good sprinkle of pepper
175 ml/6 fluid oz milk
1 beaten egg
1 tablespoon white or cider vinegar
100 g/4 oz salmon
Chopped parsley to taste (optional)
Slices of cucumber

1. Set oven at moderately hot, Gas 6, 400°F, 200°C.
2. Use a plain 18 cm/7 inch flan ring on a baking sheet.
3. Roll out pastry on a floured board to a round. The pastry should measure about 5 cm/ 2 inches more than diameter of the flan ring.
4. Follow instructions for baking 'blind' (see page 85, paragraphs 1 to 7).
5. Bake for about 20 minutes until golden brown on the edges. Remove beans and paper and put back in oven for 5 minutes more to 'dry off' centre of the flan.
6. Slide flan off baking sheet on to a cooling wire. Lift off flan ring and leave flan case to cool.

If eating it hot, keep flan-case warm.

For the filling
1. Melt margarine in a saucepan.
2. Add flour and cook for about 2 minutes.
3. In a small basin, blend mustard, sugar, salt and pepper with a little of the milk.
4. Add blended mustard mixture to remaining milk.
5. Gradually stir into pan.
6. Heat, stirring all the time, until mixture thickens.
7. Remove from heat, cool slightly

and beat in the egg. Heat again but do not allow mixture to boil or egg will curdle.
8. Lastly, add vinegar, flaked salmon and chopped parsley.
9. Pour into flan case and garnish with slices of cucumber.

**Stella Boldy,
Sykehouse, N. Humberside**

TUNA PLAIT

200 g/8 oz plain flour
Pinch of salt
50 g/2 oz lard
50 g/2 oz margarine
75 g/3 oz grated cheese
2 tablespoons cold water
175 g/7 oz tin tuna fish
1 small onion, chopped finely
Squeeze of lemon juice
A little beaten egg

1. Sift flour and salt into a bowl.
2. Rub fat into flour until mixture is like fine breadcrumbs.
3. Add 25 g/1 oz of the grated cheese and mix pastry to a stiff dough with cold water.
4. Mix together tuna, chopped onion, grated cheese and lemon juice.
5. Roll out pastry into a rectangle about 20 cm/8 inches wide and 30 cm/12 inches long. Dampen edges.
6. Pile filling down centre of pastry. Make slits on either side of filling at 2·5 cm/1 inch intervals and cross these alternately over filling to form plait. Seal top and bottom.
7. Brush with beaten egg. Bake in a hot oven, Gas 7, 425°F, 210°C, for 25 minutes.

**Janet Town,
Pudsey, Yorkshire**

CELERY AND CHEESE FLAN

175 g/6 oz wholewheat cheese pastry (see page 85) or a ready-baked 20 cm/8 inch flan case.

Filling and Sauce
1 head celery
1 onion
25 g/1 oz margarine
25 g/1 oz plain flour
Salt and pepper
150 ml/¼ pint milk
50 g/2 oz grated cheese

1. Roll out pastry, line a 20 cm/
8 inch flan ring and bake 'blind'
(see page 85).
2. Clean celery and slice it into
5 cm/2 inch lengths.
3. Peel and slice onion.
4. Cook celery and onion gently till
tender in a little water in a pan
with close-fitting lid. Drain and
reserve the liquor.
5. Melt margarine in a pan. Stir in
flour, salt and pepper. Cook
2 minutes.
6. Gradually stir in milk and
150 ml/¼ pint of celery liquor. Boil
for 2 minutes.
7. Add celery, onion and half of
grated cheese.
8. Spread filling in flan case.
Sprinkle on remaining cheese.
9. Heat through in a moderately
hot oven, Gas 6, 400°F, 200°C, for
15 minutes until golden brown on
top.

CHEESE AND EGG PIE

For 4 people

100 g/4 oz shortcrust pastry,
either white or wholewheat (see
pages 84 and 85)
200 g/8 oz Cheddar cheese
4 eggs
Salt and pepper
25 g/1 oz fresh brown
breadcrumbs
A very little butter
2 tablespoons milk

1. Line an 18 cm/7 inch flan ring or
tin with the pastry.
2. Bake it 'blind' but not brown
(see page 85). Let it cool for 5
minutes or so.

3. Place half the cheese in flan case
and make 4 small hollows. Break
an egg into each.
4. Season with salt and pepper.
5. Cover with rest of cheese and
then the breadcrumbs.
6. Dot with a little butter and
moisten all over with the milk.
7. Bake in a moderate oven, Gas 4,
350°F, 180°C, for ½ to ¾ hour until
nicely brown and set.

This is delicious served with sliced
tomatoes, either grilled or fresh.

**Judith Adshead,
Mottram St. Andrew, Cheshire**

WHOLEWHEAT CHEESE AND ONION FLAN

For 2 or 3 people

You will need a 20 cm/8 inch flan
ring on a baking sheet or flan tin
with loose bottom.

175 g/6 oz wholewheat pastry (see
page 85).

Filling
25 g/1 oz butter
1 tablespoon vegetable oil
450 g/1 lb onions
2 eggs
2 tablespoons cream or top of the
milk
Salt and pepper
Grating of nutmeg
75 g/3 oz grated cheese

1. First make the pastry, line the
flan tin and bake 'blind' for 20
minutes (see page 85). Remove
from oven, take out baking beans
and paper but leave flan in ring.
Lower oven temperature to
moderate, Gas 4, 350°F, 180°C.
2. Meanwhile, start the filling. Melt
butter with oil in a large frying
pan and fry onions gently until
soft but not brown. They will need
turning over with a spoon.
3. In a bowl, beat eggs, cream (or
milk top), a little salt, pepper and
nutmeg and mix in 50 g/2 oz of the
cheese. Add onions.

4. Pour filling into flan case.
Sprinkle with the rest of cheese.
5. Put it in moderate oven, Gas 4,
350°F, 180°C, for 30 minutes.

ALMOND TART

100 g/4 oz shortcrust pastry (see
page 84)

Filling
50 g/2 oz butter or margarine
50 g/2 oz granulated sugar
50 g/2 oz semolina
1 teaspoon almond essence
1 beaten egg
½ teaspoon baking powder
**2 tablespoons jam, apricot goes
well with this**

You can use a small or large .
sandwich tin, an 18 cm/7 inch pie-
plate or flan ring. You can make it
up as tartlets, or you can use a
small square tin and serve it in
slices.

1. Make up pastry and line the tin.
2. **For the filling:** melt margarine
and sugar in a saucepan.
3. Stir in semolina and cook for a
few minutes, stirring all the time.
4. Remove from heat, add almond
essence and stir well to cool
mixture a little.
5. Add beaten egg and baking
powder. Mix well.
6. Spread jam over pastry.
7. Pour mixture from saucepan
into pastry case and spread
evenly.
8. Bake in a moderate oven, Gas 6,
400°F, 200°C, until it is nicely
brown, about 30 minutes. Tartlets
take about 15 minutes.

**Mrs Evelyn Taylor,
Flixton, Manchester**

APPLE DAPPY

More than enough for 6. Make half
the quantities for 3 or 4.

225 g/8 oz self-raising flour
1 teaspoon baking powder
Pinch of salt

50 g/2 oz margarine
150 ml/¼ pint milk
450 g/1 lb cooking apples
1 tablespoon demerara sugar
**½ level teaspoon cinnamon,
nutmeg, ground cloves or mixed
spice**

Syrup
1 lemon or a little lemon essence
1 tablespoon golden syrup
15 g/½ oz margarine
100 g/4 oz sugar
200 ml/7 fluid oz water

1. Make syrup first. Peel a fine
strip of lemon rind and squeeze
lemon. Put rind, juice and all other
ingredients in a pan and stir over
a gentle heat until sugar is
dissolved. Remove from heat and
leave in the pan until needed.
2. Sift flour, baking powder and
salt into a bowl.
3. Rub in margarine.
4. Mix to a dough with the milk.
5. Roll out on a floured board to a
rectangle about 20 × 13 cm/8 × 5
inches, and 7 mm/¼ inch thick.
6. Peel, core and chop apples.
7. Spread them on pastry.
8. Mix sugar and spice together
and sprinkle over apple.
9. Roll up pastry and apple like a
Swiss roll. Then cut into slices
about 2·5 cm/1 inch thick.
10. Grease an ovenproof dish and
lay slices flat in it.
11. Remove lemon rind from syrup
and pour over the apple slices.
12. Bake in a moderately hot oven,
Gas 6, 375°F, 190°C, for about 30
minutes.

Serve with cream or custard.

**Joan Guy,
Tavistock, Devon**

STRUDEL FLAN

For 4 to 5

Flan
25 g/1 oz barbados sugar
150 g/5 oz wholewheat flour
150 g/5 oz butter
50 g/2 oz unblanched almonds

1 teaspoon lemon juice
1 egg-yolk
Filling
25 g/1 oz split blanched almonds
450 g/1 lb cooking apples
1 tablespoon barbados sugar
1 tablespoon raisins
1 tablespoon water
Meringue top
1 egg-white
40 g/1½ oz demerara sugar

1. **Start with pastry.** Mix sugar and flour and rub in fat.
2. Chop 50 g/2 oz unblanched almonds, add them with lemon juice and mix.
3. Bind pastry with lightly-beaten egg-yolk. Chill dough for ½ hour.
4. Oil a 20 cm/8 inch fluted flan ring and place on a lightly-oiled baking sheet.
5. Roll out pastry on a floured board to a round 25 cm/10 inches across. Fit it into flan ring, pressing it in gently. Roll off surplus pastry.
6. Bake in a moderately hot oven, Gas 6, 400°F, 200°C, for 20 minutes.
7. **Meanwhile prepare filling.** Chop blanched almonds. Peel, core and slice apples.
8. Put almonds, apples, sugar, raisins and water in a pan and simmer gently for 5 minutes. Remove from heat and allow to cool.
9. When pastry case is done, remove from oven and allow to cool.
10. Reduce oven heat to slow, Gas 2, 300°F, 150°C.
11. Fill pastry case with apple mixture.
12. **The meringue:** whisk up egg-white until stiff, then gradually whisk in sugar. Pipe in diagonal patterns across top of flan.
13. Put in cooled oven for 15 minutes or until meringue is crisp. Serve warm or cold with cream.

**Ursula Cavanagh,
author of 'The Wholefood Cookery
Book'**

SWEET POTATO PASTRY
Easy to cut down for smaller households

450 g/1 lb potatoes
25 g/1 oz butter or margarine
1 level teaspoon dark brown sugar (barbados)
100 g/4 oz wholewheat or plain flour

1. Peel potatoes and cut into even-sized pieces. Simmer in a little, lightly-salted water until tender. Drain and dry over a low heat.
2. Mash with a potato masher or fork. Mix in, a little at a time, butter or margarine, sugar and flour. Beat well after each addition.
3. Turn out pastry on to a floured board and knead until smooth.

Potato Apple Cake
Potato pastry as above
450 g/1 lb cooking apples
2 dessertspoons dark brown sugar (barbados)
25 g/1 oz butter
A little demerara sugar

1. Cut pastry into 2 pieces, one slightly larger than the other.
2. Roll out each piece to a round: one about 19 cm/7½ inches across, the other about 23 cm/9 inches across.
3. Place smaller round on a greased baking sheet.
4. Peel and thinly slice apples. Arrange sliced apples on pastry base, leaving a border about 1 cm/¼ inch wide round edge. Sprinkle apples with 1 dessertspoon of sugar.
5. Brush border of pastry with water and place larger circle of pastry over apples. Seal edges together. Make a small slit in centre of pastry to enable steam to escape.
6. Bake in centre of a moderately hot oven, Gas 5, 375°F, 190°C, for 35 to 40 minutes until cake is lightly-browned.
7. Remove from oven and, using a sharp and pointed knife, carefully

cut out a circle from top of cake about 8 cm/3 inches across. Place butter and remaining dessertspoon of sugar inside cake.

8. Replace 'lid' and return to oven for 5 minutes to allow butter to melt.

9. Lift cake on to a serving plate and sprinkle with demerara sugar.

Serve straightaway with fresh cream. Tends to go 'sad' if allowed to go cold.

BAKEWELL PUDDING

Made this way for generations.

Enough for 6 people

Shortcrust Pastry
100 g/4 oz self-raising flour
Pinch of salt
50 g/2 oz butter or margarine
1 brimming tablespoon water

Filling
50 g/2 oz butter or margarine
50 g/2 oz castor sugar
2 beaten eggs
A few drops almond essence
25 g/1 oz ground almonds (optional)
Strawberry jam

1. Sift flour and salt into a bowl.
2. Rub in butter or margarine.
3. Mix to a firm dough with water.
4. Using a floured board, roll out and line a 20 cm/8 inch flan tin.
5. **For the filling:** beat butter and sugar together until creamy.
6. Beat in eggs gradually.
7. Add essence and ground almonds, beat well.
8. Spread a little strawberry jam over pastry case.
9. Pour in egg mixture, making sure it runs to the edges otherwise jam may escape.
10. Bake in a moderately hot oven, Gas 5, 375°F, 190°C, for 25 to 30 minutes or until filling is set.

Eat hot with ice-cream, or cold with or without cream.

Jan Wilson,
Youlgrave, Derbyshire

CUSTARD TART

For this you need a pie tin or dish about 18 cm/7 inches in diameter and 4 cm/1½ inches deep. A custard tart should be deep, so an ordinary flan ring is not the best choice.

Pastry
175 g/6 oz plain flour
¼ teaspoon salt
50 g/2 oz firm margarine
35 g/1 oz lard
3 to 4 dessertspoons cold water

Filling
250 ml/8 fluid oz milk
1 rounded tablespoon sugar
2 large eggs
Nutmeg

1. Mix flour and salt in a bowl.
2. Rub in fats.
3. Mix to a firm dough with 3 or 4 dessertspoons of cold water. Leave to rest while preparing filling.
4. Warm milk, dissolve sugar in it then let it cool. Dissolving the sugar stops it falling to bottom of custard mixture in pastry case. A layer of sugar on pastry base tends to make it go rubbery.
5. Beat eggs lightly but not to a froth. Add to milk mixture.
6. Using a floured board, roll out pastry a good 25 cm/10 inches in diameter. Fit it into pie tin. Roll off surplus pastry with rolling pin.
7. Strain custard mixture into pastry case. Grate a little nutmeg on top.
8. Bake in a hot oven, Gas 7, 425°F, 220°C, for 15 minutes to set pastry. Reduce heat, if pastry is browning too quickly, to Gas 6, 400°F, 200°C, and cook for 25 minutes more or until filling is set.
9. Leave tart in tin for 5 minutes. Drop it gently out on to a clean cloth in your hand. Then immediately place cooling wire against base and turn tart right way up again.

KENTISH PUDDING

A very old Kentish recipe.

Enough for 6 people

For this you need a ready-baked 18 cm/7 inch shortcrust or sweet shortcrust flan case (see page 86).

Filling
25 g/1 oz ground rice
300 ml/½ pint milk and 1 or
2 tablespoons extra
25 g/1 oz castor sugar
Pinch of salt
15 g/½ oz butter
1 well-beaten egg
A grating of nutmeg
Grated zest of 1 lemon
1 tablespoon currants

1. Put ground rice in a basin and slake it with 2 tablespoons of the cold milk – i.e., mix it to a smooth cream.
2. Put rest of milk, the sugar and salt into a saucepan and bring to the boil.
3. Pour boiling milk on to ground rice, stirring all the time.
4. Pour mixture back into saucepan and simmer for 5 minutes, stirring occasionally.
5. Take pan off heat and let mixture cool for 2 or 3 minutes. Stir in butter, well-beaten egg, nutmeg and finely grated lemon zest. Blend well.
6. Stand pastry case on a baking sheet and fill it with the mixture. Strew the currants over the top.
7. Bake it in a moderate oven, Gas 4, 350°F, 180°C, for 20 minutes when filling will be set and slightly risen.

Mrs W. White, Mrs Sue Marshall, St. Michaels, Tenterden, Kent

LEMON MERINGUE PIE

175 g/6 oz shortcrust pastry (see page 84)

Filling
40 g/1½ oz cornflour
100 g/4 oz sugar
2 lemons
Water
15 g/½ oz butter
2 egg-yolks

Top
2 egg-whites

100 g/4 oz castor sugar
½ teaspoon cornflour
A little extra castor sugar

1. Line a 20 cm/8 inch flan ring with pastry and bake 'blind' (see page 85).
2. **For the filling:** in a pan combine cornflour, sugar, grated lemon rind and lemon juice made up to 300 ml/½ pint with water.
3. Bring to the boil, stirring. Cook for 2 minutes.
4. Remove from heat, beat in butter and then the egg-yolks.
5. Pour into hot or cold flan case.
6. **For the top:** whisk egg-whites stiffly. Whisk in 50 g/2 oz of the castor sugar until firm and shiny.
7. Sift remaining 50 g/2 oz castor sugar with the cornflour and fold into egg-whites.
8. Spread meringue on top of flan, making sure it reaches pastry all round and seals in the lemon filling.
9. Sift on a little castor sugar.
10. Bake in a slow oven, Gas 1 to 2, 275° to 300°F, 140° to 150°C, for 25 to 30 minutes, until set and just golden.

RHUBARB PLATE TART

Other fruits may be used. This pastry is quite satisfactory with a moist filling.

575 g/1¼ lb cooked rhubarb

Pastry
225 g/9 oz plain flour
75 g/3 oz self-raising flour
Pinch of salt
10 ml/2 level teaspoons castor sugar
100 g/4 oz hard margarine
50 g/2 oz Cookeen
3 tablespoons milk (use 15 ml size or a measuring spoon)

1. Sieve together dry ingredients.
2. Rub in fats until texture is like fine breadcrumbs.
3. Bind to a firm dough with milk.
4. Using a floured board, roll out half of the pastry thinly to line a

25 cm/10 inch pie-plate.
5. Roll out second half of pastry for lid.
6. Place a generous layer of drained rhubarb to within 1·5 cm/½ inch of edge of pastry.
7. Damp edge with water and put on pastry lid. Seal firmly round edge.
8. Brush top with milk. Cut 2 slits in the top to let steam out during cooking and prevent pastry from becoming soggy.
9. Bake in a moderately hot oven, Gas 5, 375°F, 190°C, for 35 to 40 minutes.

**Anne Wallace,
Dunlop, Scotland**

BANBURY CAKES

Makes 12 cakes

8 oz flaky pastry (see page 84)
Filling
100 g/4 oz currants
25 g/1 oz butter
50 g/2 oz sugar
½ a beaten egg
Pinch of cinnamon
A little grated lemon rind
25 g/1 oz cake crumbs
To finish
Egg-white
Castor sugar

1. Pick over the currants and remove any stalks, etc. Clean them either by washing in cold water and patting dry in a tea-towel, or by rubbing them in flour and sifting flour out.
2. Cream butter and sugar.
3. Add beaten egg and mix well.
4. Add cleaned fruit, cinnamon and grated lemon rind, and finally the cake crumbs, and mix well.
5. Roll out pastry on a floured board and cut into twelve 10 cm/3–4 inch rounds.
6. Place a good teaspoonful of the filling in centre of each round.
7. Damp round the edges, then join edges together in shape of a Cornish pasty.
8. Turn over with joined edges underneath and flatten gently with

rolling pin.
9. Make 3 diagonal cuts across top of each one. Place on a baking sheet.
10. Brush with lightly-beaten egg-white and dredge castor sugar over them.
11. Bake in hot oven, Gas 6, 400°F, 200°C, for about 20 minutes until risen and golden brown.
12. Remove from baking sheet on to a wire rack to cool.

**Stella Boldy,
Sykehouse, N. Humberside**

YORKSHIRE CHEESE TARTS

A recipe using cottage cheese instead of curds.

200 g/8 oz shortcrust pastry (see page 84)
50 g/2 oz butter
225 g/8 oz cottage cheese
Pinch of salt
125 g/5 oz sugar
25 g/1 oz cake crumbs
50 g/2 oz currants
Grated rind of ½ lemon
3 egg-yolks

1. Line 24 tartlet tins with the pastry.
2. Put butter in a warm place to soften and then cream it.
3. Sieve cottage cheese into a large basin.
4. Add salt, sugar, cake-crumbs, currants and lemon rind and mix well. Add the creamed butter.
5. Beat the egg-yolks and mix well into cheese mixture.
6. Spoon mixture into pastry cases.
7. Bake in a moderately hot oven, Gas 6, 400°F, 200°C, for 20 minutes until golden brown.

Uses for spare egg-white
Pavlova (page 109)
Royal icing (page 127)
Macaroons (page 135)
Meringues (page 138)
Or, 1 egg-white whisked and folded into 300 ml/½ pint cream will make it go further.

**Stella Boldy,
Sykehouse, N. Humberside**

CHAPTER 8

PUDDINGS, HOT AND COLD

ALMOND STUFFED PEACHES

For 6 people

6 large fresh peaches, or 12 halves from a can of peaches
2 sponge buns
75 g/3 oz castor sugar
40 g/1½ oz ground almonds
Grated rind of ½ large lemon
2 tablespoons sherry
1 heaped tablespoon demerara sugar
1½ sherry glasses of brandy

1. Skin and halve peaches and remove stones.
2. Remove a little flesh from each peach to make the hollow larger.
3. Crumble sponge buns into a bowl and mix in peach flesh, castor sugar, ground almonds, lemon rind and sherry.
4. Place peach halves in a flat, oven-proof dish and spoon mixture into each.
5. Sprinkle with demerara sugar.
6. Bake in a moderate oven, Gas 4, 350°F, 180°C, for 15 to 20 minutes until sugar is crisp.
7. Heat a soup ladle over a gas flame, spirit lamp or candle flame. Pour brandy into the hot ladle, allow it to heat and ignite. Pour flaming brandy quickly over all the peaches and bring dish straight to the table while flames are still flickering over it.

For maximum effect, turn off the lights.
Serve hot, with or without cream.

Shelagh Robinson, Leeds

APPLE CRUNCH

For 4 people

450 g/1 lb cooking apples
25 g/1 oz butter
2 level tablespoons granulated sugar
Grated rind of 1 lemon

Topping
3 slices brown or white bread from small loaf
50 g/2 oz butter
4 level tablespoons desiccated coconut
5 level tablespoons demerara sugar

1. Peel, core and slice apples.
2. Melt 25 g/1 oz butter in a saucepan. Add apples and granulated sugar. Cover and cook over a low heat, stirring occasionally, until soft and thick.
3. Remove from heat and stir in lemon rind.
4. Spread apple in a shallow, oven-proof dish and keep warm. Rinse out the saucepan.
5. Remove rack from grill pan and heat grill to moderately hot.
6. Cut bread into 7 mm/¼ inch cubes.
7. Melt 2 oz butter in the saucepan. Add bread cubes, coconut and demerara sugar and mix well.
8. Pile on top of apple mixture. Place dish in grill pan and grill until golden brown.

Serve immediately.

APPLE AND RAISIN CRISP

75 g/3 oz butter or margarine
40 g/1½ oz moist brown sugar
40 g/1½ oz demerara sugar
150 g/5 oz rolled oats
2 large cooking apples
50 g/2 oz seedless raisins

1. Grease a deep 22cm/8½ inch pie plate.
2. Cream butter and sugar together and work in rolled oats.
3. Peel and core apples, slice into plate and add raisins.
4. Spread mixture over apples.
5. Bake in a moderate oven, Gas 4, 350°F, 180°C for 45 minutes until crisp and golden brown.

Serve hot or cold with cream or custard.

APRICOT RICE

For 4

125 g/4 oz dried apricots
50 g/2 oz natural short grain
brown rice
2 eggs
75 g/3 oz barbados sugar
600 ml/1 pint milk
A nut of butter

1. Soak apricots overnight.Cover them with water and cook gently for about 1 hour until tender.
2. Drain liquid into a cup and put apricots at bottom of a greased, oven-proof dish.
3. Add rice.
4. Whisk eggs with sugar and pour on the milk.
5. Pour this over rice. Dot with butter.
6. Bake in a moderate oven, Gas 4, 350°F, 180°C, for 1½ hours.

Best eaten hot.

Ursula Cavanagh,
author of 'The Wholefood Cookery
Book'

APRICOT AND HAZELNUT PUDDING

For 3 to 4 people

50 g/2 oz dried apricots
50 g/2 oz soft margarine or butter
50 g/2 oz castor sugar
25 g/1 oz hazelnuts
1 large egg, separated
50 g/2 oz plain cake crumbs
Icing sugar

1. Cover apricots with cold water, leave overnight to soften. Dry thoroughly on kitchen paper.
2. Cream margarine or butter and sugar together until fluffy.
3. Grind nuts or chop finely, add to creamed mixture.
4. Chop apricots fairly small.
5. Add egg-yolk with apricots to the mixture. Beat well in.
6. Fold in cake crumbs.
7. Whisk egg-white until stiff and fold into mixture.
8. Pour into an oiled, oven-proof dish and level the surface.

9. Cook on centre shelf of oven at Gas 4, 350°F, 180°C, for 40 minutes until risen a little and fairly firm when pressed with the fingertips.
10. Sprinkle with icing sugar.

Serve hot or cold.

BAKED CUSTARD

3 eggs and 1 egg-yolk
1 heaped dessertspoon honey
450 ml/¾ pint milk
A grating of nutmeg

1. Lightly beat eggs and egg-yolk with the honey.
2. Pour on milk.
3. Strain into an oven-proof dish. Grate on fresh nutmeg.
4. Stand dish in a small roasting tin. Pour in enough cold water to come half-way up sides of dish.
5. Put in a moderate oven, Gas 3, 325°F, 160°C, for about 1 hour until firm. To test, slip a knife in diagonally. If it comes out clean, custard is cooked.

Serve hot or cold.

CHOCOLATE UP AND OVER PUDDING

A sponge top over a thick fudge sauce.

For 4 to 5 people

Pudding
100 g/4 oz margarine, soft
100 g/4 oz granulated sugar
2 eggs
75 g/3 oz self-raising flour
25 g/1 oz chocolate powder or 1
rounded tablespoon cocoa.

Topping and Sauce
1 rounded tablespoon cocoa
40 g/1½ oz chopped nuts, walnuts
or flaked almonds
100 g/4 oz demerara sugar
300 ml/½ pint hot, strong black
coffee (if using instant coffee, pour
water on to 3 teaspoonfuls)

1. Grease a deep, oven-proof, pudding dish, 1 litre/2 pint capacity.

2. Sieve flour and chocolate powder into a bowl with other pudding ingredients. This pudding is mixed by the 'all-in' method.
3. Mix up and beat well for 2 minutes with a wooden spoon to make a smooth mixture. Or use an electric mixer for $\frac{1}{2}$ minute.
4. Tip mixture into greased dish and level the top.
5. **For the topping and sauce:** mix cocoa, nuts and 50 g/2 oz of the demerara sugar together and sprinkle this over the pudding.
6. Sweeten the hot coffee with remaining 50 g/2 oz demerara and pour over the pudding.
7. Bake in a moderate oven, Gas 4, 350°F, 180°C, for 50 minutes to 1 hour. During cooking, the sponge rises up and over and the coffee mixture makes a thick fudge sauce underneath.
Serve hot with cream or ice-cream.

**Pat Dixon,
Holmfirth, W. Yorkshire**

MOTHER'S EXCELLENT RECIPE FOR A CHRISTMAS PUDDING

Makes 4 puddings weighing approx. 575 g/1$\frac{1}{4}$ lb each, but larger puddings can be made. Or, by reducing quantities of ingredients carefully, just 1 or 2 puddings can be made.
Always made in October to allow time to mature. Keep well for at least a year.

**225 g/8 oz butter
275 g/10 oz stale wholemeal or white breadcrumbs
100 g/4 oz plain flour
$\frac{1}{2}$ teaspoon ground mace
1 teaspoon ground ginger
1 teaspoon ground nutmeg
225 g/8 oz demerara sugar
100 g/4 oz chopped candied orange peel
50 g/2 oz chopped candied lemon peel
25 g/1 oz chopped candied citron peel
100 g/4 oz chopped glacé cherries
225 g/8 oz currants
450 g/1 lb chopped raisins
75 g/3 oz blanched almonds, chopped
1 grated carrot
6 beaten eggs
2 tablespoons golden syrup or black treacle
275 ml/$\frac{1}{2}$ pint ale**

1. Grease four $\frac{1}{2}$ litre/1 pint pudding basins, or two 1·2 litre/2 pint basins.
2. Put butter in warm place to melt.
3. Place breadcrumbs in a very large mixing bowl or crock.
4. Sift in the flour and spices.
5. Mix in sugar.
6. Add chopped peels and cherries.
7. Add currants and raisins and mix well.
8. Add almonds and carrot to the mixture and mix well.
9. Stir in beaten eggs and golden syrup or black treacle. Mix well.
10. Add to the mixture the melted butter and ale and stir in well.
11. Divide mixture equally between the basins.
12. Cover tightly with a layer of greased, greaseproof paper and then foil.
13. Place in a steamer, $\frac{2}{3}$ full of boiling water or in saucepan of boiling water. Water should come half-way up sides of the basin.
A pressure cooker may be used instead of a steamer. Use as directed in the instruction booklet.
14. Steam 3$\frac{1}{2}$ to 4 hours. Water should not go off the boil. When it needs replenishing, use boiling water.
If making 2 larger puddings steam for 7 to 8 hours.
15. Remove puddings from saucepan and take off the foil and paper. Allow to cool.
16. When puddings are quite cold, cover with fresh greased, greaseproof paper and foil. Store in a cool place.

17. Steam again for 1½ to 2 hours before serving.
18. Serve with Brandy Sauce (see below).

Stella Boldy,
Sykehouse, N. Humberside

BRANDY SAUCE

To serve with Christmas Pudding.

300 ml/½ pint double cream
1 tablespoon brandy
25 g/1 oz soft brown sugar
1 egg-white

1. Whisk cream until it is starting to thicken.
2. Add brandy and sugar and whisk until thick.
3. Whisk egg-white with a clean whisk in a clean basin until stiff but not dry.
4. Using a metal spoon, fold egg-white into the cream mixture.
5. Turn into a serving dish.

Stella Boldy,
Sykehouse, N. Humberside

VEGETABLE PLUM PUDDING

50 g/2 oz plain wholewheat flour
Pinch of salt
50 g/2 oz grated carrot
50 g/2 oz grated potato
50 g/2 oz barbados sugar
50 g/2 oz shredded suet
25 g/1 oz raisins
25 g/1 oz currants
1 egg
1 to 2 tablespoons milk

This pudding can be made with white flour and sugar but it looked and tasted even better as above – **Ed**.

1. Mix all ingredients thoroughly.
2. Grease a 600 ml/1 pint pudding basin and put in the mixture.
3. Cover basin with a sheet of greased, greaseproof paper, pleated across the middle. Cover that loosely with foil, securing it well under rim of basin.
4. Steam for 3 hours. If you do not have a steamer, stand basin on a trivet or upturned saucer in a saucepan. Pour in enough boiling water to come half-way up sides of basin. Keep it boiling for 3 hours. If water boils low replenish with more boiling water.

Or use a pressure cooker. Steam without pressure valve for 15 minutes. Then bring to pressure (lowest pressure) and pressure-cook for 40 minutes.

Mrs M. E. Houslay
Shiptonthorpe, York

FIG DUMPLING

175 g/6 oz dried figs
225 ml/8 fluid oz milk
150 g/5 oz self-raising flour
1 rounded teaspoon baking powder
175 g/6 oz sugar
125 g/4 oz shredded suet
50 g/2 oz fresh white or wholemeal breadcrumbs
1 beaten egg

1. Discard stalks and cut figs into small pieces.
2. Stew them gently in milk for 5 minutes.
3. Sift flour and baking powder into a mixing bowl.
4. Mix in other dry ingredients.
5. Make a well in the centre, pour in stewed figs and milk and beat well to combine thoroughly.
6. Mix in beaten egg.
7. Grease a 1·4 litre/2½ pint, heat-proof, pudding basin and put in the mixture.
8. Cover basin with a piece of greased, greaseproof paper and cover that with foil, tucking edges securely round rim.
9. Place pudding in a saucepan and pour in enough boiling water to come half-way up sides of basin.
10. Steam for 2 hours. Keep water boiling constantly and replenish if necessary with more boiling water.

Mrs Margaret Boyd,
Kirkintilloch, Glasgow

GINGER MARMALADE PUDDING

Enough for 4 to 5 people but easy to make less or more.

10 small slices or 5 large slices of wholemeal or white bread
Butter or margarine
50 g/2 oz sultanas or raisins
50 g/2 oz demerara sugar
Ginger marmalade
1 large egg
300 ml/½ pint milk
A grating of nutmeg (optional)

1. Grease a small pie dish.
2. Butter the bread.
3. Line bottom and sides of dish with bread.
4. Sprinkle on a few sultanas and some of the sugar
5. Spread next layer of bread with marmalade.
6. Make as many layers as you can, alternating fruit with marmalade between layers. Save a little sugar for the top.
7. Beat egg and milk together, strain it over the pudding and leave it for 15 minutes to soak.
8. Sprinkle top with sugar and grate on a little nutmeg.
9. Bake in a moderate oven, Gas 4, 350°F, 180°C, for 40 to 50 minutes.

**Mrs Wynne Ashby,
Gosport, Hampshire**

JAM SANDWICHES IN BATTER

An old recipe.

Batter
50 g/2 oz plain flour
Pinch of salt
2 teaspoons salad oil or melted butter
4 tablespoons luke-warm water
1 egg-white

The Sandwiches
Thin slices of bread
Margarine or butter
Raspberry jam, or your own favourite
Oil or fat for frying

1. Sift flour and salt into a basin. Make a well in the centre and add oil or butter and half of the water.
2. Beat well, then gradually beat in rest of water.
3. Make the sandwiches and cut them into triangles, removing crusts.
4. Whisk egg-white until stiff. Fold it into batter mixture.
5. Dip sandwiches in batter and fry in hot oil until nicely brown.
6. Remove from frying pan on to paper to drain and sprinkle with castor sugar.

**Mr A. J. Rayner,
Bordesley Green East, Birmingham**

ORANGE MERINGUE PUDDING

For 4 or more people

50 g/2 oz butter
300 ml/½ pint milk
75 g/3 oz fresh wholewheat breadcrumbs
75 g/3 oz barbados sugar
4 eggs, separated
3 oranges
225 g/8 oz demerara sugar

1. Put butter and milk in a saucepan and bring to the boil. Pour it over breadcrumbs. Stir in barbados sugar.
2. Beat egg-yolks and stir them in. Allow to cool.
3. Meanwhile, grate rind from oranges, then peel them and cut flesh up finely. Add to cooled mixture.
4. Pour into a greased, oven-proof dish.
5. Bake in a moderate oven, Gas 4, 350°F, 180°C, for ½ hour, until set.
6. Reduce oven temperature to low, Gas 1, 275°F, 140°C.
7. Beat up egg-whites till stiff then gradually beat in demerara sugar and beat till stiff.
8. Pile meringue on top of pudding and return to middle shelf of oven

for ½ hour or until meringue is crisp on top.

**Ursula Cavanagh,
author of 'The Wholefood Cookery
Book'**

PLUM CRUMBLE

**450 g/1 lb plums
2 tablespoons dark brown
barbados sugar**

**Crumble Top
100 g/4 oz wholewheat flour, plain
or self-raising
Pinch of salt
65 g/2½ oz brown sugar
A grating of nutmeg
50 g/2 oz butter or margarine**

1. Wash plums and put them without drying into a small, round, oven-proof dish. Make them lie as level as possible.
2. Sprinkle with 2 tablespoons sugar.
3. **For the crumble:** mix together flour, salt, sugar and nutmeg.
4. Rub in butter or margarine until mixture is like fine breadcrumbs.
5. Cover plums all over with the crumble.
6. Put at once into a moderately hot oven Gas 6, 400°F, 200°C, for 20 minutes. Then lower heat to moderate Gas 4, 350°F, 180°C, for 20 minutes more.

RHUBARB AND ORANGE MERINGUE

**450 g/1 lb young rhubarb
1 orange
50 g/2 oz demerara sugar
40 g/1½ oz cornflour
2 eggs, separated
75 g/3 oz castor sugar**

1. Wash and trim rhubarb and cut into short lengths. Place in a 1·2 litre/2 pint shallow oven-proof casserole or pie dish.
2. Grate rind and squeeze juice from orange. Place in a measuring jug and make up to 450 ml/¾ pint with water.
3. Place demerara sugar and cornflour in a saucepan and gradually blend in liquid. Bring to boil, stirring, and simmer for 3 minutes. Allow to cool slightly.
4. Stir egg-yolks into orange sauce and pour over rhubarb.
5. Cook in centre of a moderate oven, Gas 3, 325°F, 160°C, for 20 minutes. Lower temperature to cool, Gas 2, 300°F, 150°C.
6. Meanwhile, whisk egg-whites until stiff and dry, whisk in half the castor sugar and whisk until stiff again. Fold in remaining sugar.
7. Spread meringue over mixture in dish and return to oven to cook for a further 20 to 25 minutes until it is golden brown and the rhubarb is tender.

APPLE SUNDAE

For 4 people

**2 eating apples
40 g/1½ oz barbados sugar
50 g/2 oz chopped mixed nuts
300 ml/½ pint yoghurt**

1. Wash and coarsely shred unpeeled apples, discarding core.
2. Put into 4 individual glasses.
3. Sprinkle with sugar and add alternate layers of chopped nuts and yoghurt. Finish with a sprinkling of nuts.

**Ursula Cavanagh,
author of 'The Wholefood Cookery
Book'**

APRICOT AND RHUBARB REFRESHER

For 4 people

**40 g/1½ oz dried apricots
150 ml/¼ pint water
675 g/1½ lb red rhubarb
125 g/4 oz demerara or white sugar
Grated rind and juice of 1 orange
15 g/½ oz (1 envelope) gelatine
3 tablespoons single or whipping cream**

To Decorate
Angelica
Tiny pieces of rhubarb
Fine slices of dried apricot
4 tablespoons whipped cream
(optional)

1. Soak apricots in water overnight.
2. Stew them gently in a pan with a lid until tender.
3. Meanwhile, wash and trim rhubarb, slice it and put it in a casserole dish with the sugar but no water. Cover with lid and cook gently in a moderate oven, Gas 3, 325°F, 170°C, for 15 minutes. This will draw out the juice and cook the rhubarb without breaking it up.
4. Strain juice from rhubarb into a measuring jug. There should be about 450 ml/¾ pint. Allow to cool.
5. Drain apricots. Put juice with the orange juice in a small bowl and sprinkle on the gelatine. Stand bowl over a pan of hot water to melt.
6. Mix gelatine liquid with the rhubarb juice. Pour off ½ cupful to use in a moment. Pour the rest equally into 4 serving glasses. Put these in fridge, or a cold place, to set.
7. Meanwhile, rub apricots through a sieve or liquidise them. Add finely-grated orange rind, cream and reserved jelly liquid to the purée.
8. When first layer of jelly is set top with the creamy one.
9. When this has set decorate with delicate strips of angelica and fine slices of dried apricot.

The rhubarb may be used in a tart (see page 95).

Anne Wallace,
Dunlop, Scotland

BLACKBERRY AND APPLE FOOL

450 g/1 lb blackberries
450 g/1 lb cooking apples
2 tablespoons honey or barbados sugar

150 ml/¼ pint double or whipping cream

1. Wash blackberries and place in a saucepan or casserole dish with lid.
2. Wash and slice apples and add to blackberries.
3. Either simmer in pan till fruit is soft or put lid on casserole and put in a slow oven, Gas 2, 300°F, 150°C, and leave till fruit is soft.
4. Sieve fruit and sweeten to taste with honey or sugar. Leave to cool.
5. Whip cream until same thickness as purée.
6. When purée is cold fold together with cream and put in a pretty dish.

CHOCOLATE CHESTNUT DESSERT

175 g/6 oz dark cooking chocolate
75 g/3 oz butter
75 g/3 oz castor sugar
425 g/15 oz can of chestnut purée
3 tablespoons rum or brandy
½ pint thick cream

1. Put chocolate in pieces into a small bowl and stand over a pan of simmering water to melt.
2. Cream butter and sugar together. Add chestnut purée, mix thoroughly.
3. Add melted chocolate, then rum or brandy, and lastly the unwhipped cream. Pour into a nice dish.
4. Leave in fridge to set.

This is very rich and does not require any additional cream for decoration. A sprinkling of grated chocolate looks attractive.

Judith Adshead,
Mottram St. Andrew, Cheshire

CHOCOLATE MOUSSE

For at least 4 people
100 g/4 oz good plain cooking chocolate
3 to 4 eggs, separated
15 g/½ oz butter

1 teaspoon hot water
1 tablespoon brandy

To Decorate
Glacé cherries
Small carton of double or
whipping cream

1. Break up chocolate and melt in
a basin over a pan of simmering
water. Do not let basin touch
water.
2. Meanwhile, separate eggs into
different bowls. Cut up butter into
small pieces.
3. Remove pan and bowl of
chocolate from heat. Keep bowl on
pan.
4. Beat the egg-yolks and then beat
spoonfuls of it into chocolate. Beat
well after each spoonful is added
until mixture is soft and creamy.
5. Add pieces of butter one at a
time and beat in to dissolve them.
6. Beat in hot water.
7. Beat in brandy and leave to cool.
8. Meanwhile, beat egg-whites
until stiff.
9. Use a metal spoon and fold egg-
whites into chocolate mixture until
all white disappears.
10. Pour into glass bowl or
individual dishes.
11. Decorate with cherries or
cream.

Dry sherry can be used instead of
brandy but brandy is better.

**Mrs M. Lucie-Smith,
London**

COFFEE MOUSSE
WITH CRUNCHY
TOPPING

Enough for 6 people

1 large can evaporated milk
½ cup hot water
15 g/½ oz (1 envelope) gelatine
4 heaped teaspoons instant coffee
grains
175 g/6 oz granulated sugar
75 g/3 oz crisp peanut toffee

1. Put evaporated milk to chill in
refrigerator for at least 1 hour.
2. Sprinkle gelatine on to the ½ cup

of hot water and stir to dissolve it.
Stir in coffee until smooth. Allow
to cool slightly but stir frequently
so that it does not set.
3. Beat evaporated milk until very
thick and creamy. Gradually beat
in the sugar.
4. Add gelatine mixture slowly,
beating continuously. Pour
mixture into a large serving bowl.
5. Chop peanut toffee into small
bits. It tends to fly everywhere –
try using the bread saw on it with
a lever action.
6. When mousse has partly set,
sprinkle with peanut toffee. Put
dish to chill in fridge.

Serve with cream.

This dish can be made up to 48
hours before serving if kept in
refrigerator.

**Shelagh Robinson,
Leeds**

SIMPLE FRUIT SALAD

Quick to make.

Enough for 2 or 3 people

1 large orange
¼ lemon
1 tablespoon raisins
1 large banana
1 large, green eating apple
5 or 6 hazelnuts

*Try also these unusual but
delicious ingredients*
A sprinkling of sprouted seeds
(see page 65)
A teaspoon of germinated wheat
(see page 65)

To serve
4 tablespoons double or whipping
cream
1 dessertspoon honey

1. Cut top off orange about ¼ of the
way down. Squeeze juice from this
small piece into a bowl.
2. Squeeze juice from lemon
quarter into bowl.
3. Put raisins into juice.
4. Peel rest of orange and cut it
into small pieces.

5. Quarter and core unpeeled apple. Cut it into small pieces.
6. Peel and slice banana.
7. Put fruit in with raisins and juice and toss well to coat with juice.
8. Slice hazelnuts into thin slivers and sprinkle them on top.
9. Toss in sprouted seed and germinated wheat grains.
10. Whip up cream with honey and serve it in a separate bowl. This cream is very sweet so do not add sugar to fruit salad.

TO KEEP BANANAS FROM GOING BROWN

Put unpeeled bananas in cold water for 5 to 10 minutes. They may then be peeled, sliced and left for some time without going brown.   **Miss M. Owen, Elworth, Cheshire**

In our test, with firm bananas, there was only slight discoloration after 4 hours. It was 8 hours before they went brown and soft. Very ripe bananas and a warm kitchen could give less good results. – **Ed.**

HAZELNUT MERINGUE GÂTEAU

3 large egg-whites
A pinch of salt
175 g/6 oz granulated sugar
75 g/3 oz ground hazelnuts
40 g/1½ oz fine semolina (Farola is best)

To Fill and Decorate
150–200 ml/5–7 fluid oz double or whipping cream
50 g/2 oz chopped hazelnuts
A few whole hazelnuts
15 g/½ oz plain cooking chocolate
Try your own fillings, such as fresh raspberries or pears.

1. Line base of two 18 cm/7 inch sandwich tins with rounds of Bakewell paper or greased, greaseproof paper.
2. Beat egg-whites with salt till firm.

3. Add 75 g/3 oz of the sugar and beat again.
4. In another bowl, mix remaining sugar with ground hazelnuts and semolina. Fold this mixture into egg-whites.
5. Divide mixture between tins, spread it evenly and smooth the tops.
6. Bake in a moderate oven, Gas 4, 350°F, 180°C, for 25 to 30 minutes until crisp and golden.
7. Turn meringues out of tins to cool on a wire rack.
8. When quite cold, sandwich with whipped cream.
9. Spread cream round the sides.
10. Roll sides in chopped hazelnuts.
11. Pipe cream roses on top and decorate with whole hazelnuts.
12. Finish with decorations of piped chocolate.

The gâteau bases keep well in an air-tight tin before filling and decorating. Also, when filled and decorated they may be frozen successfully. Will thaw quite quickly.

Anne Wallace, Dunlop, Scotland

LEMON AND BANANA SOUFFLÉ

Enough for 4 people

3 large eggs
75 g/3 oz castor sugar
2 lemons
3 bananas
15 g/½ oz (1 envelope) gelatine
3 tablespoons very hot water
1 small carton double cream

1. Separate egg-yolks from whites, put yolks and whites in separate large bowls.
2. Add sugar to the yolks.
3. Wipe lemons, finely grate the rind and add to egg-yolks with juice of 1 lemon.
4. Place bowl over a saucepan of hot water and whisk until mixture becomes rather thick and fluffy.
5. Remove from heat and leave to

cool, whisking occasionally.

6. Keep aside ½ banana in its skin and ½ lemon for decoration later.

7. Squeeze out juice from remaining lemons and pour into goblet of an electric blender. Peel other 2½ bananas, cut up and add. Switch on and blend until creamy and smooth. (If preferred, the bananas may be thoroughly mashed with a fork and then worked into the lemon juice.)

8. Whisk banana mixture into the egg-yolks.

9. Put hot water into a small bowl and sprinkle with gelatine. Stand bowl in hot water to dissolve gelatine, stirring once to combine.

10. Cool gelatine slightly and whisk into the banana mixture.

11. Leave until cold and on the point of setting.

12. Whisk egg-whites until stiff.

13. Place cream in a small bowl and whisk until thick but soft.

14. Using a metal spoon, fold cream into the nearly-set banana mixture and lightly fold in egg-whites.

15. Turn into a glass serving dish and leave in a cold place to set.

16. Before serving, squeeze juice from remaining ½ lemon, peel and slice ½ banana and toss in the juice. Arrange round top of dish.

FLUFFY ORANGE MOUSSE

2 large oranges
½ lemon
4 tablespoons water
15 g/½ oz (1 envelope) gelatine
3 eggs, separated
75 g/3 oz castor sugar
2 tablespoons very hot water
25 g/1 oz blanched almonds

1. Finely-grate rind from one orange. Squeeze out juice from both oranges and ½ lemon.

2. Place 4 tablespoons water in a small bowl and sprinkle with gelatine. Stand bowl in hot water

to dissolve gelatine, stirring once to combine.

3. Set aside to cool slightly but do not let it set.

4. Carefully separate egg-yolks from whites and place them in separate bowls.

5. Add 2 oz sugar and the very hot water to yolks and whisk at least 5 minutes until mixture is thick and pale in colour. The mixture should be stiff enough to hold the trail of the whisk when lifted.

6. Strain in fruit juices, add orange rind and whisk to mix.

7. Pour in gelatine, stirring really vigorously.

8. Put bowl aside, but whisk occasionally until mixture is cold and beginning to thicken.

9. Beat egg-whites with a clean whisk until very stiff and dry.

10. Add remaining 25 g/1 oz of sugar to egg-whites and whisk again until stiff and glossy.

11. Lightly fold egg-whites into orange mixture until evenly-mixed.

12. Pour immediately into a serving dish and leave in a cold place to set.

13. Heat grill to moderately hot.

14. Finely shred almonds and grill until evenly-coloured, shaking occasionally.

15. Leave to cool. Sprinkle almonds round edge of mousse to decorate.

ORANGE CHEESECAKE

Needs no baking.

Makes 8 reasonable portions

Base
100 g/4 oz digestive biscuits
2 level tablespoons golden syrup
1 level tablespoon cocoa
25 g/1 oz butter

Filling
15 g/½ oz (1 envelope) gelatine
2 tablespoons hot water
2 small oranges

1 small lemon
4 level tablespoons castor sugar
450 g/1 lb cottage cheese
2 to 3 tablespoons double cream
1 tablespoon milk

Decoration
3 thin round slices from an orange,
including skin
25 g/1 oz grated plain chocolate

1. **To make base:** put biscuits
between 2 sheets of greaseproof
paper or in a polythene bag. Crush
to fine crumbs with rolling pin, or
use electric grinder to make
crumbs.
2. Measure golden syrup carefully
into a saucepan, levelling off spoon
with a knife and making sure
there is none on back of spoon.
3. Add cocoa and butter to pan.
Heat gently, stirring occasionally,
until butter has melted.
4. Remove pan from heat and stir
in biscuit crumbs.
5. Spread biscuit mixture in
bottom of a round 20 cm/8 inch,
loose-based cake tin. Level top and
press down lightly. Leave tin in a
cool place so that mixture hardens.
6. **To make filling:** measure 2
tablespoons hot water into a small
basin and sprinkle in gelatine. Stir
until gelatine has dissolved.
7. Scrub oranges and lemon. Grate
rind into a bowl.
8. Squeeze juice and pour into a
measuring jug.
9. Stir gelatine into juices and
make up to $\frac{1}{4}$ pint with cold water.
Add sugar and stir until dissolved.
10. Rub cheese through a sieve on
to grated rind. Add fruit syrup
mixture and mix well. **Or,** put
cheese with grated rind and fruit
syrup mixture into liquidiser and
switch on to blend until smooth,
then return it to bowl.
11. Put cream and milk into a
basin and whisk until just thick.
Stir into cheese mixture in bowl.
12. Pour cheese mixture over
biscuit base in tin. Leave in a cool
place to set.
13. **To decorate when cheesecake**

is set: cut each slice of orange into
6 triangular pieces.
14. An easy way to remove
cheesecake from tin: stand it on
top of a large can of fruit or
vegetables, or similar. Gently pull
cake tin down from cheesecake.
Ease cheesecake off base on to a
plate with a palette knife.
15. Arrange grated chocolate in a
pile in centre and orange triangles,
pointing inwards, around edge of
top.

Serve in slices. Will keep 2 to 3
days in refrigerator.

PLANT POT CHEESECAKE

For 6 people

For this you need a clay plant pot,
12·5 cm/5 inches diameter at top.
If you are starting with a new
plant pot, bake it in a moderate
oven, Gas 4, 350°F, 180°C, for 15
minutes. It can then be used for
this pudding or for baking bread.

50 g/2 oz maraschino cherries
50 g/2 oz mixed peel
50 g/2 oz blanched almonds
50 g/2 oz seedless raisins
Finely-grated rind $\frac{1}{4}$ lemon
Finely-grated rind $\frac{1}{4}$ orange
1 tablespoon dry sherry
350 g/12 oz cottage cheese
100 g/4 oz cream cheese
100 g/4 oz castor sugar
120 ml/4 fluid oz double cream
1$\frac{1}{2}$ tablespoons orange juice
1$\frac{1}{2}$ tablespoons lemon juice
2 level teaspoons powdered
gelatine

To Decorate
120 ml/4 fluid oz carton double
cream
A few maraschino cherries
A few orange and lemon slices

1. Finely chop cherries, mixed peel,
almonds and raisins (liquidiser
can be used) and transfer to a
small basin.
2. Stir in grated lemon and orange

rind, cover with sherry and leave until sherry is absorbed.
3. In another bowl, mix cottage cheese and cream cheese together and beat in the sugar.
4. Beat cream until thick and fold into cheese with the fruit and nut mixture.
5. Put orange and lemon juice in a small heat-proof bowl and sprinkle the gelatine over it. Leave until gelatine is spongy. Place bowl in a pan of hot water and stir over low heat until gelatine has dissolved. Remove from heat and leave to cool slightly, about 20 minutes. Fold into cheese mixture.
6. Line a 12·5 cm/5 inch clay plant pot with a large piece of muslin or a clean tea towel, spoon in cheese mixture and fold cloth over the top.
7. Cover with a saucer which will just fit inside top of pot, place weights on top (1·5 kg/3 lb is enough). Stand pot in a dish and chill in a refrigerator overnight.
8. The next day, remove weights and saucer and unfold the cloth. Place a serving dish over the pot and turn cheesecake out. Remove the cloth.
9. Whip cream for decoration and pipe over the cheesecake. Decorate with halved maraschino cherries and orange and lemon slices.

**Stella Boldy,
Sykehouse, N. Humberside**

PAVLOVA

**4 egg-whites
225 g/8 oz castor sugar
1 level teaspoon cornflour
1 teaspoon vinegar
1 teaspoon vanilla essence**

**Filling
300 ml/½ pint double or whipping cream
Fruits, such as strawberries, raspberries, bananas, fresh peaches
Juice 1 lemon
Passion fruit pulp (optional)**

1. Grease thoroughly a large, flat, round or oval heat-proof dish or tart-plate.
2. Beat egg-whites until stiff.
3. Gradually beat in sugar.
4. Mix cornflour, vinegar and vanilla and fold in.
5. Spread mixture 2·5 cm/1 inch thick on prepared plate, forming a raised edge that will contain the filling.
6. Bake in a very slow oven, Gas ½, 250°F, 120°C, for 1 hour. Switch off heat and leave pavlova in oven overnight to dry out.
7. Fill with whipped cream.
8. Top with fresh fruits well sprinkled with lemon juice to prevent discolouration. If you can get passion fruit, mix it with the lemon juice.

**Mrs Rita McEachern,
Adelaide, South Australia**

RAW FRUIT PURÉE

A refreshing and sustaining dessert.

For 4 people

Made in the liquidiser.

**50 g/2 oz dried apricots or prunes
50 g/2 oz raisins
4 dessert apples
½ lemon**

**To Decorate and Serve
1 tablespoon freshly-ground nuts
1 tablespoon dessicated coconut
Whipped cream or yoghurt**

1. Put apricots or prunes and raisins in a bowl of water. Allow to soak and plump up overnight. Remove stones from prunes.
2. Quarter, core and slice apples, but do not skin them.
3. Pour into liquidiser ½ cupful of water in which fruit has soaked. Add apples and blend until smooth.
4. Add apricots, raisins and lemon juice and blend until smooth, adding more of the fruit water if necessary.
5. Pour purée into nice glass bowls.

6. Sprinkle with nuts and coconut and top each glass with a spoonful of whipped cream or yoghurt.

**Elizabeth Shears,
author of 'Why Do We Eat'**

ICE-CREAM

**2 eggs, separated
Few drops vanilla essence
150 ml/¼ pint double cream
50 g/2 oz icing sugar**

Fresh fruit may be used to flavour ice-cream instead of vanilla essence. First make a purée of the fruit. A cupful is enough for the above quantity of ice-cream.

1. Beat egg-yolks and vanilla. (If using fruit purée it is added later; leave out vanilla.)
2. Whip the cream.
3. Beat egg-white and sugar
4. Combine all three mixtures and beat again.
5. If using fruit purée fold it in now.
6. Pour mixture into a 1 kg/2 lb margarine carton or a freezer tray with lid and freeze.

**Anne Wallace,
Dunlop, Scotland**

EGG FLIP

For 1 to 2 people

**1 egg, separated
1 or 2 teaspoons honey
300 ml/½ pint milk
Cinnamon or nutmeg**

1. Put egg-yolk, honey and half the milk in a bowl and whisk until blended.
2. Whisk in rest of milk.
3. Whisk egg-white separately until stiff. Fold it in.
4. Pour out into glasses and sprinkle with a pinch of cinnamon or a fine grating of nutmeg.

HOME-MADE YOGHURT

The easiest way to make yoghurt is to buy a kit, which is basically a temperature-controlled or insulated flask and thermometer. However, by trial and error you can make it without special equipment, especially if you have a warm place in which to set or thicken it such as an airing cupboard or gas oven with pilot light. So many factors affect yoghurt in the making that everybody has to experiment.

**600 ml/1 pint milk
1 tablespoon dried skimmed milk (optional)
1 tablespoon natural yoghurt, bought or home-made**

You can use untreated milk, pasteurised, homogenised or U.H.T., and sterilised milk. However, the flavour and thickness will vary – e.g., U.H.T. and sterilised milk give a thinner yoghurt.
The dried skimmed milk helps to make yoghurt thicker and creamier.

1. Bring milk to boiling point. If using U.H.T. milk heat it only to blood temperature and proceed straight to paragraph 4.
2. Allow to cool to 120°F, 48°C.
3. Stir in dried skimmed milk, if used.
4. Add yoghurt and whisk well.
5. Pour mixture into a clean, warm bowl, or small bowls, wide-necked jars or cartons. Cover with a plate, saucers or lids.
If you have a wide-necked Thermos flask, pre-heat it by rinsing out with boiling water, and pour in the mixture. Put on lid.
6. Containers must be put at once into a slightly warmer place, preferably 110°F, 43°C, and where temperature will remain constant for 4 to 6 hours. During this time (if you are lucky) it will turn to curd. You can wrap container in a warmed blanket or make a box for it out of polystyrene. Any device to keep temperature of yoghurt constant at not less than 110°F, 43°C, is worth trying.

7. As soon as it is set, place it in fridge. If you leave it in the warmth it will go on working and the acid flavour will become stronger, although it will also become thicker.

Save a tablespoon of your yoghurt to make the next batch. It is best to spoon it out of the middle of the container where the activity of the yoghurt-making bacteria is greater. After 3 batches of yoghurt have been made from your own culture it is advisable to buy another carton of commercially-made yoghurt to use as the next starter. Choose a brand which has as few additives as possible as this will more easily make a good new yoghurt.

Yoghurt is a soured milk product thought to have originated among the nomadic tribes of Eastern Europe. It was traditionally a drink, made by allowing the natural milk flora to ferment the milk sugar – lactose – to lactic acid. It has very high food value.

ICE-CREAM MADE WITH YOGHURT

Switch freezer or refrigerator to lowest setting about 1 hour before starting.

3 eggs, free-range if possible
2 heaped tablespoons honey
300 ml/½ pint warm milk
150 ml/¼ pint yoghurt
150 ml/¼ pint fresh double cream
½ teaspoon vanilla essence

1. Separate one of the eggs.
2. Whisk 2 whole eggs with egg-yolk and honey.
3. Pour on the warmed milk.
4. Stand bowl of egg and milk over a pan of simmering water. Stir this custard mixture until it is thick and creamy. Remove from heat and allow to cool.
5. Lightly whip yoghurt and cream.

6. Stiffly whip remaining egg-white.
7. Fold in yoghurt and cream, egg-white and vanilla.
8. Pour mixture into a shallow, square freezer box or refrigerator tray (18 cm/7 inch square is ideal).
9. Put in to freeze for 1 hour or until mixture has frozen round edges. Chill a mixing bowl at the same time.
10. Turn ice-cream into chilled bowl and whisk for 5 minutes.
11. Return mixture to freezer box for 2 hours more to freeze completely.

Fresh fruit may be added at stage 10. Raspberries, strawberries, pineapple, blackberries, blackcurrants or loganberries. Do not use vanilla if you intend to add fruit.

In winter, use soaked dried fruits – 225 g/8 oz soaked dried apricots puréed in the blender and added at stage 10 with 50 g/2 oz chopped almonds. Leave out vanilla.

Try also replacing vanilla at stage 7 with 2 level tablespoons Carob powder. Add 50 g/2 oz chopped walnuts at stage 10.

Elizabeth Shears,
author of 'Why Do We Eat'

YOGHURT AND FRUIT

For 1 or 2 people

Made in the liquidiser.

150 ml/¼ pint natural yoghurt
A handful of blackberries, black- or redcurrants, loganberries, raspberries or strawberries
1 tablespoon runny honey
A little milk
1 or 2 teaspoons wheat germ (optional)

1. Put yoghurt, fruit and honey in liquidiser and blend till mixture is consistency you like. Thin with a little milk if necessary.
2. Pour into glasses or bowls and sprinkle with wheat germ.

111

Can be made into a drink by blending until smooth, and thinning with milk.

HOME-MADE MUESLI

This can be a nourishing and satisfying meal in itself when eaten with plenty of fresh fruits and some yoghurt.

For 1 person

1 dessertspoon crushed or rolled oats
1 dessertspoon barley kernels or barley flakes
1 dessertspoon raisins or sultanas
A sprinkling of sunflower seeds and unroasted buckwheat
1 large eating apple
1 carrot
1 tablespoon lemon juice
1 tablespoon mixed nuts, freshly ground
2 to 4 tablespoons fresh plain yoghurt
1 teaspoon honey
1 tablespoon wheat germ
A sprinkling of germinated wheat (*see page 65*), **optional**

1. Soak oats, barley and raisins or sultanas in a little water overnight.
2. Soak sunflower seeds and buckwheat separately in a cup.
3. Next morning, wash apple and scrub carrot, leaving skins on, and grate coarsely on to soaked grains. Pour lemon juice over.
4. Mix well, adding nuts, yoghurt, honey and wheat germ.
5. Sprinkle with soaked sunflower seeds, buckwheat and germinated wheat.

If you like this, experiment with the wide variety of ingredients available: cereals, seeds, nuts, dried apricots, figs, prunes, coconut and sprouts such as alfalfa.

Fresh fruits can be varied according to the season. Fresh fruit and/or vegetable should ideally form over half of each helping of muesli if you want to make a balanced meal of it.

If you get seeds and cereals whole, soak them until they begin to germinate (to germinate *see pages 64–65*).

Elizabeth Shears,
author of 'Why Do We Eat'

112

CHAPTER 9

YEAST COOKERY, TEABREADS AND SCONES

WHITE BREAD DOUGH

900 g/2 lb strong plain flour
3 teaspoons salt
75 g/3 oz margarine
3 level teaspoons dried yeast, or
40 g/1½ oz fresh yeast
1 teaspoon sugar
300 ml/½ pint tepid water
300 ml/½ pint milk

This quantity makes approximately 1·5 kg/3¼ lb of risen dough.

Note: Different brands of flour require differing quantities of water to produce a good elastic dough. The quantity of water listed gives a general indication but may be modified slightly as required.

1. Mix together flour and salt and rub in the margarine.
2. Mix dried yeast and sugar into the water. Leave in a warm place until quite dissolved and frothing. If using fresh yeast, mix it and sugar into the water, stirring to dissolve yeast. It is now ready for use.
3. Add yeast mixture with milk to the flour mixture.
4. Mix to a pliable dough and turn on to a floured board.
5. Knead well until dough is no longer sticky, and is smooth and shiny. If dough is a little soft, extra flour may be added whilst kneading (up to 50 g/2 oz), but it is difficult to add water if too firm.
6. Lightly grease bowl and place dough in it. Cover, or place inside a large polythene bag. Keep away from draughts, and leave to rise (or 'prove') until doubled in size.
7. Turn on to a floured board and knead lightly to let out air and to make dough pliable again.

The dough at this stage is referred to as 'risen dough'. Cut off quantity required for shaping, final rising and baking.

Standard ½ kg/1 lb loaf
Approximately ½ kg/1 lb risen dough.

1. Grease a ½ kg/1 lb loaf tin with a little lard.
2. Lightly shape dough to fit into tin, cover with muslin or light cloth, or place in polythene bag, and leave to rise to the top of the tin.
3. Bake in a hot oven, Gas 7, 425°F, 220°C, for 40 minutes. Reduce to moderately hot, Gas 6, 400°F, 200°C, if it browns too quickly.

Cottage Loaf, Twist, Plait
About 350 g/12 oz risen dough. Hot oven, Gas 7, 425°F, 220°C, 35 minutes.

Bread Buns
Hot oven, Gas 7, 425°F, 220°C, 10 to 12 minutes.

Baps
½ kg/1 lb risen dough for 10–12 baps. Hot oven, Gas 7, 425°F, 220°C, 20 minutes.

WHOLEMEAL BREAD

675 g/1½ lb wholewheat flour
2 teaspoons sea salt
25 g/1 oz butter
1 tablespoon molasses, black treacle or honey
20 g/¾ oz dried yeast or 40 g/1½ oz fresh yeast
425 ml/¾ pint warm water
15 g/½ oz barbados sugar

If you wish to make double quantity of bread, double all ingredients **except** yeast. 50 g/2 oz fresh yeast or 25 g/1 oz dried yeast will rise 1·3 kg/3 lb flour.

1. Mix flour and salt in a large bowl and put in a warm place.
2. Melt butter slowly. Add molasses, treacle or honey.
3. In a small bowl, dissolve yeast in 2 tablespoons of the warm water with the sugar. Put mixture in a warm place for 10 to 15 minutes until it begins to froth up.
4. Add yeast liquid to flour, then add butter and molasses mixture.
5. Mix continuously while pouring in warm water. Add enough to make a soft dough. It should not be sticky.

6. Turn out on to a floured board and knead for 15 minutes. This stretches the dough, encourages the action of the gluten and the result is a strong dough that will rise well.

7. Put dough back into bowl. Cover and leave in a warm place to rise for 1 hour.

8. Turn out on floured board again and knead lightly for a few minutes.

9. Shape and place in a greased 1 kg/2 lb loaf tin. Cover and leave in a warm place to rise for 45 minutes.

10. Bake in a hot oven, Gas 7, 425°F, 220°C, for 25 minutes. Reduce temperature to moderate, Gas 4, 350°F, 180°C, for a further 25 minutes.

Ursula Cavanagh, author of 'The Wholefood Cookery Book'

WHOLEWHEAT BUN LOAF AND HOT CROSS BUNS

25 g/1 oz fresh yeast or 15 g/½ oz dried yeast
40 g/1½ oz dark brown barbados sugar
150 ml/¼ pint tepid water
450 g/1 lb plain wholewheat flour
1 level teaspoon sea salt
1 teaspoon mixed spice
½ teaspoon cinnamon
A grating of nutmeg
50 g/2 oz margarine
100 g/4 oz mixed currants, sultanas and peel
Warm milk and 1 beaten egg to make 150 ml/¼ pint bare measure

Glaze
1 tablespoon demerara sugar dissolved over low heat in 2 tablespoons milk and boiled for 1 minute

1. Mix fresh yeast with 1 teaspoon of the sugar and stir it into the tepid water.
If using dried yeast, mix 1 teaspoon of sugar into the tepid water, sprinkle in yeast, whisking with a fork to disperse the grains. Let it stand in a warm place for 10 to 15 minutes when it should be frothing well and ready to use.

2. Mix together in a large bowl flour, salt and spices.

3. Rub in margarine.

4. Mix in rest of sugar and fruit.

5. Mix to a pliable dough with yeast liquid and egg and milk mixture.

6. Knead thoroughly.

7. Place to rise in a greased bowl away from draughts. Cover with polythene or a clean tea-towel. Let it rise for about 1 hour until doubled in size.

8. Turn on to a floured board and knead well.

9. **For bun loaf:** weigh off 450 g/ 1 lb dough, shape into a loaf and put into a greased ½ kg/1 lb loaf tin, or round tin of similar capacity. Cover and leave to rise, away from draughts.

10. **For Hot Cross Buns:** divide remaining dough into 8 even pieces. Shape into buns, round or oval. Roll lightly and make a cross on top with knife.

11. Place on greased baking tray, cover, and allow to rise until puffy. **For rising:** a slightly warm atmosphere (e.g., above the stove, or the airing cupboard) is an advantage as this type of dough rises more slowly than plain bread.

12. Bake buns for approximately 15 minutes in a moderately hot oven, Gas 6, 400°F, 200°C, until nicely browned. Remove from oven and turn on to cooling rack. Brush with glaze while hot.

13. Bake loaf in a moderately hot oven, Gas 6, 400°F, 200°C, for 15 minutes. Reduce heat to moderate, Gas 4, 350°F, 180°C, for a further 25 to 30 minutes until firm. Turn out on to wire rack to cool. Glaze as for buns as desired.

These freeze very well after they are baked, but do not glaze before freezing.

115

MY GRANDMOTHER'S YULE BREAD

This bread improves with keeping. Make it 3 weeks before Christmas.

450 g/1 lb strong plain flour
Pinch of salt
15 g/½ oz fresh yeast, or
2 teaspoons dried yeast
300 ml/½ pint luke-warm water
225 g/8 oz butter
225 g/8 oz sugar
Half a grated nutmeg
350 g/12 oz currants
100 g/4 oz candied peel
2 beaten eggs

1. Put flour with a pinch of salt in a warm basin.
2. Dissolve fresh yeast in the luke-warm water. If using dried yeast, add 1 teaspoon of the sugar to the water, sprinkle yeast on top and leave it to froth up.
3. Stir yeast liquid into flour. Cover basin and let it stand 1 hour in a warm place.
4. Meanwhile, cream the butter.
5. Add butter, sugar, nutmeg, currants, candied peel and beaten eggs to flour and yeast. Mix well.
6. Pour into a 1 kg/2 lb greased loaf tin, or two ½ kg/1 lb loaf tins. Cover tins and leave to rise, about ¼ hour, until mixture just reaches top of tins.
7. Bake in a moderate oven, Gas 4, 350°F, 180°C. Large tin takes about 2 hours. Small tins take 1 hour. Should be brown and firm when done.
8. Turn out of tins on to wire rack to cool.

Keep for 3 weeks before using. This loaf is particularly nice buttered.

**Stella Boldy,
Sykehouse, N. Humberside**

MRS ZACHAROVA'S METHOD OF MAKING BREAD

The essential difference between this and other methods is that the yeast is mixed with the liquid, and the flour is added to the liquid until the desired consistency is achieved. Consequently, it requires less physical effort to get the dough right.

The second feature of Mrs Zacharova's bread-making is that it fits into her daily routine. Sometimes she lets the bread rise for 1 hour in a warm place, and sometimes all day in a cool place, or all night. The main principle is that it should at least double, if not treble, in size during the first rising.

Finally, after the first rising, the loaves are shaped and put straight out of the way into a cold oven and left for 20 to 30 minutes. The oven is then switched on and baking proceeds. So, if you have a gas or electric cooker, why not try it?

White Bread

It is better for newcomers to this method to start with white bread: with white flour it is easier to handle and learn the feel of the dough than it is with brown flours.

20 g/⅔ oz fresh yeast, or 10 g/2¼ teaspoons dried yeast
2 teaspoons sugar
450 ml/16 fluid oz luke-warm water
About 675 g/1½ lb strong plain white flour
2 teaspoons salt

1. Mix yeast, sugar, 120 ml/4 fluid oz of the warm water and 2 to 3 tablespoons of the flour to a cream. Leave in a warm place for 15 minutes until yeast is working actively and mixture is frothing. If using dried yeast, make doubly sure it is completely dissolved and frothing well.
2. Put yeast mixture, salt, and rest of water in a big mixing bowl and start mixing in the flour. Mix with dough hook on electric mixer, a big wooden spoon or clean hands.

3. Continue to add flour and mix thoroughly. This develops the gluten into stretchy, rubbery strands which will hold the gas made by the yeast.
After a while dough will become difficult to mix in the bowl, so transfer it to a well-floured board.
4. Knead, adding more flour as necessary, until dough retains its shape and no longer sticks to the board. At this point you should be able to feel the rubbery strands between your fingers and the dough should resist when you push against it. Once you recognise the feel of the dough you will know when it is kneaded enough.
5. Put dough into a large bowl, or plastic container, and cover closely with a plate, lid or sheet of polythene. Leave in a warm place, at room temperature or in the cool (depending on when you can complete the next stage) and allow it at least to double in size. It is better to let it rise to three times its original volume than not to let it rise enough. It can be pushed down in the bowl and kneaded a little (but this is not necessary) during this rising period.
6. When dough has risen sufficiently, flour your fingers and scrape and push it back into a small lump.
7. If dough has been allowed to rise for a long period in a cool place it is best to warm it up a little before it is kneaded the second time. Stand covered bowl in the sink or a basin of warm water until dough no longer feels cold. Turn it out on to a floured board. Knead a little, just enough to break down the large air bubbles.
8. Cut into two pieces, shape each piece and place in 2 greased 1 kg/2 lb loaf tins.
9. Stand tins out of your way in a cold oven on the top shelf. Leave enough headroom for rising. In 30

minutes the top of the loaf should just about reach the top of the tin. If your oven has a pilot light, look at loaves after 20 minutes.
10. Now switch on oven and set temperature at Gas 6, 400°F, 200°C. Set timer for 40 minutes. The loaves go on rising until oven is hot enough to kill the yeast. Loaves on lower shelves may need 10 minutes longer to bake.
11. Drop each loaf out of tin and knock its bottom. If it is ready it will sound hollow. If not ready, return to oven in or out of tins for another 5 or 10 minutes.
12. Turn loaves out of tins on to a wire rack to cool.

Brown Bread

You can buy wholemeal flour for bread-making and 100% extraction wholewheat. Wholemeal flour is easier to work and feels more like a white dough. 100% extraction wholewheat is coarser. The rough bits in the flour make it more difficult to form the gluten into rubbery, stretchy strands.

20 g/⅔ oz fresh yeast, or 10 g/2½ teaspoons dried yeast
2 teaspoons barbados or demerara sugar
600 ml/1 pint luke-warm water
About 675 g/1½ lb wholemeal or wholewheat flour
2½ teaspoons salt

Follow method for White Bread (see page 116), but note 3 points:
1. Dough will be stickier and it will be hard to feel the rubbery strands of gluten. It will end up feeling firmer.
2. Loaves cannot rise as much as white ones or they would be impossibly crumbly. However, dough should be allowed to double or treble in size during first rising.
3. Loaves may take 5 minutes longer to bake.

Spicey Fruit Loaf
20 g/⅔ oz fresh yeast, or 10 g/2½

117

teaspoons dried yeast
50 g/2 oz demerara or barbados
sugar
450 ml/16 fluid oz luke-warm water
About 675 g/1½ lb strong plain
white flour
2 teaspoons salt
50–75 g/2–3 oz medium oatmeal, or
rolled oats
1 rounded teaspoon mixed spice
75 g/3 oz mixed dried fruit and
chopped peel

Follow method for white bread
(see page 116) but note 3 points:
1. Add oatmeal or rolled oats and
spice at paragraph 2.
2. Add fruit just before turning
dough out on to board. Fruit will
make dough a bit more difficult to
handle.
3. Dough should be allowed to
double or treble in size during first
rising but, because of oatmeal and
fruit, it will be more like brown
dough both to handle and in the
way it rises in the tins.

Malt Bread
20 g/⅔ oz fresh yeast or 10 g/2½
teaspoons dried yeast
450 ml/16 fluid oz luke-warm milk,
milk and water or reconstituted
dried milk
2 teaspoons sugar
About 675 g/1½ lb strong plain
white flour, or white and
wholewheat flour
½ tablespoon molasses or black
treacle
1 tablespoon malt extract
½ tablespoon golden syrup
75 g/3 oz soya flour
2 teaspoons salt
100 g/4 oz mixed dried fruits and
peel
A little melted butter

1. Mix yeast, sugar, 120 ml/4 fluid
oz of the warm milk and 2 to 3
tablespoons of the flour to a
cream. Leave in a warm place for
15 minutes until yeast is working
actively and mixture is frothing. If
using dried yeast, make doubly
sure it is completely dissolved and
frothing well.
2. Mix remainder of liquid,

molasses, malt and syrup,
warming a little if necessary.
3. Put yeast liquid and malt
mixture in a large bowl and mix in
soya flour and 225 g/8 oz of the
white flour.
4. Cover bowl closely and leave it
in a warm place for 4 or 5 hours.
5. Add salt and start mixing in
rest of flour. Mix with dough hook
on electric mixer, a wooden spoon
or clean hands.
6. Mix in fruit and continue to
work in flour. After a while dough
will become too difficult to mix in
the bowl, so transfer it to a well-
floured board.
7. Follow method for White Bread
from stages 4 to 7 (see page 117,
noting dough should be rather
tight).
8. Cut it into 3 even-sized pieces,
shape and put into tins.
9. Stand tins out of your way in a
cold oven on the top shelf. Leave
enough headroom for rising. In 30
minutes the top of the loaf should
just about reach the top of the tin.
If your oven has a pilot light, look
at loaves after 20 minutes.
10. Now switch on oven and set
temperature at Gas 6, 400°F,
200°C. Set timer for 40 minutes.
The loaves go on rising until oven
is hot enough to kill the yeast.
Loaves on lower shelves may need
10 minutes longer to bake.
11. Turn loaves out of tins on to a
wire rack to cool. Brush tops
immediately with melted butter to
make them shine.

Sour Rye Bread
Start to prepare this bread 48
hours before you want to bake it.

450 ml/15 fl oz luke-warm water
350 g/12 oz rye flour

Mix these two ingredients
together, cover closely with a lid,
plate or sheet of polythene and
leave in a warm place (such as on
top of central heating boiler, or in
airing cupboard) for 48 hours. The
mixture must 'sour'. It will develop
a strong aroma.

150 ml/5 fluid oz luke-warm water
20 g/$\frac{2}{3}$ oz fresh yeast or 10 g/
2$\frac{1}{2}$ teaspoons dried yeast
1 tablespoon carraway seeds
(optional)
2 teaspoons sugar
About 450 g/1 lb strong plain
white flour, or wholewheat flour,
or a mixture of both. Up to 100 g/
4 oz rye flour could be included to
make a total of 450 g/1 lb flour
2$\frac{1}{2}$ teaspoons salt

Follow method for White Bread
(see page 116) but note 3 points:
1. Soured rye flour mixture is put
in large mixing bowl at paragraph
2, then yeast mixture salt, rest of
water and carraway seeds are
added.
2. It will seem difficult to work
because there is no gluten in rye
flour.
3. When oven is switched on, set
timer for 50 minutes.

Halla
A Continental bread made from a
rich dough and shaped in a twist
or plait.

20 g/$\frac{2}{3}$ oz fresh yeast or 10 g/2$\frac{1}{2}$
teaspoons dried yeast
2 teaspoons sugar (more if you like
a sweet loaf)
250 ml/9 fluid oz warm milk, milk and
water or reconstituted dried milk
About 675 g/1$\frac{1}{2}$ lb strong plain
white flour
2 teaspoons salt
100 g/4 oz melted margarine,
butter or half of each
2 beaten eggs

1. Mix yeast, sugar, 120 ml/4 fluid
oz of the warm milk and 2 to 3
tablespoons of the flour to a
cream. Leave in a warm place for
15 minutes until yeast is working
actively and mixture is frothing. If
using dried yeast, make doubly
sure it is completely dissolved and
frothing well.
2. Put yeast mixture, salt, rest of
milk and a little flour in a big
mixing bowl. Mix together. Add

melted fat, some more flour and
then the eggs. Eggs mix in better if
there is already some flour in
dough.
3. Continue to add flour and mix
very thoroughly at each addition.
It is important to develop all the
gluten in order to make a really
light, well-risen loaf. At some stage
it will be too difficult to mix dough
in a bowl, so transfer it to a well-
floured board.
4. Knead, adding more flour as
necessary, until dough retains its
shape and no longer sticks to the
board. Mix in plenty of flour to
make a firm dough. These loaves
are baked without the support of a
tin, and a soft dough would spread
sideways.
5. Put dough into an especially
large bowl, or plastic container,
and cover closely with a plate, lid
or sheet of polythene. Dough that
has been well-worked rises very
high. It can be punched back if it
grows too high. Leave bowl in a
warm place, at room temperature
or in the cool (depending on when
you can complete the next stage)
and allow it at least to double in
size. It is better to let it rise to
three times its original volume
than not to let it rise enough. It
can be pushed down in the bowl
and kneaded a little (but this is
not necessary) during this rising
period.
6. When dough has risen
sufficiently, flour your fingers and
scrape and push it back into a
small lump.
7. If dough has been allowed to
rise for a long period in a cool
place it is best to warm it up a
little before it is kneaded the
second time. Stand covered bowl
in the sink or a basin of warm
water until dough no longer feels
cold. Turn it out on to a floured
board. Knead a little, just enough
to break down the large air
bubbles.
8. Cut into 2 even-sized pieces.
Work each piece into a long roll,

cut into 2 or 3 strands and plait them. Place on a greased baking sheet, well apart.

9. Place baking sheet in a cold oven and leave to rise. It is not easy to judge when these loaves are ready for baking. Sometimes, if over-risen, they will collapse during baking but if you have worked hard at the mixing and kneading to develop the gluten this will help keep the air in. Look at loaves in 20 to 30 minutes. They should have begun to rise nicely before oven is switched on.

10. Just before switching on oven, gently brush tops of loaves with milk or egg-yolk and milk. This will give them a nice colour.

11. Now switch on oven and set temperature at Gas 6, 400°F, 200°C. Set timer for 40 minutes. The loaves go on rising until oven is hot enough to kill the yeast. Loaves on lower shelves may need 10 minutes longer to bake.

12. Take each loaf off baking sheet and tap its bottom. If it is ready it will sound hollow. If not ready, return to oven for another 5 or 10 minutes.

13. Turn loaves on to a wire rack to cool.

14. Handle gently when baked.

**Jeannie Zacharova,
London**

WHOLEMEAL ONION, TOMATO AND ANCHOVY FLAN

Enough for 4 for a main course
Base
100 g/4 oz wholemeal flour
½ level teaspoon salt
25 g/1 oz butter
7 g/¼ oz fresh yeast, or 1 level teaspoon dried yeast with ½ level teaspoon sugar
3 tablespoons tepid water
1 small egg or ½ large egg

Filling
450 g/1 lb onions
3 tomatoes

1 clove garlic
3 tablespoons cooking oil
Seasoning

Garnish
1 can of anchovy fillets
A few black olives

1. Mix flour and salt in bowl and rub in butter.

2. Cream fresh yeast in 1 tablespoon of the tepid water. If using dried yeast, put all the water into a small basin. Stir in dried yeast and sugar, place basin in a container of warm water and leave to stand for about 15 minutes until starting to froth.

3. Lightly beat egg.

4. Make a well in centre of flour, add yeast mixture, beat in egg and, if using fresh yeast, remaining 2 tablespoons of tepid water. Mix to a soft dough.

5. Knead dough on a floured board for 5 minutes. Put in a bowl, cover and leave in a warm place to rise until doubled in size.

6. **For the filling:** peel and slice onions finely.

7. Skin and chop tomatoes (*see page 66*). Crush garlic (*see page 66*).

8. Heat oil in a frying pan and slowly cook onions until soft but not brown.

9. Add tomatoes, garlic and seasoning.

10. Continue to cook gently until any liquid from tomatoes has evaporated. Leave to cool.

11. When dough has risen, knock it back – i.e., knead the air out of it. Then knead into a round ball.

12. Put a greased 20 cm/8 inch flan ring on to a greased baking sheet. Put ball of dough in centre of flan ring and press it out over base and up sides of ring.

13. Fill with onion mixture.

14. Drain and dry anchovy fillets and cut into narrow strips. Remove stones from olives.

15. Make a trellis pattern on top of onions with the anchovies and decorate with pieces of olive.

16. Leave to rise for 10 minutes.

17. Bake in centre of moderately hot oven, Gas 6, 400°F, 200°C, for 20 minutes. Reduce heat to moderate, Gas 4, 350°F, 180°C, for 15 to 20 minutes more.
Excellent served with green salad. Freezes well.

**Jean Welshman,
Malton, E. Yorkshire**

WHOLEWHEAT RHUM BABA

Enough for 5 to 6 people

For a 19 cm/7½ inch ring mould
225 g/8 oz wholewheat flour
Pinch of sea salt
15 g/½ oz fresh yeast, or 2 teaspoons dried yeast
15 g/½ oz barbados sugar
2 tablespoons luke-warm water
150 ml/¼ pint luke-warm milk
2 beaten eggs
75 g/3 oz melted butter

Syrup
150 ml/5 fluid oz water
125 g/4 oz demerara sugar
1 tablespoon rum

To Finish and Decorate
300 ml/½ pint fresh double or whipping cream

1. Put flour and salt in a bowl in a warm place.
2. Dissolve yeast and sugar in a small bowl with 2 tablespoons luke-warm water.
3. Add yeast mixture, beaten eggs, milk and melted butter to flour. Mix and beat with the hands for several minutes.
4. Cover basin and leave in a warm place for about 40 minutes to double in size.
5. Meanwhile, butter the ring mould.
6. Beat dough again and put into mould. Leave to rise in a warm place for 10 minutes.
7. Bake in a hot oven, Gas 7, 425°F, 220°C, for 25 minutes.
8. Turn carefully out of mould on to a warmed dish.

9. **For the syrup:** bring water to boil and remove pan from heat. Add sugar and stir carefully to dissolve. Bring to the boil and boil fast for 5 minutes.
10. Let syrup cool a little and stir in rum.
11. Spoon warm syrup over while cake is still warm.
12. At the last minute, fill the middle with whipped cream. Serve cold.

**Ursula Cavanagh,
author of 'The Wholefood Cookery Book'**

IRISH BROWN SODA BREAD

250 g/9 oz self-raising wholewheat flour
½ level teaspoon salt
½ level teaspoon barbados sugar
10 g/¼ oz butter or margarine
150 ml/¼ pint buttermilk or sour milk

1. Mix flour, salt and sugar in a large bowl.
2. Rub in butter or margarine.
3. Mix in the milk to form a soft dough.
4. Turn on to a floured surface and knead lightly to form a smooth dough. Shape into a small, round, flat loaf.
5. Place on a lightly-floured baking sheet and brush top with a little milk.
6. With a sharp knife slash a cross on the top.
7. Bake on centre shelf of a moderately hot oven, Gas 6, 400°F, 200°C, for 30 minutes. Cool on a wire rack.

Eat the same day. Easily made with double quantities, in which case bake for 40 minutes.

CHEESE AND WALNUT LOAF

225 g/8 oz self-raising flour
1 level tablespoon dry mustard, bare measure
A good pinch of salt

A shake of pepper
100 g/4 oz margarine
100 g/4 oz grated cheddar cheese
25 g/1 oz chopped walnuts
2 beaten eggs
150 ml/¼ pint milk

1. Sieve together into a bowl the flour, mustard, salt and pepper.
2. Rub in margarine.
3. Mix in cheese and walnuts.
4. Add eggs and milk and mix well.
5. Grease a ½ kg/1 lb loaf tin and line base with greased, greaseproof paper. Tip mixture in.
6. Bake just below middle of a moderately hot oven, Gas 5, 375°F, 190°C, for 1½ hours. Leave to cool for a few minutes before turning out on to wire cooling rack.
Eat cold with butter.

**Miss M. Owen,
Elworth, Cheshire**

DATE BREAD

225 g/8 oz dates
½ teaspoon bicarbonate of soda
150 ml/¼ pint milk and water mixed
40 g/1½ oz butter or margarine
225 g/8 oz self-raising flour
100 g/4 oz sugar

1. Chop dates and put in a bowl with bicarbonate of soda.
2. Heat milk and water to boiling point and pour over the dates. Leave to cool.
3. Rub butter or margarine into flour.
4. Add sugar.
5. Drain dates, saving liquid, and mix them in with enough liquid to form a fairly soft mixture.
6. Grease a ½ kg/1 lb loaf tin and line it with greased, greaseproof paper.
7. Put mixture in tin.
8. Bake just below middle of a moderate oven, Gas 3, 325°F, 170°C, for 1 hour, until well-risen, brown and firm on top.

**Mrs M. Naylor,
Manston, Leeds**

HONEY RAISIN LOAF

175 g/6 oz wholewheat flour
175 g/6 oz self-raising flour
½ teaspoon salt
40 g/1½ oz soft brown sugar
275 g/10 oz seedless raisins
50 g/2 oz chopped walnuts (optional)
40 g/1½ oz butter or margarine
10 tablespoons honey
1 beaten egg
Grated rind of 1 orange
¼ teaspoon bicarbonate of soda
150 ml/¼ pint milk

1. Mix together flours, salt and sugar in a large bowl.
2. Mix in raisins and walnuts.
3. Melt butter or margarine with honey until runny. Do not overheat. Add to bowl and mix in.
4. Add beaten egg and orange rind.
5. Mix bicarbonate of soda into a little of the milk and add with the rest of the milk.
6. Mix well together.
7. Grease and flour, or line with greased, greaseproof paper a 1 kg/2 lb loaf tin.
8. Pour in the mixture.
9. Bake in centre of a moderate oven, Gas 3, 325°F, 160°C, for 1½ hours.
This cake improves with keeping. Try and keep it a week, or at least 2 to 3 days, before cutting.

**Renée Rouston,
Kippax, W. Yorkshire**

CANADIAN MALT BREAD

375 g/13 oz sultanas
50 g/2 oz butter
350 ml/12 fluid oz hot water
375 g/13 oz self-raising flour
½ teaspoon bicarbonate of soda
250 g/9 oz sugar
2 beaten eggs

1. Put sultanas, butter and water in a pan, bring to the boil and simmer for 4 minutes. Allow to cool a little.

2. Mix together flour, bicarbonate of soda and sugar.
3. Mix warm fruit mixture into flour mixture.
4. Mix in the beaten eggs.
5. Grease two ½ kg/1 lb loaf tins and put in the mixture. Level the tops.
6. Bake in a moderately hot oven, Gas 5, 375°F, 190°C, for 1 hour.

**Mrs J. Barsby,
Kirkby in Ashfield, Notts**

WALNUT AND APPLE TEABREAD

All-in-one mix.

**1 large apple
50 g/2 oz chopped walnuts
100 g/4 oz soft brown sugar
100 g/4 oz soft margarine
100 g/4 oz sultanas or raisins
2 large eggs
1 tablespoon honey
175 g/6 oz self-raising flour
50 g/2 oz wholemeal flour
1 teaspoon mixed spice
Pinch of salt**

1. Grease a 1 kg/2 lb loaf tin or two ½ kg/1 lb loaf tins and line with greased, greaseproof paper.
2. Peel, core and chop apple.
3. Place all ingredients in a large bowl and beat well for 2 minutes.
4. Put mixture into the prepared tins.
5. Bake in a moderate oven, Gas 4, 350°F, 180°C, for 1 hour. Reduce heat to Gas 3, 325°F, 160°C, for a further 15 to 20 minutes.
6. Turn out on to a wire rack to cool.

Serve sliced with butter.

**Sybil Norcott,
Irlam, Nr. Manchester**

CHEESE OATMEAL SCONES

**100 g/4 oz plain flour
½ teaspoon bicarbonate of soda
1 teaspoon cream of tartar
½ teaspoon salt**

**25 g/1 oz margarine or lard
100 g/4 oz oatmeal
50 g/2 oz grated cheese
A little milk**

1. Sift together into a bowl the flour, bicarbonate of soda, cream of tartar and salt.
2. Rub in fat. Mix in oatmeal and cheese.
3. Add enough milk to form a stiffish dough.
4. Turn dough on to a floured board, knead lightly, roll out quite thick and cut into rounds.
5. Put scones on a greased baking sheet.
6. Bake in a hot oven, Gas 8, 450°F, 230°C, for 12 minutes.

**Mrs Margaret Hussey,
Leeds**

CHEESE AND POTATO SCONES

Makes 6 or 8 scones

**225 g/8 oz cold, cooked potato, mashed
50 g/2 oz margarine
50 g/2 oz plain flour
Salt and pepper
75 g/3 oz grated cheese
Oil, pork or bacon dripping, to fry**

1. Prepare the potato.
2. Warm margarine to soften but do not melt.
3. Mix margarine into potato with flour, a little salt and pepper and the cheese.
4. Form into rounds about 7 mm/½ inch thick on a floured board
5. Put in fridge to stiffen up.
6. Heat 2 teaspoons of oil in a frying pan and fry scones until golden brown, 3 minutes on each side. Drain on kitchen paper.

LEMON SCONES

Makes 12 to 14 scones

**225 g/8 oz plain or wholewheat flour
Pinch of salt**

1 rounded teaspoon cream of
tartar
1 level teaspoon bicarbonate of
soda
50 g/2 oz margarine
35 g/1¼ oz barbados sugar
Grated rind 1 lemon
150 ml/¼ pint milk

1. Set oven at hot, Gas 7, 425°F,
220°C.
2. Grease a baking sheet.
3. Sieve together or mix well the
flour, salt, cream of tartar and
bicarbonate of soda. Rub in the
margarine.
4. Add the sugar and lemon rind
and mix well.
5. Mix to a soft dough with the
milk.
6. Roll out lightly and quite thick
on a floured board.
7. Cut into rounds with a 5 cm/2
inch cutter. You should get 12 to
14 scones.
8. Place on greased baking sheet.
9. Brush tops with a little milk.
10. Bake for 10 to 12 minutes until
nicely-risen and golden brown.
11. Cool on a wire rack.
12. Cut scones across and spread
with lemon curd.
13. Pipe fresh whipped cream on
the top.

**Stella Boldy,
Sykehouse, N. Humberside**

YOGHURT
WHOLEMEAL SCONES

**225 g/8 oz wholewheat flour
½ teaspoon salt
1½ teaspoons baking powder
25 g/1 oz margarine
150 ml/¼ pint yoghurt**

1. Mix together flour, salt and
baking powder.
2. Rub in margarine.

3. Form into a stiff dough with the
yoghurt.
4. Turn on to a floured board and
shape with the hands until 2 cm/
¾ inch thick.
5. Cut into rounds with a pastry
cutter.
6. Place on a lightly-greased
baking tray and bake in a
moderately hot oven, Gas 6, 400°F,
200°C, for 10 to 12 minutes.
7. Serve hot with butter.

**Sybil Norcott,
Irlam, Nr. Manchester**

WHOLEMEAL
DROPPED SCONES

**225 g/8 oz wholemeal flour
1 teaspoon cream of tartar
½ teaspoon bicarbonate of soda
Pinch of salt
50 g/2 oz dark brown barbados
sugar
25 g/1 oz (1 dessertspoon) black
treacle
1 egg
200 ml/7 fluid oz milk**

1. Mix together dry ingredients
very thoroughly.
2. Beat together treacle, egg and
milk and mix into dry ingredients
to make a smooth batter.
3. Heat a girdle or heavy frying
pan. (If it is cast aluminium there
is no need to grease it.)
4. Drop dessertspoons of mixture
on to hot girdle. When scones are
full of bubbles and brown, turn
them over and bake until brown
on other side and cooked through.
5. Place on a cooling rack covered
with a clean cloth.

Freezes well.

**Anne Wallace,
Dunlop, Scotland**

CHAPTER 10

CAKES, BISCUITS AND COOKIES

BASIC WHOLEFOOD BUTTER SPONGE CAKE

175 g/6 oz butter or margarine
75 g/3 oz barbados sugar
3 beaten eggs
175 g/6 oz self-raising wholewheat flour
2 tablespoons boiling water

1. Grease a 20 cm/8 inch sandwich tin and flour it or line it with greased, greaseproof paper.
2. Cream butter and sugar until mixture is light and fluffy.
3. Add well-beaten eggs, a little at a time, alternately with small quantities of flour, beating lightly.
4. Beat in boiling water and pour mixture into prepared tin.
5. Bake in a moderate oven, Gas 4, 350°F, 180°C, for 35 minutes until firm on top.
6. Turn out of tin immediately on to a cooling wire.

Ursula Cavanagh, author of 'The Wholefood Cookery Book'

WHOLEMEAL CARROT CAKE

175 g/6 oz wholemeal flour
2 slightly-rounded teaspoons baking powder
Pinch of salt
1 level teaspoon cinnamon (optional)
100 g/4 oz grated carrot
100 g/4 oz margarine
100 g/4 oz soft, dark brown sugar
Grated zest of ½ orange
2 large eggs
About 1 tablespoon milk

1. Sift baking powder, salt and cinnamon into the flour and mix well.
2. Mix in grated carrot.
3. Cream margarine and sugar until light and fluffy. Add orange zest.
4. Add eggs one at a time, beating well, and spoon in a little of the flour mixture to prevent curdling.

5. Gradually mix in flour. Add milk a little at a time until consistency is soft but not runny.
6. Grease a 16 cm/6 inch round cake tin and line base with greased, greaseproof paper. Tip in the mixture.
7. Bake in a moderate oven, Gas 3, 325°F, 160°C, for ¾ to 1 hour.

For a special occasion, ice with orange glacé icing and decorate with pieces of walnut.

Orange Glacé Icing
125 g/4 oz sifted icing sugar
Zest of ½ orange and 4 teaspoons orange juice

1. Mix orange juice and zest with icing sugar. The mixture should evenly coat the back of a spoon.
2. Spread icing over cake, using a wet palette knife to obtain a smooth finish.

Decorate with walnut halves before icing sets.

Mrs H. D. Harvey,
Sherfield-on-Loddon, Hants

GREAT AUNT ANNIE'S CHOCOLATE COCONUT CAKE

100 g/4 oz soft margarine
100 g/4 oz castor sugar
2 large eggs
100 g/4 oz self-raising flour
1 tablespoon cocoa
¼ level teaspoon baking powder
25 g/1 oz coconut
25 g/1 oz ground almonds
A little milk, if necessary

1. Grease and flour an 18 cm/7 inch sandwich tin.
2. Cream together in a mixing bowl margarine and sugar until light and fluffy.
3. Beat eggs well in a small basin.
4. Sieve flour, cocoa and baking powder together into another basin.
5. Mix coconut and ground almonds into flour mixture.
6. Add a little of the beaten egg

and a little of the flour mixture to creamed fat and sugar. Add a little of each alternately, folding in until all ingredients are mixed.

7. Add a little milk, if necessary, to make a soft, dropping consistency.
8. Put mixture into prepared tin.
9. Bake in a moderate oven Gas 4, 350°F, 180°C, for about 40 minutes, until it is shrinking from sides of tin and feels firm to the touch.
10. Cool on a wire rack.

This cake may be decorated with chocolate glacé icing, melted chocolate and walnuts or chocolate drops. No filling is necessary. The cake can be used to make a Chocolate Easter Cake by decorating with yellow, fluffy chickens and tiny Easter eggs.

Chocolate Glacé Icing
(for top and sides of cake)
340 g/12 oz sieved icing sugar
3 to 4 tablespoons hot, not boiling, water
3 tablespoons cocoa

Never use boiling water for glacé icing or the finished icing will be dull.

1. Sieve icing sugar into a bowl.
2. Blend cocoa into hot water and beat into the icing sugar. Beat well with a wooden spoon. The icing should just coat the back of the spoon.
3. Use immediately, putting spoonfuls on top of the cake. Using a palette knife with a round blade, spread icing over top of cake and let it run down the sides. Spread evenly round sides. Dip knife in hot water if icing does not run very well. The icing should be smooth and shining.

Stella Boldy,
Sykehouse, N. Humberside

CIDER CAKE

250 g/8 oz mixed sultanas, raisins and currants
4 tablespoons sweet cider

175 g/6 oz butter or margarine
175 g/6 oz soft brown sugar
3 eggs
250 g/8 oz self-raising flour
1 teaspoon mixed spice (optional)

1. Soak mixed fruits in the cider overnight.
2. Cream butter or margarine and add sugar. Cream until fluffy.
3. Lightly beat eggs and gradually beat them into the mixture.
4. Mix in fruit and cider.
5. Sift flour and spice together.
6. Fold in half of the flour, mix well. Mix in rest of flour.
7. Grease a 20 cm/8 inch round or 18 cm/7 inch square tin and line bottom with greased, greaseproof paper.
8. Bake in a moderate oven, Gas 4, 350°F, 180°C, for 1 hour and 10 minutes.

Mrs Peggy Hughes,
Skewen, Glamorgan

CHRISTMAS CAKE WITH ALMOND PASTE AND ROYAL ICING

Bake this cake in September or October as it improves with keeping.

100 g/4 oz raisins
100 g/4 oz glacé cherries
100 g/4 oz mixed peel
450 g/1 lb currants
100 g/4 oz sultanas
2 tablespoons brandy, sherry or rum.
4 eggs
225 g/8 oz butter
225 g/8 oz soft brown sugar
225 g/8 oz plain white flour
1 teaspoon mixed spice
100 g/4 oz ground almonds

1. Chop raisins, cherries and mixed peel.
2. Put them in a bowl with currants and sultanas, pour over the brandy, sherry or rum and leave overnight.
3. Line a 20 cm/8 inch diameter round cake tin or an 18 cm/7 inch

square tin, with greased, greaseproof paper.

4. Prepare a cool oven, Gas 2, 300°F, 150°C.

5. Beat eggs.

6. Cream butter and sugar in a large bowl.

7. Sift flour and mixed spice into a separate bowl and add soaked fruit and ground almonds. Mix well together.

8. Add spoonfuls of egg then flour mixture to bowl of creamed ingredients. Mix well at each addition until all has been mixed thoroughly.

9. Put mixture into prepared tin.

10. Wrap a double thickness of brown paper or newspaper round outside of tin. Let it stand up a good 5 cm/2 inches above tin. Tie it on with string. This will protect cake from browning on the outside before middle is cooked.

11. Bake cake for 3 to 4 hours, until firm and fruit stops 'singing' and 'sissing'.

12. Remove cake from tin on to a cooling wire.

13. When cold, store in an air-tight tin and let it mature as long as possible (at least 3 months).

It will keep for a year.

Almond Paste

Makes enough to cover top and sides of a 20 cm/8 inch diameter round cake or an 18 cm/7 inch square cake.

350 g/12 oz ground almonds
175 g/6 oz sieved icing sugar
175 g/6 oz castor sugar
1 large egg and 1 egg-white
Juice of ½ lemon
A few drops ratafia essence
A few drops almond flavouring
A few drops vanilla flavouring
1 teaspoon orange flower water (buy it from a chemist)
2 teaspoons brandy, rum or sherry

1. Mix ground almonds and sugars together.

2. Beat whole egg and add lemon juice, ratafia, flavourings, orange flower water and brandy, rum or sherry.

3. Using a wooden spoon, mix liquid carefully into almond and sugar. Do not add it all at once because if mixture becomes too soft it will be difficult to roll out. Work it into a firm, but manageable paste, kneading a little with hands.

4. Brush top and sides of cake with a little beaten egg-white. This gives a tacky surface to help paste stick to cake.

5. Dredge a board with sifted icing sugar and have more icing sugar ready for the rolling pin.

6. Take off ⅔ of the almond paste for the sides of the cake.

7. Measure the circumference of your cake – a piece of string will do – and measure the height of sides. Your measurements will give a long, narrow rectangle.

8. Roll out the larger piece of paste just longer than this measurement and it will fit nicely round sides of cake. Press lightly with rolling pin at join.

9. For the top of the cake, shape remaining piece of paste into a round or a square and roll it out slightly larger than top of cake. Using the piece of string, check size of paste against size of cake top. Do not lift paste on to cake.

10. Turn cake upside-down on to the paste and trim neatly. Turn cake right side up again with paste in position. By doing it this way you get a nice flat surface to the paste.

11. Brush almond paste all over with egg-white and leave to dry.

Royal Icing

To cover the cake only, not for decoration.

Mix icing the day before you mean to ice the cake.

450 g/1 lb icing sugar
2 egg-whites
2 teaspoons glycerine (buy at a chemist)
2 teaspoons lemon juice, strained

1. Sieve icing sugar three times. This is necessary because the icing must not have any lumps in it – even tiny ones.
2. Put egg-whites into a bowl and beat, but only lightly.
3. Add icing sugar to egg-whites, a tablespoonful at a time. Beat each spoonful in quickly with a round-bladed knife.
4. Add glycerine and strained lemon juice and mix in well. Glycerine is used to stop icing going hard.
5. Put a damp cloth over bowl of icing. Put bowl into a polythene bag and leave it overnight.
6. Next day, put cake on a board that is at least 8 cm/3 inches wider than the cake.
7. Put a first coat of icing on the sides first. Use a plastic scraper, a hot knife or metal ruler. Dip it in a jug of boiling water, but wipe it dry before use. Never use a wet knife with this type of icing as it makes icing too soft and it may start to run.
8. Allow icing on the sides to dry overnight, then put a first coat on the top. It is better to use a hot knife or metal ruler for top, not a plastic scraper.
9. Allow time for icing to dry on top, then give the sides a second coat. Two coats of icing give a better finish. Finally, finish icing the top.

To Decorate Cake
225 g/8 oz icing sugar
1 egg-white
1 teaspoon strained lemon juice
Vegetable colouring

1. Prick the design on the cake-top with a darning needle or hat pin.
2. Sieve icing sugar three times to ensure there are no tiny lumps.
3. Put egg-whites into a bowl and beat, but only lightly.
4. Add icing sugar to egg-whites, a tablespoonful at a time. Beat each spoonful in quickly with a round-bladed knife.
5. Add strained lemon juice and

mix in well. Consistency should be very firm: it should form peaks in the bowl when you lift up the spoon.
6. Be very careful in colouring icing. Add colour by dipping a skewer into the bottle and shaking it into icing.
7. Use a greaseproof paper or parchment bag with icing nozzles.

To make a paper icing bag
1. Take a piece of greaseproof paper, 25 cm/10 inches square. Fold along the line A – B.

2. Twist in point A to meet point C and hold it firmly in place. Then twist point B towards point C to complete the cone.

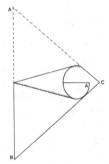

3. Fold the points over firmly to secure the cone. Then snip off the tip so that piping nozzle will project through hole.

Mrs Stella Boldy,
Sykehouse, N. Humberside

CHINCHILLA CAKE

200 g/7 oz butter or margarine
225 g/8 oz castor sugar

4 eggs
50 g/2 oz ground rice
100 g/4 oz ground almonds
50 g/2 oz chopped walnuts
50 g/2 oz split or whole blanched almonds
50 g/2 oz red glacé cherries
50 g/2 oz green glacé cherries
25 g/1 oz angelica, cut small
1 teaspoon vanilla essence
100 g/4 oz self-raising flour

1. Grease a 20 cm/8 inch round cake tin or an 18 cm/7 inch square tin and line with greased, greaseproof paper.
2. Prepare moderate oven, Gas 4, 350°F, 180°C.
3. Cream butter or margarine and sugar until light and fluffy.
4. Beat eggs.
5. Chop almonds and cherries.
6. Mix ground rice, ground almonds, chopped walnuts, almonds, cherries, angelica and flour.
7. Add half of the beaten egg and about 4 tablespoons of the fruit and flour mixture to the creamed butter and sugar, and beat in.
8. Add remaining egg, rest of dry ingredients and vanilla. Mix thoroughly.
9. Put mixture into prepared tin.
10. Bake for about 1¼ hours until firm to the touch.
11. Remove from oven and leave for 2 minutes. Carefully turn out of tin on to a cooling wire.
Will keep for about 4 weeks.

Mrs Grace Wilson,
Pudsey, W. Yorkshire

MRS ROBIN'S WHOLEWHEAT FRUIT CAKE

100 g/4 oz margarine
175 g/6 oz dark brown barbados sugar
175 g/6 oz currants
175 g/6 oz sultanas or raisins
50 g/2 oz chopped peel
25 g/1 oz chopped cherries (optional)

200 ml/8 fluid oz water
1 level teaspoon bicarbonate of soda
1 heaped teaspoon mixed spices
2 beaten eggs
100 g/4 oz plain wholewheat flour
100 g/4 oz self-raising wholewheat flour
Pinch of salt

Note: If you cannot get self-raising wholewheat flour, use 225 g/8 oz plain wholewheat flour and add ½ level teaspoon baking powder.

1. Place margarine, sugar, currants, sultanas, peel, cherries, water, bicarbonate of soda and mixed spice in a pan, bring to boil and simmer one minute. Pour into large mixing bowl. Allow to cool.
2. Line an 18 cm/7 inch square or 20 cm/8 inch round tin with greased, greaseproof paper.
3. Add eggs, flours and salt to cooled mixture. Mix well and pour into tin.
4. Bake in centre of a moderate oven, Gas 4, 350°F, 180°C, for 1¼ to 1½ hours.

SHERRY BUTTER ICING

For a fruit cake or a Christmas cake.
100 g/4 oz butter or margarine or 2 oz of each
225 g/8 oz sifted icing sugar
2 tablespoons sherry

1. Beat butter or margarine until soft.
2. Work in icing sugar and sherry.
3. Spread over cake, fork top and put in a cool place to set.

A tip
If it is to be kept for some time, cake may cause discolouration of icing. To prevent this:
1. Lightly beat white of an egg until runny but not fluffy.
2. Brush egg-white over top and sides of cake. Leave to dry before icing.

To be doubly sure, give cake a second coat of egg-white and allow to dry before icing.

4 DIFFERENT CAKES: SAME METHOD

Method
1. Grease an 18 cm/7 inch square tin or a 20 cm/8 inch round tin and line with greased, greaseproof paper.
2. Beat together fat, sugar and any zest or rind.
3. Beat in eggs, one at a time.
4. Sift flours, salt, baking powder (if used) and mix with other dry ingredients such as fruit, nuts, etc.
5. Fold dry ingredients into egg mixture.
6. Lightly mix in any other liquid.

Cherry Cake
175 g/6 oz margarine, soft type
175 g/6 oz castor sugar
3 eggs
125 g/4 oz self-raising flour
75 g/3 oz plain flour
50 g/2 oz ground almonds
175 g/6 oz glacé cherries, cut in quarters

Moderate oven, Gas 3, 325°F, 160°C, for 1¼ hours or until firm and shrinking slightly from sides of tin.

Madeira Cake
150 g/5 oz margarine, soft type
150 g/5 oz castor sugar
Zest of 1 lemon
3 eggs
175 g/6 oz plain flour
Pinch of salt
2 teaspoons cornflour
1½ level teaspoons baking powder

Moderate oven, Gas 4, 350°F, 180°C, for 1¼ hours or until firm on top and shrinking slightly from sides of tin.

Rice Cake
225 g/8 oz margarine, soft type
225 g/8 oz castor sugar
Zest of 1 lemon
3 large eggs
175 g/6 oz ground rice

150 g/5 oz self-raising flour
3 dessertspoons lemon juice

Moderate oven, Gas 3, 325°F, 160°C, for 1¼ hours or until firm and shrinking slightly from sides of tin.

Walnut Cake with Fudge Icing
175 g/6 oz margarine, soft type
175 g/6 oz castor sugar
3 eggs
225 g/8 oz plain flour
1½ level teaspoons baking powder
75 g/3 oz chopped walnuts
2 tablespoons milk

Moderate oven, Gas 3, 325°F, 160°C, for 1¼ hours or until firm on top and shrinking slightly from sides of tin.

Fudge Icing
75 g/3 oz margarine
3 dessertspoons milk
1 dessertspoon water
1 dessertspoon instant coffee
350 g/12 oz icing sugar

1. Warm together margarine, milk, water and coffee. Allow to cool.
2. Beat in icing sugar.
3. Swirl over cake when cool.

SOFT GINGERBREAD

This cake will bake in a 23 cm/9 inch square tin, a 19 × 29 cm/7½ × 11½ inch dripping tin, or in two 1 kg/2 lb loaf tins.
100 g/4 oz butter
100 g/4 oz golden syrup
125 g/5 oz dark treacle
100 g/4 oz granulated sugar
275 g/10 oz plain flour
¼ teaspoon salt
1 level teaspoon bicarbonate of soda
2 teaspoons ground ginger
1 teaspoon cinnamon
1 beaten egg
225 ml/7 to 8 fluid oz sour milk

1. Grease tin and line with greased, greaseproof paper.
2. Melt butter, syrup, treacle and sugar gently in a pan. Allow to cool.
3. Sieve together flour, salt, ginger cinnamon and bicarbonate of soda.

4. Pour contents of pan into flour.
5. Beat in egg and milk.
6. Pour into prepared tin(s).
7. Bake in a moderate oven, Gas 3, 325°F, 160°C, for about 1 hour. Could take 15 minutes longer in the loaf tins.
8. Turn out of tin on to wire rack to cool.

WHOLEWHEAT MINCEMEAT CAKE

100 g/4 oz butter
100 g/4 oz barbados sugar
3 large eggs
300 g/12 oz mincemeat
175 g/7 oz self-raising wholewheat flour
About 4 tablespoons milk

1. Grease an 18–20 cm/8 inch round cake tin and line bottom with greased, greaseproof paper.
2. Cream butter and sugar well.
3. Beat in eggs, one at a time. If it begins to curdle add a little of the flour.
4. Stir in mincemeat and fold in flour, adding milk to obtain a moist mixture.
5. Bake in a moderate oven, Gas 3, 325°F, 160°C, for 10 minutes. Lower heat to slow, Gas 2, 300°F, 150°C, for about 1¼ hours, until cake is firm on top and shrinking slightly from edge of tin.

Keeps well for several weeks.

Stella Boldy,
Sykehouse, N. Humberside

LEMON CUSTARD CAKE

Custard Filling
25 g/1 oz cornflour
250 ml/½ pint milk
2 egg-yolks
2 dessertspoons sugar
Rind and juice of ½ lemon
3 dessertspoons lemon curd

Cake
225 g/8 oz self-raising flour
100 g/4 oz margarine
75 g/3 oz sugar

1 beaten egg
¼ teaspoon vanilla or almond essence
A little milk
A little egg-white

Make the filling first
1. Blend cornflour in a cup with a little of the milk.
2. Mix egg-yolks and sugar with a fork. Add blended cornflour and gradually mix in rest of the milk.
3. Put in a pan over a low heat and, stirring continuously, bring to the boil. If mixture goes lumpy whisk vigorously.
4. Remove from heat, beat in lemon rind, juice and lemon curd. Leave this custard to cool.

For the cake
5. Put flour in a bowl and rub in margarine.
6. Mix in sugar, beaten egg, vanilla or almond essence. Add a little milk, a tablespoonful at a time, and mix to a stiff, scone-like consistency.
7. Grease a 20 cm/8 inch cake tin with removable base. Line base with greased, greaseproof paper.
8. Roll out just over half the mixture to a round about 27 cm/10½ inches across.
9. Fit this into the tin and fill with cooled custard mixture.
10. Brush top edges of cake base with a little egg-white.
11. Roll out remaining cake mixture and fit on top, pressing lightly round edges to seal it in place. Brush top with egg-white.
12. Bake in centre of a moderate oven, Gas 4, 350°F, 180°C, for about 30 minutes until quite firm and golden on top.
13. Lift out of tin on removable base and slide off base on to a cooling wire.

Serve warm or cooled as a sweet course or at tea-time. When cool, serve with a little cream.

Mrs Carol Goldsmith,
Beccles, Suffolk

TANGY LEMON CAKE

100 g/4 oz butter
150 g/6 oz castor sugar
Grated rind and juice 2 lemons
2 beaten eggs
150 g/6 oz self-raising flour
A little milk
50 g/2 oz granulated sugar

1. Cream butter, castor sugar and lemon rind until fluffy.
2. Gradually beat in eggs.
3. Mix in flour and add about 4 tablespoons milk to soften mixture. It should be soft enough to drop off end of spoon when shaken gently.
4. Grease a 1 kg/2 lb loaf tin.
5. Bake in a moderate oven, Gas 4, 350°F, 180°C, for 45 to 50 minutes until risen and golden, firm on top and shrinking from sides of tin.
6. Just before cake is ready to come out of oven, prepare the lemon syrup. Heat lemon juice and granulated sugar gently until sugar is dissolved.
7. As soon as cake is out of oven, while still in tin, pierce top all over with a skewer. Pour over the lemon syrup. Leave cake in tin until cold.

**Mrs Judith Perry,
Sutton St. Nicholas, Hereford**

ORANGE SPONGE CAKE

75 g/3 oz barbados sugar
3 eggs, separated
100 g/4 oz ground almonds
2 oranges
100 g/4 oz self-raising wholewheat flour

Icing
75 g/3 oz butter
75 g/3 oz barbados sugar
50 g/2 oz powdered milk
1 orange

1. Use a tin approximately 20 cm/8 inches in diameter and 6 cm/2½ inches deep. Grease and flour it, or line with greased, greaseproof paper.
2. Beat sugar and egg-yolks together.
3. Beat in ground almonds and grated rind and juice of 2 oranges.
4. Fold in flour, then stiffly-beaten egg-whites.
5. Pour into prepared tin.
6. Bake in a moderately hot oven, Gas 5, 375°F, 190°C, for 35 minutes.
7. Turn straight out on to a wire rack to cool.
8. Make butter icing by beating together butter and sugar, adding powdered milk and grated rind and juice of half an orange.
9. When cake is cool, slice in half and sandwich together with half the icing.
10. Spread rest of icing on top of cake and decorate with fine strips of thinly-pared orange rind.

**Ursula Cavanagh,
author of 'The Wholefood Cookery, Book'**

SULTANA CAKE

A moist cake. Keeps well.

225 g/8 oz sultanas
100 g/4 oz butter, or firm margarine, cut in small pieces
175 g/6 oz sugar
2 small beaten eggs
A little almond essence
175 g/6 oz self-raising flour
Pinch of salt
50 g/2 oz chopped nuts (optional)

Note: If using nuts reduce quantity of sultanas to 175 g/6 oz.

1. Cover sultanas with water and soak overnight. Next day, bring to the boil.
2. Strain sultanas and mix them, while hot, into butter or margarine.
3. Add sugar, eggs and almond essence.
4. Sift in flour and salt.
5. Lastly, add chopped nuts, if desired. Mix well.
6. Grease a 20 cm/8 inch round tin and line bottom with greased, greaseproof paper. Tip cake

mixture in and smooth the top.
7. Bake in a moderate oven, Gas 4, 350°F, 180°C, for 30 minutes. Lower heat to slow, Gas 2, 300°F, 150°C, until firm to touch in centre.

Mrs C. M. Armstrong, Canonbie, Dumfriesshire

TIPSY CAKE

Fatless Sponge Base
2 large eggs
75 g/3 oz vanilla sugar or castor sugar
75 g/3 oz soft plain flour (sometimes called super-sifted)

To finish the Tipsy Cake
250 ml/½ pint white wine (home-made wine is ideal)
150 g/5 oz carton double cream
2 tablespoons top of the milk
3 tablespoons strawberry jam
A little grated chocolate

1. Grease a 1 litre/1½ pint pudding basin which is suitable for the oven. Preheat oven to moderately hot, Gas 5, 375°F, 190°C.
2. Using a mixing bowl, whisk eggs and sugar together until pale in colour and creamy in texture, holding the impression of the whisk. The eggs should be at room temperature, not straight from the fridge. The whisking can be done in an electric mixer, first warming the bowl. If using a rotary whisk, place the bowl over a saucepan of hot water. Do not let the bowl touch the water.
3. Carefully fold in sifted flour.
4. Pour mixture into greased pudding basin and level the top.
5. Put straight into oven and bake for 25 to 35 minutes, until shrinking from sides of bowl and feeling firm.
6. Turn cake out of basin on to a cooling wire and wait until cold.
7. Whip cream until stiff and smooth, adding top of the milk.
8. Slice cake across into three round layers of even depth.
9. Place bottom largest layer on

plate from which cake is to be served.
10. Pour a little of the wine over.
11. Spread on a layer of jam and place middle layer on top.
12. Pour wine over middle layer of cake. Spread with jam. Put on top layer of cake and pour wine over this.
13. Spread cream all over and round the cake.
14. Sprinkle a little grated chocolate over top to decorate, or invent your own decoration.

Leave cake to stand in a cool place for about an hour before it is to be served.

WALNUT AND CHOCOLATE GÂTEAU

Base
100 g/4 oz margarine
200 g/8 oz crushed digestive biscuits
50 g/2 oz chopped walnuts

Cake
200 g/8 oz castor sugar
100 g/4 oz margarine
100 g/4 oz plain chocolate
2 eggs
175 g/7 oz self-raising flour
½ teaspoon cinnamon
¼ teaspoon salt
150 ml/¼ pint soured or single cream, or top of milk
150 ml/¼ pint strong, black coffee

Decoration
150 ml/¼ pint double cream
150 ml/¼ pint single cream
50 g/2 oz walnuts

Start with the base
1. Melt margarine in pan, add biscuits and chopped walnuts. Press into a greased 20 cm/8 inch loose-bottomed cake tin.

For the cake
2. Beat margarine and castor sugar together.
3. Melt chocolate in a small basin over a pan of simmering water. Add to the creamed mixture.

4. Beat eggs into the mixture.
5. Sift together flour, cinnamon and salt.
6. Mix together cream and coffee.
7. Fold flour, and the cream and coffee alternately into egg mixture.
8. Pour cake mixture on to base.
9. Bake in a moderate oven, Gas 4, 350°F, 180°C, for 1¼ hours.
10. Leave cake in tin until cold, then turn out carefully.

To decorate
11. Whip single and double cream together until thick. Coat top and sides of cake. Decorate with walnuts.

Freezes well – thaw for 2 hours.

**Janet Town,
Pudsey, Yorkshire**

OAT CRISP

For decorating cakes. An economical replacement for chopped nuts.

**40 g/1½ oz margarine
100 g/4 oz porridge oats
50 g/2 oz brown sugar**

1. Melt fat in large pan over very gentle heat.
2. Add oats and sugar. Mix well.
3. Spread mixture loosely on a baking tray. Do not press down.
4. Toast in a moderate oven, Gas 4, 350°F, 180 °C, for 15 to 20 minutes or until golden brown. Stir with a fork several times during cooking.
5. Cool and stir again.
6. When cold, store in an air-tight container.

Will keep several months.

**Sybil Norcott,
Irlam, Nr. Manchester**

ALMOND MACAROONS

You need rice paper on which to bake these.

**60–75 g/2½–3 oz ground almonds
75 g/3 oz castor sugar
1 teaspoon ground rice or rice flour**

**1 egg-white
A few drops orange flower water**

**To finish
Another egg-white
Split blanched almonds**

1. Prepare a moderate oven, Gas 4, 350°F, 180°C.
2. Place rice paper on a baking sheet.
3. Mix ground almonds, sugar and ground rice or rice flour.
4. Beat one egg-white stiffly and fold into almond mixture.
5. Mix in orange flower water.
6. Roll mixture into small balls. Place on the prepared baking sheet. Flatten slightly.
7. To finish, brush with lightly-beaten egg-white and put a split almond on top of each.
8. Bake for 15 to 20 minutes until golden brown.
9. Cool on a wire rack.
10. Trim off rice paper neatly round each macaroon while still warm.

**Stella Boldy,
Sykehouse, N. Humberside**

BARBADOS MACAROONS

**50 g/2 oz ground almonds
1 teaspoon ground rice
100 g/4 oz barbados sugar
Few drops of almond essence
1 egg-white, free-range if possible
Whole almonds, to decorate
Sheets of rice paper**

1. Mix ground almonds, ground rice and sugar.
2. Add essence and some of unbeaten egg-white. Mix to a stiff paste, adding more egg-white as necessary. Beat well.
3. Lay sheets of rice paper on baking trays.
4. Take out teaspoonfuls of the mixture, roll into neat balls and place on to prepared baking trays. Press down a little.
5. Brush lightly with water to give a gloss.

6. Put an almond on top of each macaroon.
7. Bake in a moderate oven, Gas 4, 350°F, 180°C, for about 20 minutes.

BANANA AND NUT FINGERS

225 g/8 oz porridge oats
225 g/8 oz sugar
225 g/8 oz wholewheat flour
½ teaspoon bicarbonate of soda
225 g/8 oz butter or margarine
2 beaten eggs
4 bananas
A few chopped nuts (optional)

1. Mix all dry ingredients together.
2. Rub in butter or margarine.
3. Mix to a stiff dough with the beaten eggs.
4. Divide into 2 equal portions.
5. Grease a shallow tin, 23 cm/ 9 inches square
6. Line tin with half the mixture.
7. Cover with finely-sliced bananas and chopped nuts.
8. Spread remainder of mixture over and press down firmly.
9. Bake in a moderately hot oven, Gas 5, 375°F, 190°C, for 20 to 25 minutes until golden brown.
10. Cut into fingers while still warm and leave to cool in the tin.

Sybil Norcott,
Irlam, Nr. Manchester

CHOCOLATE COCONUT SLAB

160 g/5½ oz margarine
175 g/6 oz self-raising flour
1 good dessertspoon cocoa
100 g/4 oz coconut
75 g/3 oz brown sugar
100 g/4 oz cooking chocolate
A walnut of butter

1. Melt margarine in a large pan. Remove from heat.
2. Sift together flour and cocoa and add it, with the coconut and sugar, to the margarine. Mix well.
3. Grease a shallow, flat tin (a

Swiss roll tin is suitable).
4. Spread mixture in the tin.
5. Bake in middle of a moderate oven, Gas 4, 350°F, 180°C, for 20 to 25 minutes.
6. Remove from oven and leave in tin to cool.
7. Meanwhile, melt cooking chocolate and butter in a bowl over a pan of simmering water. Do not let bowl touch water.
8. Spread chocolate mixture evenly over top of cooked coconut slab. Leave until chocolate is set and cake is cold then cut into desired shapes.

J. M. Klüver,
Hillingdon, Middlesex

COCONUT BUNS

Makes about 16 buns

100 g/4 oz self-raising white or wholewheat flour
100 g/4 oz desiccated coconut
75 g/3 oz sugar, either white or dark brown barbados
100 g/4 oz margarine
1 beaten egg

Using wholewheat flour and barbados sugar gives good flavour, but buns are not so light and tend to dry out a bit after 3 or 4 days.

1. Mix flour, coconut and sugar in a bowl.
2. Rub in margarine.
3. Use a fork and mix thoroughly with beaten egg.
4. Fork out rough heaps of the mixture on to a greased baking sheet.
5. Bake towards top of a moderately hot oven, Gas 5, 375°F, 190°C, for 10 to 15 minutes.

Margaret Heywood,
Todmorden, Yorkshire

MATRIMONIAL CAKE

This cake keeps very well. It has a rough, crunchy top, a smooth filling and a firm base. Its old-fashioned name seems entirely suitable: you take the rough with the smooth.

100 g/4 oz porridge oats
75 g/3 oz wholewheat flour
50 g/2 oz barbados sugar
75 g/3 oz butter

Filling
250 g/8 oz stoned dates
25 g/1 oz barbados sugar
100 ml/4 fluid oz water

1. **Start with the filling:** chop dates and cook gently with the sugar and water until like a paste, soft but not sloppy. Leave to cool.
2. Mix oats, flour and sugar.
3. Rub in butter until it is like a 'crumble' mixture.
4. Put half this mixture into a greased tin, about 18 cm/7 inches square. Pat down firmly.
5. Spread with the date paste.
6. Cover with rest of crumble mixture and pat down gently.
7. Bake just above middle of a moderately hot oven, Gas 4, 350°F, 180°C, for 15 to 20 minutes until golden brown.
8. Cut into squares while still hot, then leave to cool in tin. Lift slices out when cool.

Margaret Heywood,
Todmorden, Yorkshire

FLAPJACKS

Makes 15 flapjacks

75 g/3 oz margarine
2 tablespoons golden syrup or black treacle
75 g/3 oz barbados sugar
150 g/5 oz porridge oats

1. Lightly grease a shallow 18 cm/7 inch square tin.
2. Put margarine and syrup or treacle in a saucepan. Heat gently until margarine has melted. Remove from heat.
3. Stir in sugar and rolled oats. Mix well.
4. Spread mixture evenly into tin.
5. Bake in centre of moderate oven, Gas 4, 350°F, 180°C, for 20 minutes.
6. Remove from oven. Leave to cool in tin for 5 minutes.
7. Cut into 5 strips down tin and into 3 across, to make 15 bars. Leave in tin until cold. Break into bars.

Flapjacks improve with keeping. Store in an air-tight tin for up to 4 weeks.

Try these variations
1. Add 2 rounded teaspoons grated orange rind and 50 g/2 oz currants to mixture at stage 3 of recipe.
2. Top flapjack mixture with 100 g/4 oz halved glacé cherries before baking.
3. Replace 25 g/1 oz of the rolled oats with 25 g/1 oz desiccated coconut.

FLORENTINES

225 g/8 oz plain cooking chocolate
50 g/2 oz margarine
100 g/4 oz soft brown sugar
1 egg
5 heaped tablespoons desiccated coconut
3 heaped tablespoons chopped nuts
2 heaped tablespoons chopped glacé cherries
2 heaped tablespoons mixed peel
2 heaped tablespoons sultanas

1. Melt chocolate in a small bowl over a pan of simmering water.
2. Spread melted chocolate in bottom of a Swiss roll tin. Leave to set.
3. Beat together margarine and sugar.
4. Beat in the egg.
5. Add all other ingredients.
6. Spread mixture over the chocolate.
7. Bake in moderate oven, Gas 3, 325°F, 170°C, for 30 to 40 minutes.
8. Leave to cool. Cut into slices.
9. Remove from tin when quite cold.

10. Store in an air-tight tin in a cool place.

Sybil Norcott,
Irlam, Manchester

GINGER BISCUITS

Makes about 40 biscuits

225 g/8 oz sugar
100 g/4 oz golden syrup
100 g/4 oz margarine
350 g/12 oz self-raising flour
2 teaspoons ginger
¼ teaspoon cinnamon (optional)
1 level teaspoon bicarbonate of soda
1 beaten egg
A little butter (optional)

1. Put sugar, syrup and margarine in a pan and melt over a very low heat.
2. Sift flour, spices and bicarbonate of soda into a bowl.
3. Mix in the melted ingredients and add beaten egg. Mix again well.
4. Roll teaspoonfuls of the mixture into little balls and place them well apart on a buttered or greased baking sheet.
5. Bake in moderate oven, Gas 4, 350°F, 180°C, for about 20 minutes until they are golden and 'crazed' all over.
6. Leave on baking sheet for 1 to 2 minutes to firm up, then remove on to a wire rack to cool.

Mrs Boyer recommends buttering the baking sheets as the resulting flavour suggests biscuits have been made with butter instead of margarine.

Mrs Ruth Boyer,
Cononley, W. Yorkshire

MERINGUES

2 egg-whites
125 g/4 oz demerara sugar

1. Line a greased baking tray with double thickness of greaseproof paper. Oil top sheet with a little vegetable oil.

2. Beat egg-whites until stiff.
3. Gradually beat in the sugar and whisk until mixture is really stiff and shiny.
4. Place mixture in mounds on to prepared baking tray.
5. Dry off in a very slow oven, Gas ¼, 225°F, 110°C, for 3 hours.
6. Store in air-tight tins. This way meringues will keep for weeks.

To serve, sandwich together with whipped cream.

Ursula Cavanagh,
author of 'The Wholefood Cookery Book'

CRUNCHY OAT COOKIES

Makes 14 cookies

75 g/3 oz porridge oats
50 g/2 oz plain flour
50 g/2 oz margarine
50 g/2 oz granulated sugar
1 level tablespoon golden syrup
½ level teaspoon bicarbonate of soda

1. Mix together porridge oats and flour.
2. Melt margarine in a large pan with sugar and syrup.
3. Stir bicarbonate of soda into mixture in pan.
4. Add flour and oats and mix well.
5. Make walnut-sized balls of mixture and place them, well apart, on well-greased baking sheets.
6. Bake in a moderate oven, Gas 4, 350°F, 180°C, for 11 to 15 minutes.
7. Let cookies cool slightly on baking sheet before removing them to a cooling wire.

Mrs J. M. Bell,
Macclesfield, Cheshire

PEANUT BISCUITS

50 g/2 oz shelled peanuts
100 g/4 oz butter
75 g/3 oz barbados sugar
1 small beaten egg

100 g/4 oz self-raising wholewheat flour

1. Chop peanuts.
2. Cream butter and sugar.
3. Add beaten egg gradually. Add the nuts, saving a few for sprinkling on top.
4. Fold in flour to make a stiff dough.
5. Put small mounds 5 cm/2 inches apart on a greased baking tray. Sprinkle a few chopped peanuts on top of each.
6. Bake in a moderate oven, Gas 4, 350°F, 180°C, for 15 minutes.
7. Leave on baking sheet for 1 to 2 minutes to firm up then slide on to cooling wire.

**Ursula Cavanagh,
author of 'The Wholefood Cookery Book'**

GINGER SHORTCAKE

Shortcake
225 g/8 oz plain flour
1 teaspoon ground ginger
75 g/3 oz sugar
175 g/6 oz margarine or butter

Topping
1 tablespoon golden syrup
50 g/2 oz butter or margarine
2 tablespoons icing sugar
1 level teaspoon ginger

1. Sieve flour and ginger into a bowl and stir in the sugar.
2. Rub in the margarine or butter until mixture works into a ball.
3. Press mixture into a Swiss roll tin or a shallow tin measuring about 18 × 28 cm/7 × 11 inches. Level top with a palette knife.
4. Bake in moderate oven, Gas 4, 350°F, 180°C, for 40 minutes. The mixture will still be slightly soft when it comes out of oven.
5. Meanwhile, mix the topping. Melt syrup and butter in a pan and stir in icing sugar and ginger.
6. Pour topping over shortcake while both are still hot.

7. Allow to cool slightly, then cut into fingers.

**Pat Dixon,
Holmfirth, W. Yorkshire**

WHOLEWHEAT SHORTBREAD

225 g/8 oz wholewheat flour
Pinch of sea salt
175 g/6 oz butter
125 g/4 oz demerara sugar

1. Put flour and salt into a bowl.
2. Rub in butter.
3. Add sugar.
4. Knead with hands until mixture is soft.
5. Using a floured board, roll out 1·5 cm/½ inch thick.
6. Cut into fingers and put these on a lightly-greased baking tray. Prick each slice once or twice with a fork.
7. Bake on middle shelf of a moderately hot oven, Gas 5, 375°F, 190°C, for 25 minutes until golden brown.

**Ursula Cavanagh,
author of 'The Wholefood Cookery Book'**

CURRY BISCUITS

250 g/8 oz wholewheat flour
2 level teaspoons curry powder
Pinch of salt
Pepper
125 g/4 oz finely-grated cheese
175 g/6 oz margarine
2 egg-yolks

1. Mix flour, curry powder, salt and pepper together.
2. Rub in margarine. Mix in cheese.
3. Mix to a stiff dough with egg-yolks.
4. Using a floured board, roll out about 7 mm/¼ inch thick. Stamp into small biscuits with a cutter.
5. Place on a lightly-greased baking sheet.
6. Bake in moderately hot oven, Gas 5, 375°F, 190°C, for 20

minutes until golden brown.

7. Leave on baking sheet for 1 to 2 minutes to firm up, then slide carefully on to a cooling wire.

**Ursula Cavanagh,
author of 'The Wholefood Cookery Book'**

NORFOLK RUSKS

**175 g/6 oz self-raising flour
A good pinch of salt
70 g/2½ oz margarine
1 beaten egg**

1. Sift flour and salt into a bowl.
2. Rub in margarine.
3. Mix to a firm dough with the egg.

4. Roll out on a floured board to 7 mm/¼ inch thick, cut into rounds and place on a baking sheet.
5. Bake in moderately hot oven, Gas 6, 400°F, 200°C, for 15 to 20 minutes until golden.
6. Remove from oven and, when cool enough to handle, split in half with a sharp knife.
7. Return rusks to oven, cut side up, for 5 minutes longer to dry and colour a little.
8. Turn on to a cooling wire.

Keep in an air-tight tin.
Delicious spread with butter, and served with cheese.

**Mrs E. M. Bettell,
Bedford**

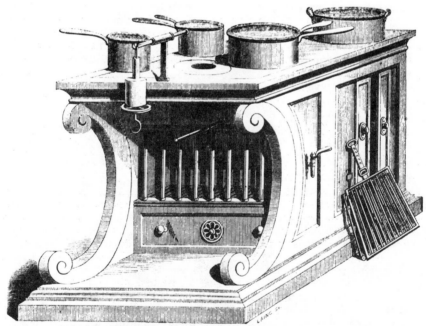

SOYER'S MODERN HOUSEWIFE'S KITCHEN APPARATUS.

CHAPTER 11

PRESERVES

SOME METHODS OF TESTING FOR SETTING POINT

For jams, jelly and marmalade.

Flake Test

Dip a clean, cold, wooden spoon into the jam. Lift up a spoonful and let it cool for 4 or 5 seconds. Then, holding spoon horizontally, tip it so that jam drips off side (see picture). When setting point has been reached the drops will run together and set in a 'flake' which hangs below spoon, then snaps off cleanly under its own weight.

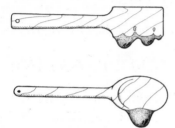

Cold Plate Method

1. Take saucepan off the heat.
2. Take out no more than a teaspoonful of the preserve on to a cold plate. Allow it to cool (in refrigerator to save time).
3. The surface should set and wrinkle when pushed with finger.

Note: Do not allow the preserve to boil while making this test or setting point may be missed.

Temperature Test

Setting point is usually regarded as 220°F or 105°C. If using a thermometer it should be put into very hot water immediately before and after testing the temperature of the jam. Stir jam thoroughly before taking temperature. Make sure thermometer bulb is well immersed but do not let it rest on the bottom of the jam pan.

PECTIN TEST

1. Put 3 teaspoonfuls of methylated spirits into a small jar or tumbler.

2. Add to this 1 teaspoon of the juice.
3. Swirl the meths around gently and leave it for 1 minute.
4. If there is plenty of pectin in the fruit a transparent jelly-like lump is formed. This means good setting quality so use 675 g/1½ lb sugar to each 600 ml/1 pint of juice.
5. If the pectin content is moderate the clot of jelly is not very firm and may be broken into two or three lumps. This means fair setting quality so use 450 g/1 lb sugar to each 600 ml/1 pint of juice.
6. If very little pectin is present the clot is broken into numerous small pieces. This means poor setting quality so use 350 g/12 oz sugar to each 600 ml/1 pint of juice.

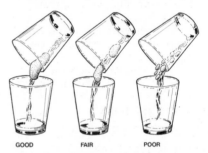

GOOD   FAIR   POOR

BLACKBERRY JAM

Made from a purée. No pips. Goes well with bread and butter, hot sponge puddings, milk puddings and ice-cream.

Blackberries
Sugar

1. Pick over the blackberries and rinse them in a colander.
2. Tip blackberries into a large pan.
3. Cover pan and put on a low heat. There will be enough moisture from washing fruit, provided heat is kept low. Bring slowly to boil and simmer gently for 15 minutes.
4. Press berries through an ordinary nylon kitchen sieve.
5. Measure the purée and pour into a large pan.
6. For every 600 ml/1 pint of purée

allow 450 g/1 lb of sugar. (Or for every ½ litre of purée allow 400 g sugar.)
7. Warm sugar in a very slow oven, Gas ¼, 225°F, 110°C.
8. Heat purée to boiling point, remove from heat and add the warm sugar. Stir over low heat until sugar is completely dissolved.
9. Bring jam to the boil and boil rapidly until setting point is reached (see opposite page).
10. Meanwhile, put clean jam pots in the oven to warm.
11. While jam is hot, fill the pots to the brim. Put on the waxed paper discs, waxed side down. Put jam pot covers on at once or leave till jam is quite cold. Never put covers on while jam is between hot and cold.
12. Label pots with name and date.
13. Store in a cool, dark, dry, well-ventilated cupboard.

Mrs Patricia Sweetland, Milton Keynes

BLACKBERRY, ELDERBERRY AND APPLE JAM

½ kg/1 lb elderberries
½ kg/1 lb blackberries
½ kg/1 lb apples
A little water
Juice of 1 lemon
1½ kg/3 lb sugar

1. Remove elderberries from stalks. To do this, hold them over a large bowl and strip off berries with a table fork. (A large bowl is necessary because berries tend to fly everywhere.)
2. Pick over the blackberries.
3. Peel and core apples and chop them as small as the blackberries.
4. Put less than 1 cm/½ inch water in a large saucepan and tip in the fruit.
5. Cover pan and gently simmer fruit until it is soft.
6. Meanwhile, put sugar in a very cool oven, Gas ¼, 225°F, 110°C.

7. When fruit is soft add lemon juice and sugar and stir over a low heat until it is completely dissolved.
8. Bring jam to the boil and boil rapidly until setting point is reached (see opposite page).
9. Meanwhile, put clean jam pots to warm in oven.
10. Pot the jam straight away, filling each pot to the brim. Put on the waxed paper discs, waxed side down and leave to cool.
11. When pots of jam are quite cold put on the jam pot covers and label pots with name and date.
12. Store in a cool, dark, dry, well-ventilated cupboard.

Mrs Lynda M. White, Sturton by Stow, Lincoln

BLACKCURRANT JAM

Yields about 6 kg/13–14 lb
Easy to make half the quantity.

1·8 kg/4 lb blackcurrants
2 litres/3½ pints water
3·2 kg/7 lb sugar

1. Remove stems and wash fruit in plenty of cold water. Strain in a colander.
2. Put fruit in a preserving pan with the water.
3. Bring to the boil and simmer gently until skins are quite tender. Stir from time to time in case fruit begins to stick and burn. Contents of pan will be reduced considerably.
4. Meanwhile put sugar into a bowl and warm it in a very cool oven, Gas ¼, 225°F, 110°C.
5. Prepare clean jars and put them in coolest part of the oven to warm.
6. When fruit is broken down and skins are tender, add the warmed sugar and stir until it is dissolved. Do not let it boil again before sugar is dissolved.
7. Bring to the boil and boil rapidly until setting point is reached. This may take only ¼ hour.

143

Setting point can be determined by temperature (220°–221°F or 105°C). The Flake Test or Cold Plate Test also may be used (see page 142).
8. Remove scum from top of jam with a metal spoon.
9. Fill warmed jars to the brim. Put on waxed paper disc straight away, waxed-side down. This seals the jars and protects them from the atmosphere.
10. Wipe the jars. Either put outer covers on while jam is hot or when it is quite cold, never in between.
11. Label with name and date and store in a cool, dark, dry, well-ventilated place.

Sybil Norcott,
Irlam, Nr. Manchester

DAMSON JAM

Yields 4·5 kg/10 lb
Easy to make half the quantity

2·2 kg/4¾ lb damsons
700 ml–1·1 litre/1¼–2 pints water
2·7 kg/6 lb sugar

1. Pick over the fruit, removing stems. Wash if necessary and drain well.
2. Put fruit in preserving pan or very large saucepan and add water. If fruit is ripe use the smaller quantity of water. If it is not very ripe it will need to boil longer to make it tender, so use the larger quantity of water.
3. Simmer fruit gently until quite tender (contents of pan will be reduced considerably). Stir from time to time to make sure it does not stick and burn.
4. Meanwhile, put sugar in a bowl to warm in a very cool oven, Gas ¼, 225°F, 110°C.
5. Prepare clean jars and put them in coolest part of oven to dry and warm.
6. Add warmed sugar and stir until dissolved. Do not let it boil again before sugar is dissolved.
7. Bring to the boil and boil rapidly until setting point is

reached. This may take only ¼ hour.
Setting point can be determined by the temperature (220°–221°F or 105°C), by the Flake Test or Cold Plate Test (see page 142).
During the boiling the stones will start rising to the surface. Remove as many as you can before potting the jam.
8. Fill warmed jars to the brim. Put on well-fitting waxed tissues immediately, waxed side down. This seals the jam and protects it from the atmosphere.
9. Wipe jars and put on outer covers while jam is hot or cold, but never in between.
10. Label with the name and date and store in a cool, dark, dry, well-ventilated place.

GREEN GOOSEBERRY AND ELDERFLOWER JAM

Has a delicate flavour.

Yields about 3·6 kg/8 lb

1·8 kg/4 lb green gooseberries
½ to 1 teacup elderflowers
600 ml/1 pint water
2·3 kg/5 lb sugar

Use flowers from the green-leaved elder which has small flower heads. The big heads from the yellow-leaved shrub have a pungent, if not rank, flavour.

1. Top and tail gooseberries and wash them, if necessary.
2. Tie elderflowers into a piece of muslin.
3. Put fruit, flowers and water in a preserving pan or large saucepan and bring to the boil. Simmer for about 20 minutes or until fruit is soft. Contents of pan will be reduced considerably.
4. Meanwhile, put sugar in a bowl to warm in a very cool oven, Gas ¼, 225°F, 110°C.
5. Prepare clean jars and place in

coolest part of oven to dry and warm.

6. Lift out bag of elderflowers and squeeze juice into pan.

7. Now add the warmed sugar and stir until it is dissolved. Do not let it boil again before sugar is dissolved.

8. Bring to the boil and boil rapidly until setting point is reached. This may take 15 to 20 minutes.

Setting point can be determined by temperature (220°–221°F or 105°C), by the Flake Test or Cold Plate Test (see page 142).

9. Fill warmed jars to the brim. Put on well-fitting waxed tissues immediately, waxed side down. This seals the jam and protects it from the atmosphere.

10. Wipe jars and put on outer covers, either while jam is hot or cold, but *never* in between.

11. Label with name and date and store in a cool, dark, dry, well-ventilated place.

Sybil Norcott,
Irlam, Nr. Manchester

GOOSEBERRY AND ORANGE JAM

Yields about 2·7 kg/6 lbs

1·35 kg/3 lb gooseberries
2 oranges
450 ml/¾ pint water
1·6 kg/3½ lb sugar

1. Top and tail gooseberries and wash them, if necessary.

2. Wash oranges, cut them in halves and squeeze out juice. Put the peel through mincer.

3. Put gooseberries, minced orange peel, juice and water in preserving pan or large saucepan. Bring to the boil and simmer until fruit is tender.

4. Meanwhile, put sugar in a bowl to warm in a very slow oven, Gas ¼, 225°F, 110°C.

5. Prepare clean jars and put them

in coolest part of oven to dry and warm.

6. Add warmed sugar to pan and stir until it is dissolved. Do not let it boil again before sugar is dissolved.

7. Bring to the boil and boil rapidly for 8 to 10 minutes or until setting point is reached.

Setting point can be determined by temperature (220°–221°F or 105°C), by the Flake Test or Cold Plate Test (see page 142).

8. Fill warmed jars to the brim. Put on well-fitting waxed tissues immediately, waxed side down. This seals the jam and protects it from the atmosphere.

9. Wipe jars and put on outer covers either while jam is hot or cold, but *never* in between.

10. Label with name and date and store in a cool, dark, dry well-ventilated place.

Mrs Doreen Allars,
Welbourn, Nr. Lincoln

RAW RASPBERRY JAM

A very old Scottish recipe. Tastes delicious and has a lovely bright-red colour.

½ kg/1 lb raspberries
½ kg/1 lb castor sugar

1. Crush fruit slightly.

2. Put sugar to warm in a very cool oven, Gas ¼, 225°F, 110°C. Put clean jars to warm in oven also.

3. Put fruit in a saucepan over very low heat. Stir continously until just boiling.

4. Take pan off heat and stir in warm sugar.

5. Return pan to low heat and stir until sugar is completely dissolved. Stir until jam reaches boiling point.

6. If there are some whole fruits in the jam allow it to stand in the pan for a short time until a thin skin forms. Stir skin in gently and pour jam into pots, filling each one to the brim. This method ensures that

the larger pieces of fruit remain suspended in the jam instead of floating to the top.

7. Put waxed paper discs on at once, waxed side down. Put on the jam pot covers immediately, or wait until jam is quite cold. Never put the top covers on when jam is half-way between hot and cold. Condensation can form and this can lead to mouldy jam.

8. Label jam pots with the name and date and store in a cool, dry, dark, well-ventilated cupboard.

**Mrs W. White and Mrs S. Marshall,
St. Michaels, Kent**

GREEN TOMATO JAM

**2·7 kg/6 lb green tomatoes
2 lemons
1 teaspoon citric acid
2·7 kg/6 lb sugar**

1. Remove skins from tomatoes (see page 67).
2. Slice tomatoes and put them in a large pan.
3. Squeeze juice from lemons and add with citric acid to pan.
4. Tie pips and peel of lemons in a piece of muslin and put this in pan.
5. Simmer until fruit is well broken down.
6. Meanwhile, put sugar to warm in a very slow oven, Gas ¼, 225°F, 110°C.
7. Put clean jam jars to dry and warm in oven.
8. Add warmed sugar to pan, stir over gentle heat until dissolved. Bring to the boil.
9. Boil rapidly until setting point is reached (see page 142).
10. Pour into warm jars. Place waxed paper tissue on at once.
11. Cover with jam pot covers at once, or leave until quite cold – never in between. Label with name and date.
12. Store in a cool, dark, dry, well-ventilated place.

**Sybil Norcott,
Irlam, Nr. Manchester**

PEAR AND GINGER JAM

Yields about 4·5 kg/9 to 10 lb

This makes use of every bit of the fruit, so don't throw away peel and cores.

**3·2 kg/7 lb pears
3 lemons
1 piece fresh root ginger, approx.
2·5 cm/1 inch is enough
1·15 litres/2 pints water
2·3 kg/5 lb sugar**

1. Peel, quarter and core pears. Slice them and put them in a preserving pan with the water.
2. Thinly peel yellow rind from lemons. Squeeze the juice.
3. Peel ginger and bruise it. To do this, put it on a chopping board and bang it with the rolling pin.
4. Tie pear peelings and cores, with lemon and ginger rinds in a large piece of muslin and put in preserving pan.
5. Bring to the boil and simmer pears for 30 minutes or until soft.
6. Meanwhile put the sugar in a bowl to warm in a very slow oven, Gas ¼, 225 °F, 110°C, and prepare clean jam jars. Put them to dry and warm in coolest part of oven.
7. Lift out the bag and with the back of a wooden spoon press it against side of pan and squeeze out as much juice as possible.
8. Add the warmed sugar and stir without boiling until dissolved.
9. Add the lemon juice.
10. Increase heat and bring jam to the boil. Boil for 15 minutes or until setting point is reached.

Setting point can be determined by temperature (220°–221°F or 105°C), by the Flake Test or Cold Plate Test (see page 142).

11. Skim off scum and let jam stand for 5 minutes. This will prevent pieces of pear rising in the jars.
12. Fill warmed jars to the brim. Immediately put on well-fitting waxed tissue, waxed side down. This seals the jam and protects it

from the atmosphere.
13. Wipe jars and put on outer covers either while jam is hot or cold, but never in between.
14. Label with name and date and store in a cool, dry, dark, well-ventilated place.

Mrs Doreen Allars,
Welbourn, Nr. Lincoln

PLUM, ORANGE AND WALNUT JAM

Any plums may be used, including greengages.

Yields about 1.6 kg/3½ lb

1.4 kg/3 lb plums
2 oranges
1 small cupful of water
1.1 kg/2½ lb sugar
225 g/8 oz shelled walnuts

1. Wash plums in case they have been sprayed. Stone them and tie stones in a piece of muslin.
2. Wash oranges, cut them in halves and squeeze out juice. Put peel through mincer.
3. Put plums, stones, minced orange peel, juice and water in preserving pan or large saucepan. Bring to the boil and simmer until fruit is soft (about 1 hour). Stir occasionally to see that it is not sticking and add a little more water if necessary.
4. Meanwhile, put sugar in a bowl to warm in a very slow oven, Gas ¼, 225°F, 110°C.
5. Prepare clean jars and place in coolest part of oven to dry and warm.
6. Roughly chop walnuts.
7. Add warmed sugar to pan and stir until dissolved.
8. When sugar is completely dissolved, bring to the boil and add walnuts.
9. Boil jam rapidly until setting point is reached (see page 142).
10. Fill warmed jars to the brim. Put on well-fitting waxed tissues immediately, waxed side down.

This seals the jam and protects it from the atmosphere.
11. Wipe jars and put on outer covers, either while jam is hot or cold, but never in between.
12. Label with name and date and store in a cool, dark, dry, well-ventilated place.

Mrs Doreen Allars,
Welbourn, Nr. Lincoln

ORANGE AND CIDER MARMALADE

Yields about 2.3 kg/5 lb

700 g/1½ lb Seville oranges
Juice of 2 lemons
1.15 litres/2 pints dry cider
600 ml/1 pint water
1.4 kg/3 lb sugar

1. Wash oranges and cut them in half.
2. Squeeze out juice and pips and cut peel into thin strips.
3. Squeeze lemon.
4. Put orange peel, orange and lemon juice into a large pan with the cider and water.
5. Tie pips in a muslin bag and put in pan.
6. Cook gently for 1½ hours or until peel is soft.
7. Meanwhile, put sugar in a bowl to warm in a very slow oven, Gas ¼, 225°F, 110°C. Prepare clean jars and put them to dry and warm in coolest part of oven.
8. Lift out bag of pips and squeeze juice out by pressing it against side of pan with a wooden spoon.
9. Add warmed sugar and stir without boiling until completely dissolved.
10. Bring to the boil and boil rapidly until setting point is reached.
Setting point can be determined by temperature (220°–221°F or 105°C) by the Flake Test or Cold Plate Test (see page 142).
11. Remove scum with a metal spoon.
12. Allow marmalade to cool for

$\frac{1}{2}$ hour. This will prevent the peel rising in the jars.

13. Fill warmed jars to the brim. Immediately put on well-fitting waxed tissues, waxed side down. This seals the jam and protects it from the atmosphere.

14. Wipe jars and put on outer covers, either while jam is hot or cold, but *never* in between.

15. Label with name and date and store in a cool, dark, dry, well-ventilated place.

**Mrs Doreen Allars,
Welbourn, Nr. Lincoln**

SEVILLE ORANGE MARMALADE

Made in the pressure cooker. The following recipe may be used with fresh or frozen fruit. If you can get a case of Sevilles, or share a case with someone, wash and dry them and pack in large polythene bags in the freezer. Marmalade can then be made in small batches as and when required.

**1·4 kg/3 lb Seville oranges
Juice of 2 lemons, or 1 teaspoon citric or tartaric acid
1·2–1·7 litres/2–3 pints water
2·7 kg/6 lb sugar**

1. Put fruit in pressure cooker (trivet not required) with lemon juice or acid. Add 1·2 litres/2 pints or more water until pressure-cooker pan is not more than half full of liquid.

2. Put lid on pressure cooker, keeping vent open. Heat gently until steam comes out of vent. Close vent and bring to 15 lb or high pressure. Keep at pressure for 20 minutes, then remove from heat and cool in the air for 10 minutes. Open vent and remove lid from pressure cooker.

3. Lift out fruit on to a large plate and allow to cool for a few minutes.

4. Divide sugar, putting 1·4 kg/3 lb each into two separate containers. Put in oven on lowest heat to warm through, Gas $\frac{1}{4}$, 225°F, 110°C. Put clean jars in oven also, to dry and warm.

5. Cut fruit in half and, using a teaspoon, take out pips and return them to liquid in the pressure-cooker pan.

6. Boil pips in open pressure cooker for 5 minutes. Strain liquid into a measuring jug and discard pips.

7. Meanwhile, divide oranges into 2 equal portions. Cut them up, small or chunky, as preferred. Fruit, sugar and liquid are divided because pressure-cooker pan is not large enough to boil up full quantity.

8. As soon as you have cut up one portion of fruit, put it with half of liquid in measuring jug back into the pressure cooker pan and bring to boil. The rest may be boiled up simultaneously in a separate large pan to save time.

9. Lower heat and add 1·4 kg/3 lb sugar. Stir with wooden spoon over very low heat until sugar is completely dissolved.

10. Bring up to the boil and boil rapidly until setting point is reached. This may take only a few minutes because pressure cooker method requires much less water than conventional methods.

11. Test for setting point (see *page 142*). Test frequently.

12. When it is ready, remove scum from surface with a metal spoon.

13. Allow pan of marmalade to cool for a bit. This prevents peel rising to top of jars.

14. Pour into warmed jars and cover with waxed paper discs while still hot.

15. Cover with jam-pot covers when quite cold.

16. Label with name and date and store in a dry, dark, cool, ventilated cupboard.

GRAPEFRUIT JELLY

Yields about 2·3 kg/5 lb

**2 grapefruit, 2 lemons, 1 orange
(combined weight 1 kg/2 lb)
2·5 litres/4½ pints water
1·35 kg/3 lb sugar**

1. Score skins of grapefruit into 4 segments. Put them in a bowl and scald them by pouring over boiling water. Leave them for 10 minutes.
2. Remove peel, cut away the thick pith and shred the yellow part finely. Keep shreds until later.
3. Cut up coarsely the pith and rest of the fruit, including lemons and orange.
4. Put pith and fruit in a pan with a lid, add 1·5 litres/2½ pints of the water, cover pan and simmer for 2 hours.
5. In a separate pan with a lid, simmer shreds in 600 ml/1 pint water for 1½ hours or until tender.
6. Drain off liquid from shreds, add it to the pulp and tip it all into a scalded jelly bag. Let it drip into a bowl for 10 to 15 minutes.
7. Return pulp to preserving pan, add remaining 600 ml/1 pint water, simmer for a further 20 minutes, and strain through jelly bag again. Let it strain without squeezing the bag.
8. Meanwhile, put sugar in a bowl to warm in a very slow oven, Gas ¼, 225°F, 110°C. Put clean jars to warm in coolest part of oven.
9. Combine 2 extracts of juice and take a pectin test (*see page 142*). If pectin quality is poor, simmer juice again without the lid for about 10 minutes to drive off some of the excess water, then test again.
10. Add warmed sugar. Stir without boiling until sugar is dissolved.
11. When sugar is completely dissolved, add shreds of grapefruit rind, bring to the boil and boil rapidly until setting point is reached.

Setting point can be determined by temperature (220°F—221°F, 105°C), by the Flake Test or Cold Plate

Test (*see page 142*).
12. Skim off scum quickly with a metal spoon.
13. Leave jelly to cool slightly, for 10 to 15 minutes. This ensures that shreds will be suspended evenly in the jelly when potted. If it is potted hot, shreds tend to rise to surface.
14. Fill warm jars to the brim and immediately put on well-fitting waxed tissues, waxed side down. This seals the surface of the jelly and protects it from the atmosphere.
15. With jelly it is easier to put outer covers on jars when it is set, but wait until it is quite cold.
16. Label with name and date and store in a cool, dark dry, well-ventilated place.

REDCURRANT JELLY

A mixture of red and white currants may be used.
If you cannot make this jelly when fruit is ripe, put fruit in polythene bags and freeze it. No preparation of fruit is needed. Small stems, etc., will be disposed of in the jelly bag.
This recipe may also be used for blackcurrant jelly.

**2·7 kg/6 lb red and/or white currants
1·7 litres/3 pints water
Sugar**

1. Wash fruit and put in preserving pan.
2. Add 1·2 litres/2 pints of water and simmer until fruit is tender.
3. Mash fruit down, then tip it into a scalded jelly bag and let it drain for 10 to 15 minutes into a bowl.
4. Now remove pulp from jelly bag, return it to the pan, add the remaining 500 ml/1 pint of water and simmer again for about ½ hour.
5. Tip all this into a jelly bag and let it drain into another bowl. Do not squeeze the bag or the jelly may not be clear.
6. Mix together the two extracts of

juice. Then make a pectin test to ascertain the setting quality of the jelly. This test will also tell you how much sugar to use (see page 142).

If pectin test shows very poor setting quality, it is advisable to return juice or both juice and pulp to the pan and simmer again to drive off some of the excess water content. Then test again.

7. Measure juice and, according to the result of pectin test, weigh out the sugar.

8. Put sugar in a bowl to warm in a very slow oven, Gas ¼, 225°F, 110°C. Put clean small jars to warm in coolest part of oven.

9. Bring juice to the boil, add warmed sugar and stir, without boiling, until dissolved.

10. When sugar is completely dissolved bring to the boil and boil rapidly until setting point is reached.

11. **Setting point** can be determined by temperature (220°F–221°F, 105°C), by the Flake Test or Cold Plate Test (see page 142).

12. Skim off scum with a metal spoon. Fill jars without delay before jelly starts to set.

13. Put on well-fitting waxed tissues immediately, waxed side down. This seals the jelly and protects it from the atmosphere.

14. With jelly it is easier to put outer covers on jars when it is set, but wait until it is quite cold.

15. Label with name and date and store in a cool, dark, dry, well-ventilated place.

ROSEMARY JELLY

Use with lamb instead of mint sauce. Made with fresh, not dried, rosemary.

Yields about 3 kg/7 lb

2·3 kg/5 lb cooking apples
600 ml/1 pint water

4 tablespoons fresh rosemary leaves
200 ml/8 fluid oz cider vinegar or malt vinegar
Sugar
Green vegetable colouring (optional)

1. Wash apples. Cut them up but do not peel or core.

2. Put apple in preserving pan with water and rosemary.

3. Bring to the boil and simmer for 40 minutes or until soft.

4. Add vinegar and boil for 5 minutes.

5. Tip all into a scalded jelly bag and allow to drip. To ensure jelly is clear do not squeeze the bag. It will take about 12 hours to drip through.

6. Meanwhile, measure the juice. For each 600 ml/1 pint of juice weigh out 450 g/1 lb sugar. Put sugar in a bowl to warm in a very slow oven, Gas ¼, 225°F, 110°C.

7. Put clean small jars to warm in coolest part of oven.

8. Put sugar and juice in pan, place over low heat and stir until sugar is dissolved.

9. When sugar is completely dissolved bring to the boil and boil rapidly until setting point is reached.

Setting point can be determined by temperature (220°–221°F, 105°C), by the Flake Test or the Cold Plate Test (see page 142).

10. Skim off scum with a metal spoon.

11. Stir in a few drops of colouring, just enough to give it a delicate tint. Do not stir too hard or you may get bubbles in the jelly.

12. Fill warmed jars without delay before jelly starts to set.

13. Put on well-fitting, waxed tissues immediately, waxed side down. This seals the jelly in the jam and protects it from the atmosphere.

14. With jelly it is easier to put outer covers on jars when it is set, but wait until it is quite cold.

15. Label with name and date and

store in a cool, dark, dry, well-ventilated place.

Mrs Doreen Allars,
Welbourn, Nr. Lincoln

SPICED VINEGAR FOR PICKLES

Either brown or white vinegar can be used, depending on type of pickle. White vinegar is more expensive, but looks better with onions and cauliflower.

1·1 litres/2 pints best vinegar (use bottles for your finished product)
$\frac{1}{4}$ oz cinnamon bark
$\frac{1}{4}$ oz whole cloves
12 peppercorns
$\frac{1}{4}$ oz whole mace
$\frac{1}{4}$ oz whole allspice
1 or 2 bay leaves

Tie spices in a small piece of muslin and put them with the vinegar into a wide-necked jar. Cover jar with a vinegar-proof lid, or a saucer, and let the spices steep in the vinegar for 1 to 2 months for a good flavour.

Quick method
Place vinegar and spices in a glass or china bowl (not metal or polythene) standing on a pan of water. Cover bowl, bring water slowly to boil. Remove from heat. Allow to get quite cold – at least 2 hours.
Spiced vinegar need not be used at once. Remove bag of spices or strain vinegar and pour back into original bottles.
Spiced vinegar is used for most pickles. Those to be kept crisp should be covered with cold vinegar, softer types with hot vinegar.

APPLE, ONION AND MINT PICKLE

225 g/8 oz onions
450 g/1 lb hard cooking apples
2 teaspoons lemon juice
3 to 4 tablespoons finely-chopped, fresh mint leaves
200 ml/$\frac{1}{3}$ pint white vinegar or cider vinegar
75 g/3 oz castor sugar
2 teaspoons mustard
$\frac{1}{4}$ level teaspoon ground ginger
2 level teaspoons salt

1. Mince onions and apples. Add lemon juice.
2. Mix mint thoroughly with apples and onions.
3. Dissolve sugar, mustard, ground ginger and salt in a little of the vinegar. Simmer for 10 minutes.
4. Bring rest of vinegar to boil and pour over sugar mixture.
5. Allow vinegar mixture to get cold and mix it into the mint, apple and onions.
6. Put into clean jars with vinegar-proof lids. Coffee jars with plastic lids are ideal.
7. Store for 1 month before using to allow pickle to mature and flavour to mellow. This preserve will keep for up to 3 months.

Stella Boldy,
Sykehouse, N. Humberside

APPLE AND SAGE PRESERVE

Not a long keeping preserve.

Yields about 1·4 kg/3 lb

Can be made at any time of year if apples are cheap. Good with pork, duck or sausages, particularly spread over a sausage pie.

1 onion
1·8 kg/4 lb cooking apples
150 ml/$\frac{1}{4}$ pint water
225 g/8 oz castor sugar
50 g/2 oz butter
2 teaspoons salt
1 teaspoon pepper
3 teaspoons dried sage
1 teaspoon Worcestershire sauce
3 tablespoons vinegar

1. Peel and chop up onion.
2. Wash apples. Do not peel or

core but remove damaged parts and cut fruit roughly into quarters.
3. Put onion, apple and water into a pan, put lid on and simmer gently until soft.
4. Rub mixture through a nylon sieve to make a purée.
5. Return purée to the pan and cook without the lid until it is a thick pulp. Stir from time to time.
6. Stir in all remaining ingredients and continue to cook gently, stirring often, until no excess liquid remains.
7. Meanwhile, prepare clean jars with vinegar-proof lids. Coffee jars with plastic lids are ideal. Paper covers are not satisfactory because vinegar can evaporate through them and preserve will dry out. Plain metal lids should not be used because vinegar corrodes the metal.
Put clean jars into a very slow oven to dry and warm, Gas $\frac{1}{4}$, 225°F, 110°C.
8. Fill warm jars nearly to the brim with hot mixture. Put lids on at once.
9. Label and date jars. Store in a cool, dark place.
Should be used within 8 to 10 weeks.

Mrs Doreen Allars,
Welbourn, Nr. Lincoln

PICKLED BABY BEETS

To Cook the Beetroot
Baby beetroot
Vinegar
Salt
Water

For the Pickle
Spiced vinegar (see page 151)
Sugar

1. Wash young beetroots carefully. Do not break the skins.
2. Put them in a saucepan. Measure water into the pan and for every quart of water add 1 dessertspoon vinegar and 1 teaspoon salt.

3. Boil the beets for 30 minutes or until tender.
4. Prepare clean, dry, wide-necked jars with vinegar-proof lids.
5. Dip cooked beets in cold water. It will make them easier to handle. Rub off the skin and grade them into sizes.
6. Pack into jars.
7. Now mix sugar into the spiced vinegar. Allow 6 teaspoons sugar per pint of vinegar.
8. Bring spiced vinegar to the boil, stirring to dissolve the sugar.
9. Pour the hot, sweet, spiced vinegar into the jars to cover beetroot.
10. Put lids on at once and screw up tightly.

Mrs Doreen Allars,
Welbourn, Nr. Lincoln

SWEET CUCUMBER PICKLE
Yields about 1·5 kg/3$\frac{1}{2}$ lb

900 g /2 lb cucumbers
2 large onions
1 large green pepper
25 g/1 oz salt
600 ml/1 pint cider vinegar
450 g/1 lb soft brown sugar
$\frac{1}{2}$ level teaspoon ground turmeric
$\frac{1}{4}$ level teaspoon ground cloves
1 level teaspoon mustard seed
$\frac{1}{2}$ level teaspoon celery seed

1. Wash and dice cucumber but do not peel it.
2. Peel onions and slice them finely.
3. Cut core out of green pepper, knock out seeds and shred flesh.
4. Put cucumber, onion and green pepper into a large mixing bowl with the salt. Mix well, cover the bowl with a plate and leave for 2 hours.
5. Rinse vegetables thoroughly under cold running water. Drain well and put in a large pan.
6. Add vinegar and bring to the boil.

7. Simmer gently for 20 minutes or until vegetables are soft.
8. Add sugar and spices and stir over a low heat to dissolve sugar. Bring to the boil and remove pan from heat.
9. Tip it all into a large mixing bowl and set it aside until cold.
10. Meanwhile, prepare clean, dry jars with vinegar-proof, screw-top lids. Coffee jars with plastic lids are ideal.
11. Pour into jars and put on the tops.

Mrs Doreen Allars,
Welbourn, Nr. Lincoln

SWEET MIXED PICKLE

Use pears, peaches, apricots, damsons
Very good with curry or cold meats.

1·8 kg/4 lb fruit
900 g/2 lb sugar
600 ml/1 pint spiced vinegar (see page 151)
1 teaspoon coriander seeds
1 teaspoon lemon juice

1. Prepare the fruit.
Pears: Peel,core and cut in quarters or eighths.
Peaches: Skin, halve, or quarter and remove stones.
Apricots: Skin, halve and remove stones.
Damsons: Wash, and remove stalks.
2. Prepare clean, wide-necked jars with vinegar-proof lids. Put jars to dry and warm in a very slow oven, Gas ¼, 225°F, 110°C.
3. Dissolve sugar in vinegar, add coriander seeds, lemon juice and fruit.
4. Simmer very carefully until fruit is tender. Do not allow to boil hard or fruit may go ragged at edges and damsons may burst, which would spoil the appearance of the finished product.
5. Strain fruit, returning liquid to the pan.
6. Pack fruit into warmed jars and keep hot while you finish the vinegar syrup.
7. Re-boil vinegar liquid in pan until it is thick and syrupy.
8. Pour over the fruit and while it is hot put vinegar-proof lids on jars.
9. Label jars with name and date and store for 3 months before use. Store in a cool, dark, dry place.

Mrs Doreen Allars,
Welbourn, Nr. Lincoln

PICKLED RUNNER BEANS

A sweet pickle – delicious served with cold beef or cheese.

675 g/1½ lb runner beans
Salt
600 ml/1 pint good malt vinegar
675 g/1½ lb granulated sugar
1 level teaspoon ground allspice
Pepper

1. String and slice beans.
2. Cook in boiling, slightly-salted water for 8 to 10 minutes until tender.
3. Meanwhile, put vinegar, sugar, allspice and pepper into a pan over a low heat. Stir until sugar dissolves. Bring to the boil.
4. Drain beans, add them to the spiced vinegar and simmer for 5 minutes. Pour off vinegar into a jug.
5. Pack beans into clean jars and pour over the vinegar to completely cover them.
6. Put on vinegar-proof lids immediately.
7. Store in a cool, dark, dry place for a fortnight to mature before eating.

Mrs Susan Crawford,
Thorpe Bay, Nr. Southend-on-Sea

APPLE AND RAISIN CHUTNEY

An excellent chutney, particularly good with cheese dishes.

Yields about 3 kg/6 lb
Possible to make half the quantity
but, if you do, keep to the 100 ml/
4 fluid oz of vinegar.

2·3 kg/5 lb apples
Juice and finely-chopped rind of
2 oranges
100 g/4 oz chopped walnuts or
almonds
900 g/2 lb granulated sugar
275 g/10 oz raisins
⅓ teaspoon ground cloves
100 ml/4 fluid oz distilled vinegar

1. Peel and core apples and cut
into small pieces.
2. Prepare oranges and nuts.
3. Put all ingredients into a pan,
stir well and simmer with lid on
until tender.
4. Remove lid and simmer, stirring
often until chutney is thick. It is
thick enough when a spoon drawn
through it leaves its mark without
at once filling with excess liquid.
5. Meanwhile, choose jars with
vinegar-proof lids. Coffee jars with
plastic lids are ideal. Paper covers
are not satisfactory because
vinegar can evaporate through
them and chutney will dry out.
Plain metal lids should not be
used because vinegar corrodes the
metal.
Put clean jars into a very slow oven
to dry and warm, Gas ¼, 225°F,
110°C.
6. Fill warm jars nearly to the brim
with hot chutney. Put lids on at
once.
7. Label and date the chutney.
Store in a cool, dark place. Can be
eaten at once. Does not keep as
long as other chutneys because of
low vinegar content.

Mrs Doreen Allars,
Welbourn, Nr. Lincoln

DATE AND BANANA CHUTNEY

Can be made at any time of year.
Good with curry.

Yields 1·3 kg/3 lb
Easy to make double quantity.

450 g/1 lb onions
225 g/8 oz dates
100 g/4 oz crystallised ginger
2 level teaspoons salt
300 ml /½ pint vinegar
6 bananas
225 g/8 oz treacle
1 teaspoon curry powder

1. Peel and chop onions finely.
2. Chop up dates and crystallised
ginger.
3. Put these in a saucepan with
salt and half the vinegar. Cover
pan and simmer until soft.
4. Peel and chop up bananas and
add them to the pan with the
treacle, curry powder and rest of
vinegar.
5. Simmer until all is soft and
consistency is thick. When you
draw the spoon through it the trail
should remain and not at once fill
with excess liquid.
6. Meanwhile, choose jars with
vinegar-proof lids. Coffee jars with
plastic lids are ideal. Paper covers
are not satisfactory because
vinegar can evaporate through
them and chutney will dry out.
Plain metal lids should not be
used because vinegar corrodes the
metal.
Put clean jars into a very slow
oven to dry and warm, Gas ¼,
225°F, 110°C.
7. Fill warm jars nearly to the brim
with hot chutney. Put lids on
immediately.
8. Label and date chutney. Store in
a cool, dark place. Let it mature for
at least 3 months before eating.

Sybil Norcott,
Irlam, Nr. Manchester

ELDERBERRY CHUTNEY

A sharp chutney.

Yields about 675 g/1½ lb

1·2 litres/2 pints elderberries
100 g/4 oz seedless raisins
100 g/4 oz demerara sugar
50 g/2 oz onions

15 g/½ oz salt
Pinch cayenne pepper
Pinch allspice
600 ml/1 pint cider vinegar or good
malt vinegar

1. Wash elderberries if necessary.
Remove them from stalks by
running a fork down the stems.
2. Put all ingredients into a large
saucepan and stir over low heat
until sugar is dissolved.
3. Cook until ingredients are soft.
Stir from time to time. Continue
cooking until consistency is thick.
When you draw a spoon through
it the mark should remain without
filling at once with liquid.
4. Meanwhile, choose small jars
with vinegar-proof lids. Jars with
plastic lids are ideal. Paper covers
are not satisfactory because
vinegar can evaporate through
them and chutney will dry out.
Plain metal lids should not be
used because vinegar corrodes the
metal.
Put clean jars into a very slow
oven to dry and warm, Gas ¼,
225°F, 110°C.
5. Fill warmed jars nearly to the
brim with hot chutney. Put lids on
at once.
6. Label and date jars. Store in a
cool, dark place. Let chutney
mature for 3 months before eating.
It will keep for years if correctly
covered and stored.

Mrs Doreen Allars,
Welbourn, Nr. Lincoln

MARROW AND RED TOMATO CHUTNEY

Makes about 1·8 kg/4 lb

450 g/1 lb marrow (weighed after
peeling and removing seeds)
450 g/1 lb tomatoes
225 g/8 oz onions
1 clove garlic
1 tablespoon pickling spice
1 teaspoon ground ginger
225 g/8 oz sultanas
175 g/6 oz white sugar

175 g/6 oz brown sugar
2 teaspoons salt
300 ml/½ pint malt vinegar

1. Peel marrow, remove seeds and
cut flesh into small cubes.
2. Skin the tomatoes (*see page 66*).
Cut them up roughly.
3. Peel and chop onion small.
4. Crush garlic (*see page 66*).
5. Tie pickling spice in a piece of
muslin.
6. Put all ingredients in a saucepan
and stir over low heat until sugar
is dissolved.
7. Allow to simmer, stirring
occasionally until mixture is thick
(about 1 hour). Chutney is thick
enough when a spoon drawn
through it leaves a trail which
does not at once fill with excess
liquid.
8. Meanwhile, prepare clean jars
with vinegar-proof lids. Put jars to
dry and warm in a cool oven,
Gas ¼, 225°F, 110°C.
9. Pour hot chutney into warmed
jars, put on waxed tissues
immediately, waxed side down.
This seals surface of chutney and
protects it.
10. When cold, put on vinegar-
proof lids.
11. Label with name and date and
store for a few weeks in a cool,
dark, dry place. Let it mature
before eating.

Mrs A. E. Phillips,
Selsey, W. Sussex

RHUBARB AND ORANGE CHUTNEY

Yields about 1·8 kg/4 lb

900 g/2 lb rhubarb (weighed after
trimming)
3 onions
2 oranges
450 g/1 lb raisins
900 g/2 lb demerara sugar
900 ml/1½ pints good malt vinegar
1 tablespoon mustard seed
1 tablespoon white peppercorns
1 level teaspoon powdered allspice

1. Wash and wipe rhubarb, cut it into short pieces and put in preserving pan or large saucepan.
2. Peel and chop onions and add to pan.
3. Finely shred yellow rind from the oranges, squeeze out juice and discard pith. Add to pan.
4. Add raisins, sugar and vinegar.
5. Tie up the 3 spices in a piece of muslin and put this into the pan.
6. Bring to the boil and simmer gently until thick. It is thick enough when a spoon drawn through the chutney leaves its mark and does not immediately fill with excess liquid.
7. Meanwhile, choose jars with vinegar-proof lids. Coffee jars with plastic lids are ideal. Paper covers are not satisfactory because vinegar can evaporate through them and chutney will dry out. Plain metal lids should not be used because vinegar corrodes the metal. Put clean jars to dry and warm in a very cool oven, Gas $\frac{1}{4}$, 225°F, 110°C.
8. Remove muslin bag from chutney.
9. Fill warmed jars nearly to the brim with hot chutney. Put lids on at once.
10. Label and date chutney. Store in a cool, dark place. Let it mature for 3 months before eating.

**Mrs Doreen Allars,
Welbourn, Nr. Lincoln**

PLUM SAUCE

This sauce keeps well and does not need sterilizing.

Yields about 1 litre/nearly 2 pints

**1·8 kg/4 lb damsons
100 g/4 oz currants
225 g/8 oz onions
25 g/1 oz mixed pickling spice
$\frac{1}{4}$ teaspoon mustard
600 ml/1 pint vinegar
450 g/1 lb sugar
25 g/1 oz salt**

1. Cut up plums and finely chop onions. Put them in a large pan with the currants and spices and half the vinegar.
2. Cover pan and allow contents to simmer for half an hour.
3. Rub it all through a nylon sieve, returning the purée to the pan.
4. Add sugar and remaining vinegar, stir until sugar is dissolved and allow to simmer without a lid for about 1 hour, or until consistency is like thick cream. Stir often to stop it sticking.
5. Meanwhile, prepare clean bottles or jars with vinegar-proof lids. Put bottles to dry and warm in a very cool oven, Gas $\frac{1}{4}$, 225°F, 110°C.
6. Fill bottles almost to the brim with the hot sauce and put on lids immediately.
7. When bottles have cooled, label them with name and date and store in a cool, dark, dry place. Let sauce mature for 2 months.

**Sybil Norcott,
Irlam, Nr. Manchester**

RIPE TOMATO SAUCE

Choose really red, ripe tomatoes.

Yields about 2·3 kg/5 lb

As this sauce has to be sterilised to ensure it keeps, you need bottles of roughly the same height with vinegar-proof tops or new corks, and a pan or a tin deep enough to contain water up to the necks of the bottles.

**2·7 kg/6 lb tomatoes
20 g/$\frac{3}{4}$ oz salt
A small pinch of cayenne
4 g/$\frac{1}{8}$ oz paprika
$\frac{1}{2}$ teaspoon ground ginger
225 g/8 oz sugar
300 ml/$\frac{1}{2}$ pint spiced vinegar** (see page 151)

1. Wash and cut up tomatoes. Place in a pan over gentle heat. Cook until skins are free and they have softened.

2. Rub tomato pulp through a sieve and return purée to the pan.
3. Add salt, cayenne, paprika and ginger and cook gently until it begins to thicken.
4. Add sugar and spiced vinegar and cook gently until the consistency of thick cream. Stir from time to time.
5. Meanwhile, prepare clean bottles with vinegar-proof, screw caps or new corks and put them to dry and warm in a very slow oven, Gas ¼, 225°F, 110°C. Put caps or corks to sterilise for 15 minutes in a small pan of boiling water.
6. Pour hot sauce into warmed bottles. Leave 5 cm/2 inches between sauce and top of bottle. Put in the sterilised corks and tie them down with string.
If using screw tops, screw them on but not too tightly.
7. Stand bottles on a trivet or a folded cloth in the pan or tin. Support them with folds of newspaper. Pour in water to just under the lower level of corks. Heat water just to simmering point and keep it, just simmering, for 25 minutes.
8. Lift bottles out of pan. Tighten screw tops and push corks right in as soon as sauce has cooled enough to allow this. Re-tie the strings to ensure corks stay right in.
9. When bottles have cooled and corks are dry, dip tops in melted paraffin wax to make an air-tight seal. Screw caps do not need dipping in wax.
10. Label bottles with name and date and store in a cool, dark, dry place. Let sauce mature for 1 to 2 months.

**Sybil Norcott,
Irlam, Nr. Manchester**

BLACKBERRY OR RASPBERRY VINEGAR

An old-fashioned remedy for sore throats. Good to eat with a plain steamed pudding. Sometimes served in the North poured over hot Yorkshire Puddings and eaten as a sweet course.

**450 g/1 lb fruit
600 ml/1 pint best cider vinegar or malt vinegar (keep bottle for finished product)
450 g/1 lb granulated sugar (optional)**

1. Put fruit and vinegar into a glass or china bowl. Cover with a cloth and allow to stand for 3 to 5 days, stirring occasionally.
2. Strain off liquid into a saucepan. Set it over a low heat and add sugar, if used. Stir until dissolved.
3. Boil mixture for 10 minutes, then pour it into the bottle.

If you prefer not to sweeten the vinegar at paragraph 2, then sugar may be added to taste when vinegar is used.

CANDIED GINGER MARROW

**1 well-ripened marrow
Water
Sugar
To every 450 g/1 lb marrow allow 15 g/½ oz root ginger and 1 lemon**

**Crystallizing Sugar
450 g/1 lb castor sugar
½ teaspoon bicarbonate of soda
½ teaspoon cream of tartar**

1. Peel marrow, cut it in half lengthways and scoop out pips. Cut flesh into even-sized cubes, about 2·5 cm/1 inch.
2. Cover marrow with water and soak for 12 hours. Strain well.
3. Weigh marrow to calculate quantity of sugar, ginger and lemon.
4. Strew marrow with equal weight of sugar. Leave for 12 hours.
5. Tie bruised ginger and finely-pared lemon rind in a piece of muslin.
6. Tip marrow, sugar and liquid it

has made into a pan and simmer until sugar is dissolved. Add muslin bag and lemon juice. Simmer until marrow is clear and syrup thickens.

7. Pour into a jar, cover and leave to soak for 1 week.

8. Strain off syrup.

9. Place marrow on greaseproof paper on a cake rack and leave it in a warm place to dry.

10. Mix and sieve castor sugar, bicarbonate of soda and cream of tartar.

11. Roll marrow pieces in sugar mixture to coat it completely.

12. Pack in greaseproof paper in an air-tight box.

**Sybil Norcott,
Irlam, Nr. Manchester**

CHAPTER 12

HOME-MADE SWEETS

EQUIPMENT FOR SIMPLE SWEET-MAKING

You may have most of the following in the kitchen already:

Large strong saucepan with thickish base
Wooden spoon
Metal spatula (a clean paint scraper is ideal)
Tins for setting toffee, etc. (roasting, dripping, or Swiss roll tins will do)
Large crockery meat platter or marble slab

Sugar Thermometer

It is helpful to have a sugar thermometer. When using one, have it beside the pan in a saucepan of very hot water. Do not put it cold into a pan of hot mixture. While using thermometer, always replace in very hot water. Never cool it too quickly or allow even a few grains to adhere to it after use as they might spoil future batches of sweets.

GUIDE to stages in boiling sweets mixtures for those without a thermometer: to test, drop a teaspoonful in a cup of cold water. Always remove pan of mixture from heat when conducting the test:

Soft ball (240°F/116°C): when you remove from water and feel it between fingers and thumb it is like a soft ball.
Hard ball (265°F/130°C): when you remove from water and feel it between fingers and thumb it is a hard ball, but still chewy.
Soft crack (280–285°F/140–142°C): when you remove from water and feel it between fingers and thumb it is hard but not brittle.
Hard crack (300°F/150°C): when you remove from water and feel it between fingers and thumb it is brittle.
Caramel (310–320°F/155–160°C):

this is not tested in water. If you test for hard crack you will know when it has reached 300°F, 150°C. Then you must watch mixture closely, taking care it does not burn. It will turn a deep brown colour.

APRICOTINES

Makes about 300 g/11 oz

A 450 g/1 lb can apricots
175 g/6 oz granulated sugar
A squeeze of lemon juice
Granulated sugar, to coat

1. Sieve or liquidise fruit with about ⅓ of the syrup.
2. Put pulp, sugar and lemon juice in a pan. Bring to the boil.
3. Stand pan on an asbestos mat, if you have one. Boil apricot mixture very carefully, stirring most of the time so that it does not burn. Because this mixture is so thick a thermometer cannot be used. Boil until a little tested in a cup of cold water forms a really firm ball. This sweet is rather like overboiled jam.
4. Pour mixture into a wetted, round tin, 13 cm/5 inches diameter. Allow to set.
5. When set, cut into rounds and crescents and toss in granulated sugar.

This sweet is delicious and really enhances a box of assorted sweets.

FONDANT

Makes about 450 g/1 lb

For this it is helpful to have a sugar thermometer (see this page).

450 g/1 lb granulated sugar
150 ml/¼ pint water
25 g/1 oz powdered glucose (buy from a chemist)

1. Dissolve sugar completely in

water, stirring over a low heat. Do
not let it boil until every grain of
sugar is dissolved.
2. Boil to soft ball stage (see page
160).
3. Add glucose and boil until it is
dissolved.
4. Dampen a meat platter slightly
with water and pour on to it the
transparent fondant mixture.
Allow to cool until a skin has
formed (about 5 minutes).
5. Beat with a metal scraper or
spatula, or palette knife, until a
white mass forms. Leave it until
cold.
6. When cold, work it by hand,
like kneading, until smooth. Press
into a jar with a good lid.
7. Store in the store-cupboard and
use as required. It will keep for
many months.

Uses of Fondant

1. Colour and flavour to make
centres for chocolates. Shape by
hand, or roll out and cut pretty
shapes with tiny cutters. Dip in
melted chocolate and put on
waxed paper to set.
2. Flavour with instant coffee
dissolved in a very little hot water.
Work in chopped walnuts. Roll in
finely-chopped walnuts.
3. Knead in some fine coconut: 1
part coconut to 4 parts fondant.
Make into log shapes and roll
them in coconut.
4. A simple way to make coconut
ice: knead in 50 g/2 oz coconut to
200 g/7 oz fondant. Colour half of
it pink. Roll both colours out to
even thickness. Press the two
colours together, then cut into
bars.
5. Melt down, flavour, colour and
pour into fancy moulds. Or roll
out, cut into pretty shapes and
leave on waxed paper to dry off.
(Paper from a cornflakes packet is
useful.)
6. Work in a nut of butter to a
small quantity of fondant and use
as a filling for small biscuits.
7. Try, also, next recipe for
Chocolate Fudge, using fondant.

CHOCOLATE FUDGE

Makes about 700 g/1½ lb

50 g/2 oz butter
100 g/4 oz granulated sugar
50 g/2 oz dark cooking chocolate
1 large can condensed milk
2 tablespoons golden syrup
75 g/3 oz fondant

1. Put butter, sugar, chocolate,
condensed milk and syrup in a
large saucepan and melt gently
over a low heat, stirring until
sugar is dissolved and all is well
mixed.
2. Bring to the boil and boil gently,
stirring constantly, until it reaches
soft ball stage (see page 160),
240°F, 116°C. Remove pan from
heat.
3. Mix in fondant, and stir gently
until melted.
4. Pour into a greased 18 cm/7 inch
square tin.
5. Cut into cubes when cold.

NOUGAT

Makes about 500 g/1¼ lb

For this it is advisable to have a
sugar thermometer (see page 160).

50 g/2 oz blanched almonds
25 g/1 oz glacé cherries
25 g/1 oz angelica
**50 g/2 oz powdered glucose (buy at
a chemist)**
350 g/12 oz granulated sugar
100 g/4 oz honey
150 ml/¼ pint water
1 egg-white

You need 2 sheets of rice paper
and some waxed paper or cling
film for wrapping sweets.

1. Butter an 18 cm/7 inch square
tin and line it with rice paper.
2. Chop almonds, cherries and
angelica.
3. Put glucose, sugar, honey and
water in a large pan and stir over
gentle heat until sugar is
completely dissolved.

4. Boil carefully to 290°F, 145°C. It burns readily towards end of boiling time and tends to froth up. If you do not have a thermometer, put a teaspoonful in a cup of cold water. If it is ready it will go into brittle threads.
5. Meanwhile, beat egg-white in a heat-proof bowl until it is stiff and stands up in peaks.
6. When contents of pan reach the correct temperature, pour it slowly over the beaten egg-white, beating all the time.
7. When mixture thickens as you beat it, beat in the fruit and nuts.
8. Pour into prepared tin and place a piece of rice paper on top. Texture is improved if a weight is placed on top for a few hours.
9. Leave it to set overnight. Cut into bars and wrap in waxed paper or cling film wrap.

SWISS MILK TABLET

For this it is helpful but not essential to have a sugar thermometer (see page 160).

900 g/2 lb granulated sugar
200 ml/7½ fluid oz fresh milk
75 g/2 oz butter
1 small can condensed milk (200 g/7 oz)
¼ teaspoon vanilla essence

1. Put sugar, fresh milk and butter in a large pan over a low heat and stir until sugar is completely dissolved.
2. Bring to the boil and add condensed milk.
3. Boil carefully (i.e., stir occasionally so that it does not catch or burn) to soft ball stage (see page 160), 240°F, 116°C.
4. Remove from heat and when bubbles subside add vanilla essence.
5. Beat thoroughly until mixture begins to sugar on pan bottom.
6. Pour into an oiled Swiss roll tin, a shallow tin about 18 × 28 cm/ 7 × 11 inches.

7. When it is set, mark into squares. When cold it should break apart neatly.

TOFFEE HUMBUGS

Fun to make because of pulling and shaping required.

Makes about 500 g/1¼ lb

For this it is helpful, but not essential, to have a sugar thermometer (see page 160)

450 g/1 lb soft, dark brown barbados sugar
50 g/2 oz butter
150 ml/¼ pint water
1 tablespoon golden syrup
¼ teaspoon cream of tartar
2 drops of oil of peppermint or clove oil

You need some butter to oil tin, and a scraper and scissors. Humbugs are usually wrapped in cellophane paper to stop them sticking to each other in the tin, but it is not essential if your tin is absolutely air-tight.

1. Put sugar, butter, water and syrup into a large pan over a low heat. Stir until sugar is dissolved. Do not let it boil before sugar is completely dissolved.
2. Bring to the boil, add cream of tartar and boil to soft crack stage (see page 160), 280–285°F, 140–142°C.
3. Pour into oiled tin or on to oiled marble slab. Add essence.
4. Leave until it forms a skin, then start turning edges to centre with an oiled, metal spatula or scraper.
5. When cool enough to handle, start pulling and folding until it begins to harden and has a good sheen.
6. Quickly pull into a rope about 2 cm/¾ inch thick. It will pull out to 1 metre/1 yard in length, so make 2 ropes.
7. Cut with oiled scissors, half-turning the rope each time so that there is a twist in each sweet.
8. When they are quite cold, wrap

each sweet in cellophane paper and store in an air-tight tin.

TREACLE TOFFEE

Makes about 1 kg/2 lb

For this it is helpful, but not essential, to have a sugar thermometer (*see page 160*).

450 g/1 lb barbados sugar
450 g/1 lb black treacle or molasses
2½ tablespoons cider vinegar
100 g/4 oz butter

1. Put sugar, treacle or molasses and vinegar in a large saucepan and stir over a low heat until sugar is completely dissolved.
2. Bring very slowly to boiling point. Keep it boiling for 10 minutes, stirring occasionally.
3. Carefully and gradually stir in the butter, in thin pieces, piece by piece.
4. Continue to boil to 284°F, 142°C, soft crack stage (*see page 160*).
5. Remove from heat and allow toffee to settle a minute. Pour gently into a well-greased tin. A tin 2·3 cm/9 inches square gives pieces just over 1·2 cm/½ inch thick.
6. When cool, mark into squares. When cold, break into pieces.
7. Wrap in waxed paper or store in an air-tight container.

For a good variation of this, substitute half of the treacle with honey.

CHOCOLATE COCONUT BALLS

Makes 775 g/1¾ lb

225 g/8 oz desiccated coconut
100 g/4 oz icing sugar
1 small can condensed milk (200 g/7 oz)
A 250 g/9 oz block of plain or milk cooking chocolate, for coating

You need some waxed paper on which to set finished sweets. (Paper from a cornflakes packet is ideal.)

1. Mix coconut and sugar into milk. If coconut is very dry use less than the quantity given, otherwise sweets may go hard.
2. Make small balls from the mixture.
3. Melt chocolate in a small basin over a pan of simmering water.
4. To coat the balls, drop them into the melted chocolate, lift each one out with a fork and tap it on the edge of the bowl to allow excess chocolate to drop off.
5. Put the balls on waxed paper to set.

UNCOOKED MARZIPAN

Makes about 300 g/11 oz

1 egg
225 g/8 oz ground almonds
225 g/8 oz icing sugar
A few drops almond essence
¼ teaspoon orange flower water (optional)

To finish
Vegetable colourings
Chocolate powder
Melted chocolate
Cherries
Dates
Walnuts

1. Beat the egg.
2. Mix all the other ingredients together and add enough beaten egg to make a pliable paste.

Marzipan can be used in many ways. Colour green, pink, yellow, orange, etc. Or use a little chocolate powder. Build into striped sweets, make scraps into harlequin balls. Cut out shapes with small cutters to dip in melted chocolate. Use to stuff cherries, dates or walnuts. Make marzipan fruits.

UNCOOKED RAISIN FUDGE

Makes 900 g/2 lb

163

75 g/3 oz butter
100 g/4 oz plain cooking chocolate
1 egg
450 g/1 lb icing sugar
75 g/3 oz chopped walnuts
50 g/2 oz raisins
2½ tablespoons condensed milk
(100 g/3½ oz)
A few drops vanilla essence

It is useful to have some waxed paper to line the tin.

1. Oil an 18 cm/7 inch square tin or line it with waxed paper.
2. Put butter and chocolate to melt in a bowl over a pan of simmering water. Do not let water touch the basin.
3. Beat the egg.
4. Remove bowl of chocolate and butter from heat and add to it the beaten egg and all the other ingredients. Beat well together.
5. Smooth mixture into prepared tin and leave to set.
6. Cut it into squares.

RICH RUM TRUFFLES

No cooking required.

Makes about 12 truffles

75 g/3 oz dark cooking chocolate
1 teaspoon cream
1 egg-yolk
15 g/½ oz butter
Rum to taste (1 to 2 teaspoons)
Chocolate vermicelli

1. Break chocolate into a small basin. Stand basin over a pan of simmering water. Do not let water touch basin. Allow chocolate to melt, then remove from heat.
2. Add cream, egg-yolk, butter and rum and beat mixture until thick and like a paste.
3. Form little balls of the mixture and roll them in chocolate vermicelli.

(This chapter has been contributed by Mrs Anne Wallace, Dunlop, Scotland.)

CHAPTER 13

WINE, BEER AND OTHER DRINKS

YEAST STARTER

175 ml/6 fluid oz water
1 dessertspoon malt extract
1 dessertspoon sugar
A pinch citric acid
A pinch yeast nutrient
The yeast, as indicated in recipe

1. Put water in a small pan, stir in malt extract, sugar and citric acid. Bring to the boil, then turn off heat.
2. Cool this solution a little, then pour it into a small pop bottle, 300 ml/½ pint. Plug neck of the bottle with cotton-wool and cool to below 70°F, 21°C.
3. Add yeast. If it is a liquid yeast culture, shake the phial before emptying it into bottle. Replace cotton-wool plug and leave in a warm place.
4. The yeast will ferment vigorously and be ready to use in 2 to 3 days.

FRESH OR DRIED APRICOT WINE

A dry wine. Peach wine may be made in the same way, using fresh or dried peaches.

Makes 4·5 litres/1 gallon

1·8 kg/4 lb fresh apricots or
450 g/1 lb dried apricots
Pectin-destroying enzyme*
Rohament P*
Yeast nutrient*
½ teaspoon citric acid
¼ teaspoon tannin
900 g/2 lb sugar
1 Campden tablet
Water to 1 gallon (4·5 litres)
*Use quantity recommended by supplier

Yeast
Hock

Note: Alan Briggs sterilizes his equipment with a product called Chempro SDP.

1. 48 hours before you start to make the wine, prepare a yeast starter (*see this page*) so that yeast is actively working when it is required for the wine.
2. **For the wine:** halve apricots and remove stones (if using fresh fruit). Cut up the fruit and put in a sterilized polythene bucket.
3. Add pectin-destroying enzyme and Rohament P and pour on 2·8 litres/5 pints cold water.
4. Cover bucket and leave for 36 hours, stirring occasionally.
5. Add yeast nutrient, citric acid, tannin and 900 g/2 lb sugar. Stir until sugar is dissolved.
6. Make up quantity to 4·5 litres/ 1 gallon by adding cold water.
7. Add actively-working yeast starter.
8. Stir well, cover bucket and leave to ferment for 48 hours, stirring twice daily.
9. Strain liquid into a sterilized 4·5 litre/1 gallon fermenting jar and insert an air-lock.
10. Leave in a fairly warm place about 75°F, 24°C, to ferment to dryness (about 6 to 8 weeks). Sediment will collect during this fermentation. Rack the wine – i.e., syphon it off the sediment into a sterile jar from time to time, topping up jar with fresh, cold water. It is unwise to leave the wine on the lees (sediment) for any length of time.
11. When all ferment is finished, rack into a sterile jar and add one Campden tablet. This acts as an anti-oxidant. Top up jar with cold water.
12. Set it aside to clear. This could take 2 to 3 months.
13. When wine is brilliantly clear, bottle it and leave it in a cool, dark place to mature for at least 6 months. **Alan Briggs, Batley, W. Yorkshire**

BEETROOT AND PARSNIP WINE

A sweet, tawny dessert wine. Improves if allowed to mature for a year or two.

Makes 4·5 litres/1 gallon

1·35 kg/3 lb beetroot
Water
1·35 kg/3 lb parsnips
225 g/8 oz raisins or dates
1·7 kg/3¾ lb sugar
1 teaspoon citric acid
Yeast
Sherry

1. Yeast must be actively working before you start making the wine. 2 or 3 days before you begin the wine, make up the yeast starter (*see opposite page*) using the sherry yeast.
2. **For the wine:** wash beetroots and cut into 1·3 cm/½ inch cubes.
3. Cook in 2·3 litres/½ gallon of water until almost tender.
4. Pour off beetroot water into a large polythene bin or bucket, 22·7 litre/5 gallon capacity.
5. Prepare and cook parsnips in exactly the same way, pouring liquid into bin with beetroot water. Leave to cool to 18°–20°C, 65°–70°F.
6. Meanwhile, chop up raisins or dates. When temperature of liquid in bin has dropped sufficiently, add them with 450 g/1 lb of the sugar, the citric acid and the actively-working yeast.
7. Cover bin loosely with a cloth or lid. This keeps dust and flies out but lets air in. Leave in a warm place for 21 days. Stir wine carefully every day. It has a tendency to froth excessively when stirred. That is why a large bin is essential or it may froth over the top of the bin.
8. On fifth or sixth day, add another 450 g/1 lb sugar.
9. On tenth or eleventh day, add another 450 g/1 lb sugar.
10. On fifteenth or sixteenth day, add remaining 350 g/12 oz sugar.
11. After another 5–6 days, strain through a muslin or nylon cloth laid in a sieve, into a 4·5 litre/ 1 gallon dark-glass jar. Fill jar to 2·5 cm/1 inch from top. Put any left-over liquid into a small dark-glass

bottle. Top jar up with water if necessary.
12. Fit an air-lock, or cover top with a piece of polythene secured with a rubber band. Cover the small bottle in the same way.
13. Keep jar and bottle in a warm place, 18°–20°C, 60°–65°F, for 2 to 3 months.
14. After 2 to 3 months rack off i.e., syphon wine off the sediment into a clean jar. Top up jar with spare wine from bottle or with cold water to 2·5 cm/1 inch from top. Re-fit air-lock or cover as before. Be sure to taste wine in small bottle before using in case it has gone off.
15. Rack again every 3 to 4 months.
16. Bottle the wine when a year or more old and when it is stable and clear. Wash thoroughly 6 wine bottles. Syphon wine into the bottles. If you want to keep the wine, cork bottles with straight-sided corks and lay them on their sides. If it is going to be used in a few months, use flanged-type corks, but leave bottles standing upright.
17. It improves outstandingly if kept to mature for a few years.

Dennis Rouston,
Kippax, W. Yorkshire

BLACKBERRY AND ELDERBERRY WINE

A medium-sweet, red wine. The two hedgerow fruits balance each other nicely. However, as blackberries usually ripen 2 or 3 weeks before elderberries, pick both when really ripe, weigh up 900 g/2 lb lots and put them in the freezer. You can then make wine at your leisure.

Makes 4·5 litres/1 gallon

900 g/2 lb blackberries
900 g/2 lb elderberries
Boiling water
225 g/8 oz dates, or 125 g/4 oz red-grape concentrate

15 g/½ oz citric acid
1·35 kg/3 lb sugar

Yeast
Port

1. Yeast must be actively working before you start making the wine. 2 or 3 days before you begin the wine, make up the yeast starter (*see page 166*) using the Port yeast.
2. **For the wine:** thaw the fruit first.
3. Put blackberries into a large basin and pour over them ½-1 litre/1-2 pints boiling water.
4. Put on rubber gloves and squeeze berries.
5. Strain juice through a piece of muslin or net curtain, laid in a nylon strainer, into a polythene fermenting bin or bucket of at least 13·7–22·7 litre/3–5 gallon capacity. It is wise to measure the 4·5 litre/1 gallon level and mark it on the side of bin.
6. Pour another ½–1 litre/1–2 pints of boiling water over blackberries, squeeze again and strain juice into the bin.
7. Do exactly the same with the elderberries. Then throw pulp away on to the compost heap.
8. Make the volume of juice in bin up to 4·5 litres/1 gallon with cold water. Let it cool to 18°–20°C, 65°–70°F.
9. Meanwhile, chop dates and, when temperature of juice has dropped sufficiently, add them, or the grape concentrate, with the citric acid, 450 g/1 lb of the sugar and the actively-working yeast starter.
10. Cover bin loosely with cloth or lid. This keeps out dust and flies but allows air in. Keep in a warm place for 7 to 10 days, stirring daily.
11. On third day, add another 450 g/1 lb sugar.
12. On fifth day, add the last 450 g/1 lb sugar.
13. After another 2 or 3 days pour the juice—through a piece of muslin and a strainer if you have used dates—into a 4·5 litre/1 gallon

glass jar. Fill jar to 2·5 cm/1 inch from top. Put any left-over juice into a small bottle. Top jar up with cold water if necessary.
14. Fit an air-lock, or cover top with a piece of polythene secured with a rubber band. Cover small bottle in the same way.
15. Leave jar (and bottle) in a warm place for 3 months.
Note: do not put it in airing cupboard. It usually becomes too hot.
16. After about 3 months, rack off into a clean jar – i.e., syphon liquid off the sediment. Top up with spare wine from bottle, or with water, to 2·5 cm/1 inch from top of jar. Be sure to taste wine in small bottle before using in case it has gone off. Re-fit air-lock or cover.
17. After 6 to 8 months rack again.
18. When wine is stable and clear it can be bottled. Thoroughly wash 6 bottles. Syphon wine into the bottles. If you want to keep the wine, cork bottles with straight-sided corks and lay them on their sides. If it is going to be used in a few months, use flanged-type corks, but leave bottles standing upright.
19. This wine is usually ready to drink in about 1 year.

Dennis Rouston,
Kippax, W. Yorkshire

DANDELION WINE

This is an inexpensive, easily-made wine with an attractive yellow colour, nice bouquet and a pleasant flavour. Medium sweet. If you pick the dandelions on the traditional day – St George's day (23rd April), the wine should be ready at Christmas.

Makes 4·5 litres/1 gallon

2·3 litres/2 quarts dandelion
flowers
4·5 litres/1 gallon boiling water
1 orange
1 lemon
125 g/4 oz dates

1·3 kg/3 lb sugar
1 heaped teaspoon yeast nutrient

Yeast
Sauternes

1. Yeast must be actively working before you start making the wine. 2 or 3 days before you begin the wine, make up the yeast starter (see page 166), using the Sauternes yeast.
2. **For the wine:** pick the flowers on a sunny day so that they are open, but not from a busy roadside where they will have been sprayed with mud and dosed with exhaust fumes.
3. Pull off the green calyx from most of the flowers and discard.
4. Put flowers into a polythene fermenting bin or bucket. Pour over the boiling water. Let the flowers soak for 4 days, stirring daily.
5. Strain liquid, discarding the flowers.
6. Slice orange and lemon, chop dates and add them to the liquid with 450 g/1 lb of the sugar, yeast nutrient and the actively-working yeast.
7. Cover bin loosely with cloth or lid. This keeps out dust and flies but lets air in. Leave it in a warm place for 7 days, stirring daily.
8. On third day, add second 450 g/1 lb sugar.
9. On fifth day, add remaining 450 g/1 lb sugar.
10. On seventh day, strain through a muslin or net curtain and a nylon strainer into a 4·5 litre/ 1 gallon jar. Fill jar to the neck. Put any left-over juice into a small bottle. Top up jar with water if necessary.
11. Fit an air-lock or cover top with a piece of polythene secured with a rubber band. Cover small bottle in the same way.
12. Keep jar (and bottle) in a warm place, 18°–20°C, 60°–65°F, for 2 to 3 months.
13. After 2 to 3 months, rack off into a clean jar – i.e., syphon the wine off the sediment. Top up jar with spare wine from the bottle, or with cold water. Re-fit air-lock or cover as before. Be sure to taste wine in small bottle before using in case it has gone off.
14. Rack again after another 2 to 3 months.
15. By Christmas, or approximately 8 months after making wine, it should be ready to drink.
16. When the wine is stable and clear it can be bottled. Thoroughly wash 6 bottles. Syphon wine into the bottles. If you want to keep the wine, cork the bottles with straight-sided corks and lay them down on their sides. If it is going to be used in a few months, use flanged-type corks but leave bottles standing upright.

Dennis Rouston,
Kippax, W. Yorkshire

PEACH WINE

A sweet wine with a pleasant bouquet. Easy-to-make, especially for beginners.

Makes 4·5 litres/1 gallon

800 g/1¾ lb canned peaches
125 g/4 oz dates
1 heaped teaspoon citric acid
900 g/2 lb granulated sugar
450 g/1 lb demerara sugar
4·5 litre/1 gallon cold water

Yeast
Sauternes *or* 1 level tablespoon dried wine-making yeast

1. If using the Sauternes yeast starter, it must be 'working' before you start making the wine. 2 or 3 days before you want to begin the wine, make up the yeast starter (see page 166).
2. **For the wine:** empty tinned peaches, with their syrup, into a polythene bucket or bin.
3. Chop dates and put them into bucket with citric acid and 450 g/ 1 lb of the granulated sugar.

4. Pour over the water.
5. Add the actively-working yeast starter, or the dried yeast.
6. Cover bin loosely with cloth or lid. This keeps out dust and flies but lets air in. Leave in a warm room for 7 days, stirring it up at least twice daily.
7. On third or fourth day, add remaining 450 g/1 lb granulated sugar.
8. On fifth or sixth day, add the 450 g/1 lb demerara sugar.
9. On seventh day, strain liquid through a piece of muslin and a nylon strainer into a 4·5 litre/ 1 gallon jar. Fill jar to 2·5 cm/ 1 inch from the top. If there is any left-over liquid put it into a small bottle.
10. Fit an air-lock in jar, or cover top with a piece of polythene secured with a rubber band. This simple cover will also do for the small bottle.
11. Leave jar (and bottle) in a warm place, 18°–20°C, 65°–70°F, for 2 or 3 months.
12. Syphon liquid off the sediment into a clean jar every 2 to 3 months. Always top up jar with spare wine or with water. Always taste wine in the topping-up bottle before using in case it has gone off.
13. Ready to drink in 6 to 9 months.
14. When the wine is stable and clear it can be bottled. Thoroughly wash 6 bottles. Syphon wine into the bottles. If you want to keep the wine, cork the bottles with straight-sided corks and lay them down on their sides. If it is going to be used in a few months, use flanged-type corks but leave bottles standing upright.

Dennis Rouston,
Kippax, W. Yorkshire

WHITE DESSERT WINE

Can be made at any time of year.

Makes 4·5 litres/1 gallon

900 g/2 lb wheat
450 g/1 lb raisins
1 orange
1 lemon
1·3 kg/3 lb sugar
Water
½ teaspoon citric acid
1 teaspoon yeast nutrient salts

Yeast
Sauternes

Note: Alan Briggs sterilizes his equipment with a product called Chempro SDP.

1. 48 hours before you begin to make the wine, prepare a yeast starter with the Sauternes yeast (*see page 166*).
2. Wash wheat and put in a sterilized polythene bucket.
3. Wash and mince raisins and put them in bucket.
4. Wash orange and lemon. Slice thinly and add to bucket.
5. Add sugar and enough water to bring contents of bucket up to 4·5 litres/1 gallon. Stir to dissolve sugar.
6. Add citric acid, yeast nutrient salts and actively-working yeast starter. Cover bucket well and allow contents to ferment for 72 hours. (This is called fermenting on the pulp.) Stir, if possible, twice daily.
7. Strain into a sterile 4·5 litre/ 1 gallon jar, top up with cold boiled water, fit an air-lock and let wine ferment out. This could take 6 to 8 weeks.
8. Rack off the wine – i.e., syphon it off the sediment. Add 1 Campden tablet and replace air-lock.
9. Leave wine to clear. This could take 3 to 4 months.
10. Syphon the wine into sterile bottles, cork them and leave to mature for at least 12 months.

Alan Briggs,
Batley, W. Yorkshire

RED TABLE WINE

Makes 4·5 litres/1 gallon

450 g/1 lb runner beans
900 g/2 lb fresh elderberries
1 kg/2¼ lb sugar
1 teaspoon yeast nutrient
Pectin-destroying enzyme (use
quantity indicated on packet)
½ teaspoon citric acid
1 Campden tablet

Yeast
Burgundy or Bordeaux

Note: Alan Briggs sterilizes his
equipment with a product called
Chempro SDP.

1. 48 hours before you begin to
make the wine, prepare a yeast
starter with the Burgundy or
Bordeaux yeast (see page 166).
Wait until it is actively working
before going on.
2. **For the wine:** prepare runner
beans as for table use. Boil them
for 30 minutes, but no salt must be
used.
3. Meanwhile, wash elderberries,
put them in a sterilized polythene
bucket and crush them with hands.
4. Strain off liquid from runner
beans and pour into bucket of
elderberries. (Eat beans later.)
5. Add sugar, yeast nutrient,
pectin-destroying enzyme and
citric acid. Stir to dissolve sugar.
6. Add cold water to bucket to
make quantity up to 4·5 litres/
1 gallon.
7. When wine 'must' is cool add
actively-working yeast starter.
Cover bucket and allow to ferment
on the pulp for 48 hours.
8. Strain into a sterile 4·5 litre/
1 gallon jar, fit an air-lock and let
wine ferment out. This could take
from 6 to 8 weeks.
9. When all ferment has ceased,
syphon liquid off sediment into a
sterile jar and top up with cold
boiled water.
10. Leave wine to clear. This could
take about 3 months.
11. Syphon wine into sterile
bottles, cork them and leave the
wine for 12 months to mature.
Alan Briggs,
Batley, W. Yorkshire

LIGHT MEAD

A light type of mead, good to drink
with dinner. Serve chilled.

Makes 4·5 litres/1 gallon

For this mead, use clover honey or
similar. Do not use oil seed rape,
which looks like lard: it is no
good for mead.

4·5 litres/1 gallon water
1·15 kg/2½ lb light honey
15 g/½ oz citric acid
2 teaspoons yeast nutrient
1 heaped tablespoon light, dried
malt extract
¼ teaspoon grape tannin

Yeast
Sauternes

1. 48 hours before you begin the
mead, make up a yeast starter,
using the Sauternes yeast, so that
it is actively working when
required (see page 166).
2. Heat the water to 57°–60°C,
135°–140°F. Stir in the honey.
Keep at this temperature for 5
minutes.
3. Pour honey water into a bin.
Cover bin. Let it cool to about
30°C, 70°F.
4. Add other ingredients, including
actively-working yeast. Stir well.
Cover the bin and leave it in a
warm place, about 18°–20°C,
65°–70°F, for 4 to 5 days. Stir it
daily.
5. After 4 to 5 days, syphon liquid
off sediment into a 4·5 litre/
1 gallon jar. Fit an air-lock, or
cover top with a piece of polythene
secured with a rubber band.
6. Keep jar in a warm place. Rack
every 2 or 3 months – i.e., syphon
mead off the sediment into a clean
jar, replacing air-lock or polythene
cover until fermentation has
ceased completely.
7. When mead is stable and clear
it can be bottled. Thoroughly wash
6 bottles. Syphon mead into the
bottles. If you want to keep the
wine, cork the bottles with
straight-sided corks and lay them

down on their sides. If it is going to be used in a few months, use a flanged-type cork but leave bottles standing upright.

Should be ready to drink in 9 to 12 months.

**Dennis Rouston,
Kippax, W. Yorkshire**

MEDIUM SWEET MEAD

A medium to sweet mead.

Makes 4.5 litres/1 gallon

**4.5 litres/1 gallon water
900 g/2 lb Australian or
Tasmanian Leatherwood honey
900 g/2 lb general flower honey,
English or clover
15 g/½ oz citric acid
7 g/¼ oz tartaric acid
½ level teaspoon grape tannin
3 teaspoons yeast nutrient
2 tablespoons light, dried malt
extract**

**Yeast
Sauternes**

1. 48 hours before you begin the mead, make up a yeast starter, using the Sauternes yeast, so that it is actively working when required (*see page 166*).
2. Heat water to 57°–60°C, 135°–140°F. Stir in the honey. Keep at this temperature for 5 minutes.
3. Pour honey water into a bin. Let it cool to about 20°C, 70°F.
4. Add other ingredients, including actively-working yeast. Stir well. Cover bin and leave in a warm place, about 18°–20°C, 65°–70°F, for 4 to 5 days. Stir it daily.
5. Follow method for Mead from stages 5 to 7 (*see page 171*).
Should be ready to drink in 9 to 12 months, but if kept it will improve and mature.

**Dennis Rouston,
Kippax, W. Yorkshire**

WATER TREATMENT

Water can be roughly divided into

two types: soft and hard.
Soft is ideal for Brown Ales, Mild Ales and Stouts – i.e., the sweeter types of beer.
Hard is ideal for Bitters, Pale Ales and Light Ales – i.e., the dry, bitter, hop-flavoured beers.
You must therefore use water treatment to adjust your water supply for the type of beer you wish to make.
Soft to hard: add 1 to 2 teaspoons gypsum and ½ teaspoon Epsom salts.
Hard to soft: add 1 teaspoon bicarbonate of soda and 1 teaspoon salt. If very hard, it may be a good idea to boil water first, let it go cold and then syphon off the top ¾ of it, discarding what is left.

A NOTE ON HYDROMETERS

An hydrometer is an instrument for measuring the density of water mixtures.
When an hydrometer is put into pure water at 15°C, 60°F it gives a reading of 0. This is sometimes expressed as 1·000 or 1000.
Whenever wine or beer is made, sugar is added in some form.
When you put the hydrometer into the solution you will find that it does not sink as much as it does in plain water.
The reading is taken where the level of the solution cuts the stem – this first reading is usually called Original Gravity and should be noted down.
When yeast is added to either the 'must' or 'wort' it ferments using the sugar and producing carbon dioxide and alcohol.

If the sugar is added in stages you must always remember to take a reading before adding sugar *and* after the sugar has been stirred in. The first reading is deducted from the second, showing the increase in gravity. For example:

Day 1: Original Gravity   1035

Day 3: Gravity: 1028 ⎫
Gravity after adding
1 lb sugar   1063 ⎬   35
             1070

Day 5: Gravity   1060 ⎫
Gravity after adding
1½ lb sugar   1112 ⎬   52
Total gravity   1122

For wine-making: when wine becomes stable take a final gravity reading. In the example above, subtract final reading, say 1005, from total gravity:

1122 − 1005 = 117

Most hydrometers have two or three scales: gravity, alcohol and sugar-per-gallon. Find 117 on the gravity scale. It equals approximately 15·5% alcohol.

For beer-makers: the hydrometer is essential for your own safety. You measure Original Gravity just the same as in wine-making—e.g. 1042, but this must drop for malt-extract beers to 1005 or less, and for mashed beers (using pale malt) to 1012 or less. If you bottle the beer before it gets down to these gravities the tops may be forced out. At worst, they can explode, possibly causing injury and damage. This is due to the very high pressure that can build up in a bottle if too much sugar is present. So, be warned – buy an hydrometer for your own safety and, most important, use it to produce first-class brews.

BITTER

Makes 18·2 litres/4 gallons

Water
900 g/2 lb malt extract
350 g/12 oz cracked crystal malt
85 g/3 oz Golding hops
Water treatment (use a proprietary brand) *or* **1 teaspoon gypsum**
¼ teaspoon Epsom salts
1·35 kg/3 lb sugar

Yeast
British Ale yeast

For Priming
Granulated sugar
Original gravity 1·044 (see page 172, Hydrometers)

1. 48 hours before you begin the brew make up a starter bottle with the British Ale yeast (*see page 166*) so that yeast will be actively working when it is required.
2. Bring 9·1 litres/2 gallons water to the boil.
3. Add all ingredients, except yeast and priming sugar. Do not use water treatment if your water is very hard already (*see page 172*).
4. Boil for 45 minutes.
5. Strain through a nylon sieve into a bin. Before you start, put a mark on bin at 18·2 litre/4 gallon level.
6. Rinse hops with a kettleful of boiling water and strain liquid into bin.
7. Make up to 18·2 litres/4 gallons with cold water and let it cool to 18°–20°C, 65°–70°F.
8. When cool, add yeast.
9. Cover bin and leave in a warm place so that brew can ferment until gravity is 1·005 or less.
10. Syphon liquid off sediment into beer bottles. Be sure to use real beer bottles. Any other type of bottle may burst with build up of gas during secondary fermentation.
11. Prime bottles with ½ teaspoon sugar per pint (560 ml) and screw in stoppers tightly, or fix new crown corks.
12. Keep in a warm place for 3 to 4 days.
13. Ready to drink 4 weeks after bottling. Will go on improving up to 6 months.

                 Dennis Rouston,
           Kippax, W. Yorkshire

TED'S BITTER BEER

A simple recipe.

Makes 23 litres/5 gallons

75 g/3 oz dried hops
50 g/2 oz black patent malt
Water
1·4 kg/3 lb dried malt extract
1 kg/2·2 lb bag of sugar
1 pkt beer yeast
Extra sugar, to prime bottles

1. Place hops and black patent malt in muslin bag (these can be obtained at any wine supply shop). Place bag in large pan of water, at least 5·7 litres/10 pints, and bring to boil. Simmer for ½ hour.
2. Meanwhile, place malt extract and sugar in a 23 litre/5 gallon bin and pour over boiling water (2 kettles). Stir until dissolved.
3. Add hop liquid and top up with cold water to 23 litre/5 gallon level.
4. When it has cooled to lukewarm, sprinkle yeast on top and cover.
5. Leave for 7 days.
6. Have ready 38 clean 560 ml/ 1 pint beer bottles. Do not use pop bottles or screw cap bottles. Put 1 level teaspoon sugar in each bottle.
7. Syphon beer into bottles leaving about 2·5 cm/1 inch air space.
8. Cap with crown corks.
Ready to drink in 3 weeks and guaranteed to be crystal clear. Be careful, when pouring, to leave sediment in the bottle.

**Judith Adshead,
Mottram St. Andrew, Cheshire**

Original gravity 1·036 (see pages 172/3, A Note on Hydrometers)

1. Boil all ingredients, except the yeast and priming sugar, in 4·5 litres/1 gallon of water for at least 1 hour, stirring occasionally so that sugars do not stick.
2. Strain into fermenting vessel through fine muslin or similar.
3. Wash grains and hops by pouring over pre-boiled cold water, until volume in fermenting vessel reaches 9 litres/2 gallons.
4. When cool, below 21°C, 70°F, pitch with a top-fermenting beer yeast and cover brew with lid or towels to exclude dust, flies, bacteria, etc.
5. Ferment 4 or 5 days, at room temperature, skimming froth from surface after first 24 hours.
6. Skim again, then syphon liquid off into closed container (gallon jars may be used). Fit air-lock. Leave further 7 days to allow ferment to finish and until hydrometer reads 1·002. Allow yeast to settle before bottling.
7. Bottle into beer bottles, priming each 1 pint with ½ teaspoon castor sugar. Screw stoppers in tightly or fit crown corks to ensure bottles are thoroughly sealed.
8. Leave at room temperature for 7 days, then leave to mature for at least 14 days.

**Alan Briggs,
Batley, W. Yorkshire**

BROWN ALE

Makes about 9 litres/2 gallons

565 g/1¼ lb dried malt extract
125 g/4 oz crushed crystal malt
50 g/2 oz crushed black malt
225 g/8 oz soft brown sugar
225 g/8 oz brewing sugar
20 g/¾ oz hops
Water

Yeast
Top-fermenting beer yeast

For Priming Bottles
Castor sugar

BARLEY WINE BEER

Makes about 9 litres/2 gallons

900 g/2 lb light, dried malt extract
225 g/8 oz crystal malt
40 g/1½ oz black malt
450 g/1 lb glucose chips
450 g/1 lb brewing sugar
225 g/8 oz soft brown sugar
125 g/4 oz soluble dextrin
70 g/2½ oz hops
Water

Yeast
General purpose beer yeast

For Priming Bottles
Castor sugar

Original gravity 1·083 (see pages 172–3, A Note on Hydrometers)

1. Boil all ingredients, except the yeast and priming sugar, in a minimum of 4·5 litres/1 gallon of water, stirring occasionally so that the glucose chips and sugars do not stick.
2. Strain into fermenting vessel through fine muslin, or similar.
3. Wash grains and hops by pouring on pre-boiled cold water until volume in fermenting vessel reaches 9 litres/2 gallons.
4. When cold, below 21°C, 70°F, pitch with a general-purpose beer yeast and cover brew with lid or towels to exclude dust, flies, bacteria, etc.
5. Ferment 4 or 5 days, at room temperature, skimming froth from surface after first 24 hours.
6. Skim again, then syphon liquid off sediment into closed container (gallon jars may be used). Fit air-lock. Leave until fermentation has ceased and hydrometer reads about 1·008. This may take 6 to 8 weeks.
7. Bottle into beer bottles, priming each 1 pint with ½ teaspoon castor sugar. Screw stoppers in tightly, or fit crown corks, to ensure bottles are thoroughly sealed.
8. Leave at room temperature for 7 days. Leave to mature for at least 12 months before drinking. Will keep and improve for 2 or 3 years.

**Alan Briggs,
Batley, W. Yorkshire**

LAGER

Makes 22·7 litres/5 gallons

Water
1·6 kg/3½ lb liquid light malt extract
900 g/2 lb sugar
225 g/8 oz cracked crystal malt
60 g/2 oz Hallertauer hops
1 level teaspoon salt
1 level teaspoon citric acid

Yeast
Lager

For Priming Bottles
Granulated sugar

Original gravity 1·042 (see page 172, Hydrometers)

1. 48 hours before you begin the brew, make up a starter bottle using the Lager yeast (see page 166) so that yeast will be actively working when it is required.
2. Heat 9·1 litres/2 gallons water until warm enough to dissolve malt extract and sugar. Stir well, making sure they dissolve and do not stick on bottom of pan and burn.
3. When they are dissolved, add rest of ingredients, except yeast and priming sugar.
4. Bring to the boil and boil hard for 45 minutes.
5. Strain through a nylon sieve into a bin. Mark bin beforehand at the 22·7 litre/5 gallon level.
6. Make up volume of liquid in bin to 22·7 litres/5 gallons with cold water. Let it cool to about 18°–20°C, 65°–70°F.
7. When it is cool, add the actively-fermenting lager yeast starter.
8. Cover bin loosely with a cloth or loose lid. Leave in a warm place and let it ferment for about 36 hours.
9. If the bin has an air-tight lid with an air-lock use this. Otherwise, syphon lager into containers, such as 4·5 litre/1 gallon jars or larger vessels, if you have them, to which an air-lock can be fitted.
10. Leave containers in a warm place and let lager ferment to a gravity of 1·005 or less.
11. Syphon into proper beer bottles. Be sure to use real beer bottles. Other bottles are not strong enough to take the build up of gas during the secondary fermentation.
12. Prime bottles with ½ teaspoon sugar per pint (560 ml) and screw

175

in stoppers tightly or fit new crown corks.

13. Keep in a warm place for 3 to 4 days to allow priming sugar to ferment and so give the lager condition.

14. Ready to drink 3 to 4 weeks after bottling but improves if kept for 4 to 6 months.

Serve chilled.

Dennis Rouston,
Kippax, W. Yorkshire

LIGHT ALE

Easy to make. An ideal thirst-quencher after a day in the garden.

Makes 18·2 litres/4 gallons

Water
Water treatment (see page 172)
1·8 kg/4 lb crushed pale malt
675 g/1½ lb glucose chippings
70 g/2½ oz Golding hops

Yeast
British Ale

For Priming Bottles
Granulated sugar

Original gravity 1·035 (see page 172)

1. 2 or 3 days before you begin the brew make up a small starter bottle using the British Ale yeast (see page 166) so that yeast will be actively fermenting when it is required.

2. Heat 12·4 litres/2¼ gallons water to 74°C, 165°F.

3. Dissolve in this the water treatment, if used. Use water treatment for this ale if your water supply is very soft. Hard water makes good light ales.

4. Add crushed pale malt. Stir in carefully so that no dry lumps form.

5. The temperature should now drop to 65·5°C, 150°F. This should be maintained, as near as possible, for 2 hours, during which time saccharification of the starch takes place.

6. At the end of 2 hours, strain the liquid off the grain, and spray or wash the grain with water at 76°C, 170°F until volume reaches 18·2 litres or 4 gallons.

7. Return all liquid to boiler or pan and bring to the boil. Throw away the grain.

8. Boil until frothing ceases, then add glucose chippings and hops. Stir to dissolve glucose.

9. Boil for 1½ hours. Then switch off heat. The volume will now be about 13·6 litres/3 gallons.

10. Allow hops to sink to bottom of boiler or pan, then drain off into a polythene fermenting bin or bucket. Pour a kettleful of boiling water over hops to wash them. Drain off into bin.

11. Make up volume of 'wort' in fermenting vessel to 18·2 litres/ 4 gallons with cold water. Cool as rapidly as possible to 21°C, 70°F.

12. Pitch yeast – i.e., empty bottle of actively-working yeast starter into wort.

13. After 12 hours, skim off any scum, stir, and leave at room temperature for about 5 days or until an hydrometer reading gives a gravity of 1.010.

14. Then skim off yeast head.

15. Syphon ale off the sediment into proper beer bottles. Other bottles are not strong enough to take the build-up of gas during the secondary fermentation.

16. Prime bottles with ½ teaspoon sugar per pint (560 ml) and screw in stoppers tightly, or fit new crown corks.

17. Keep in a warm place for 6 to 7 days, then put in a cool place.

18. Ready to drink in 4 to 6 weeks after bottling.

Dennis Rouston,
Kippax, W. Yorkshire

STOUT: IRISH TYPE

Makes 18·2 litres/4 gallons

Water
3 kg/6¼ lb crushed pale malt
275 g/10 oz cracked crystal malt

176

275 g/10 oz cracked black malt
125 g/4 oz wheat flour
125 g/4 oz East Kent Golding hops
15 g/½ oz Northern Brewer hops
½ teaspoon citric acid
1 teaspoon salt
Sugar

Yeast
Stout or British Ale Yeast

For Priming Bottles
A little castor sugar

Original gravity 1·055/7 (see page 172)

1. 2 or 3 days before you start the main brew make up a yeast starter (*see page 166*) so that the yeast is actively working when required in the brew.
2. Heat 11·5 litres/2½ gallons water to 74°C, 165°F.
3. Add pale malt, crystal malt and black malt. Stir in carefully so that no lumps form.
4. Put wheat flour in a basin and mix with cold water until like a creamy liquid. Then stir it into brew.
If you add wheat flour straight to a hot brew it tends to turn to lumps.
5. The temperature will now have dropped to 65·5°C, 150°F. This temperature should now be maintained, as near as possible, for 2 hours, during which time saccharification of the starch takes place.
6. At the end of 2 hours, strain the liquid, known as 'wort', off the grain and sparge with water at 76°C, 170°F until volume reaches 18·2 litres/4 gallons.
(To sparge is to spray or wash the grain with water at a given temperature.)
7. Return all liquid to boiler or pan and bring to the boil. Boil until frothing ceases. Add the hops.
8. Boil for 1½ hours. Switch off heat. Volume of brew will now be about 13·6 litres/3 gallons.
9. Allow hops to sink to bottom of boiler. Drain the liquid off into fermenting bin. Pour a kettleful of boiling water over hops to wash them. Drain off into bin.
10. Make up volume of wort in fermenting bin to 18·2 litres/ 4 gallons with cold water. Cool as rapidly as possible to 15°C, 60°F. Take an hydrometer reading and slowly add sugar, continuously stirring until gravity reaches 1·055 to 1·057.
11. Pitch yeast – i.e., empty bottle of actively-working yeast starter into the wort.
12. After 12 hours, skim off the dark brown scum on the yeast head and stir up contents of bin.
13. Leave it at room temperature, 18°–21°C, 65°–70°F, for about 5 days. Stir daily, until hydrometer reading reaches a gravity of approximately 1·020.
14. Syphon into containers, such as 4·5 litre/1 gallon jars, fitted with corks and air-locks. Or cover tops with a piece of polythene secured with a rubber band.
15. Leave jars at room temperature for 7 days, or until gravity reaches 1·012 or less.
16. Bottle the stout into proper beer bottles. **Do not** use non-returnable bottles. These are made of very thin glass and can explode during secondary fermentation in bottle.
Put ½ teaspoon castor sugar into each 560 ml/1 pint bottle. This is known as 'priming'. Screw in the stoppers firmly, or fix crown corks.
17. Leave in a warm place for 7 days. Then store in a cool place for 6 to 8 weeks.

**Dennis Rouston,
Kippax, W. Yorkshire**

LEMON CORDIAL

**2 thin-skinned lemons
1·1 litre/2 pints water
450 g/1 lb sugar
1 level teaspoon citric acid**

1. Cut lemons into quarters and place in liquidiser with 300 ml/ ½ pint of the water. Switch to

maximum speed for 10 seconds
only.
2. Pour into a pan, add remaining
water, sugar and citric acid and
bring to boil, stirring to dissolve
sugar.
3. Remove from heat, allow to cool,
strain and bottle. Dilute to taste
with water or soda water.
Store in fridge. Will keep for 2 or 3
weeks.

Judith Adshead,
Mottram St. Andrew, Cheshire

ORANGE CORDIAL

Juice and zest of 2 oranges
850 ml/1½ pints water
350 g/12 oz sugar
1 level teaspoon citric acid
¼ teaspoon orange food colouring

1. Prepare oranges, discarding
pith.
2. Dissolve sugar in water and
simmer 5 minutes.
3. Add citric acid to zest and juice
of oranges. Pour on the hot syrup.
4. Add colouring carefully.
5. Allow to cool slightly, strain and
bottle.
6. Store in refrigerator. Dilute
with water or soda water to taste.
Will keep up to 3 weeks in fridge.

Judith Adshead,
Mottram St. Andrew, Cheshire

COLD MILK DRINKS

Made in the liquidiser.

Banana
Makes 3 glasses
1 pint milk
1 banana
1 level tablespoon clear honey
A grating of whole nutmeg
3 tablespoons whipped cream

1. Pour milk into liquidiser.
2. Peel and chop banana and add
the pieces with the honey and
nutmeg.
3. Switch on the machine for about
1 minute, or until banana has

blended completely with the milk.
4. Pour into three glasses and top
each with a spoonful of whipped
cream and a fine grating of
nutmeg.
Drink at once.

Chocolate
Makes 3 glasses
1 pint milk
2 level tablespoons drinking
chocolate
1 tablespoon boiling water
4 tablespoons vanilla ice-cream
A little grated chocolate

1. Pour milk into liquidiser.
2. Dissolve drinking chocolate in
the water and add it to the milk
with 2 tablespoons of the ice-
cream.
3. Switch machine on for a minute.
Pour into the glasses, spoon on top
the rest of the ice-cream and
sprinkle each with a little grated
chocolate.
Drink at once.

APRICOT NECTAR

Made in the liquidiser.

125 g/4 oz dried apricots
15 g/½ oz sunflower seeds
1 tablespoon honey
300 ml/½ pint coconut milk
15 g/½ oz desiccated coconut
15 g/½ oz chopped almonds

1. Soak apricots in water overnight.
2. Keep a few of the sunflower
seeds aside for decoration. Soak
rest with the apricots.
3. Next day, strain apricots and
sunflower seeds and put them into
liquidiser with honey, coconut
milk, coconut and almonds. Blend
until smooth, adding apricot liquid
or milk if it is too thick.
4. Serve in tall glasses with the
unsoaked sunflower seeds
sprinkled on top.

Elizabeth Shears,
author of 'Why Do We Eat'

A HOP-GARDEN.

INDEX

185